CLEOPATRA'S DAUGHTER

WOMEN IN ANTIQUITY

Series Editors: Ronnie Ancona and Sarah B. Pomeroy

This book series provides compact and accessible introductions to the life and historical times of women from the ancient world. Approaching ancient history and culture broadly, the series selects figures from the earliest of times to late antiquity.

Cleopatra
A Biography
Duane W. Roller

Clodia Metelli
The Tribune's Sister
Marilyn B. Skinner

Galla Placidia
The Last Roman Empress
Hagith Sivan

Arsinoë of Egypt and Macedon
A Royal Life
Elizabeth Donnelly Carney

Berenice II and the Golden Age of Ptolemaic Egypt
Dee L. Clayman

Faustina I and II
Imperial Women of the Golden Age
Barbara M. Levick

Turia
A Roman Woman's Civil War
Josiah Osgood

Theodora
Actress, Empress, Saint
David Potter

Hypatia
The Life and Legend of an Ancient Philosopher
Edward Watts

Boudica
Warrior Woman of Roman Britain
Caitlin C. Gillespie

Sabina Augusta
An Imperial Journey
T. Corey Brennan

Cleopatra's Daughter
and Other Royal Women of the Augustan Era
Duane W. Roller

CLEOPATRA'S DAUGHTER

AND OTHER ROYAL WOMEN OF THE AUGUSTAN ERA

Duane W. Roller

OXFORD
UNIVERSITY PRESS

OXFORD
UNIVERSITY PRESS

Oxford University Press is a department of the University of Oxford. It furthers
the University's objective of excellence in research, scholarship, and education
by publishing worldwide. Oxford is a registered trade mark of Oxford University
Press in the UK and certain other countries.

Published in the United States of America by Oxford University Press
198 Madison Avenue, New York, NY 10016, United States of America.

First issued as an Oxford University Press paperback, 2021

CIP data is on file at the Library of Congress
ISBN 978-0-19-061882-7 (hardback)
ISBN 978-0-19-760415-1 (paperback)

1 3 5 7 9 8 6 4 2

Paperback printed by Marquis, Canada

Contents

List of Illustrations   vii
Preface   ix
Genealogical Chart   xiii

Introduction   1
1   Queens and Royal Women   7
2   Cleopatra's Daughter   27
3   Glaphyra of Cappadocia   49
4   Salome of Judaea   59
5   Dynamis of Bosporos   79
6   Pythodoris of Pontos   99
7   Aba of Olbe and Mousa of Parthia   121
8   Royal Women and Roman Women   129

Appendix 1. A Note on Flavius Josephus and Nikolaos of Damascus   147
Appendix 2. The Girl Who Danced for the Head of John the Baptist   149
Abbreviations   153
Notes   155
Bibliography   177
List of Passages Cited   187
Index   197

List of Illustrations

Maps

1. The allied states with prominent royal women during the Augustan period   xii
2. Mauretania at the time of the allied monarchy   28
3. The southern Levant after the death of Herod the Great, showing the estates of Salome   60
4. The Bosporan kingdom   80
5. The eastern Mediterranean during the Augustan period   130

Figures

1. Portrait of Marcus Antonius in green basalt. Kingston Lacey, Dorset   25
2. Cleopatra Selene and Alexander Helios in chariot with Octavian in triumph of 27 BC; relief from Nikopolis in Epeiros   33
3. General view of Iol-Caesarea (modern Cherchel in Algeria)   38
4. Cleopatra Selene silver crocodile coin. British Museum RPK, p. 218.1.JubII   39
5. Petubastes IV, from Cherchel. Cherchel Museum S75   41
6. Gilded silver dish from Boscoreale, perhaps representing Cleopatra Selene. Louvre Bj 1969   42
7. Mauretanian Royal Mausoleum   47
8. Elaioussa-Sebaste   52
9. View of ancient Marisa. Shutterstock 630021467   61
10. View of ancient Askalon. Shutterstock 248945809   62
11. Pantikapaion. Shutterstock 365774894   80
12. Miniature glass portrait of Livia, from Nymphaion in Bosporos. The State Hermitage Museum, St. Petersburg, NF.83.235   92
13. Bronze bust of a Bosporan queen, from Shirokaya Balka. The State Hermitage Museum, St. Petersburg, PAN.1726   94
14. Ara Pacis in Rome, perhaps showing Dynamis   97
15. Coin of Pythodoris. British Museum 1893,0406.2   115
16. Coin of Thea Mousa and Phraatakes. British Museum 1918,0501.23   125

17. Portrait of Livia. Musée du Louvre   138
18. Cast of portrait of Octavia. Museo dell'Ara Pacis, Rome   139
19. Portrait of Antonia the Younger, from Leptis Magna   141
20. Lovis Corinth, *Salome II*. Museum der Bildenden Künste, Leipzig   150

Preface

By the last third of the first century BC, the Roman Empire had come to rule much of the Mediterranean world. Yet various regions, especially in the East, were still under the control of indigenous royalty, which existed in a symbiotic relationship with the Roman government. Even though royalty might have seemed an anachronism in the new Roman world, the kings and queens ruled large territories and wielded great power. Inevitably, studies of this period have focused on the kings—personalities such as Herod the Great and Juba II of Mauretania—and have paid little attention to the queens, whether as companions to their husbands or as independent monarchs in their own right. But they were also an essential part of the contemporary political environment.

This volume examines in detail several royal women of the era of Augustus (ruled 27 BC–AD 14), all of whom were powerful leaders. Emphasis is on Cleopatra Selene of Mauretania (40-5 BC), Glaphyra of Cappadocia (ca. 35 BC–AD 7), Salome of Judaea (ca. 57 BC–AD 10), Dynamis of Bosporos (ca. 63 BC–AD 7), and Pythodoris of Pontos (ca. 35 BC–AD 33). They were contemporaries, were related through marriage to one another, and were closely allied with the imperial family in Rome and its own women, such as Livia and the younger Antonia, who themselves took on many of the characteristics of Hellenistic queens. The most famous was Cleopatra Selene, the daughter of Cleopatra VII and the triumvir Marcus Antonius (Mark Antony), but the others were also of great importance in their own territories. Some ruled alone, and others were important partners of their husbands. They wielded power within their environments and beyond. In modern diction they are called "queens" (with the exception of Salome), an inadequate translation of the Greek words *basileia* and *basilissa*. Their role models went back to the heroic age as well as various prototypes from the late Classical and Hellenistic periods, and the concept of "queen" had developed as an important royal dynamic in the generations before the accession of Augustus, in 27 BC.

In the evolving world of the Augustan period, these women were major players in the relationships between the diverse populations of the new Roman Empire and its central government. One (and perhaps another) was a descendant of Antonius, who was also personally involved in the destiny of the others or their families: thus the queens represent an element of the survival of his ambitions in the Augustan world, even though he was a member of the discredited older Roman regime. The women could offer greater political stability and status than their husbands, who might be subject to sudden death while on campaign, and their closeness to the imperial family provided precedents for the role of Roman aristocratic women. Cleopatra Selene was a cousin of members of the ruling Julio-Claudian family and was thus related to three Roman emperors. Others had personal contact with the imperial elite in Rome. Cleopatra Selene and Pythodoris were patronesses of intellectual culture and implemented the work of major scholars. And the descendants of the queens held royal power on the borders of the Roman Empire for generations thereafter.

This contribution to the Women in Antiquity series relies on the author's long acquaintance with the world of the queens, the transitional years from the Hellenistic kingdoms to the Roman Empire. An essential part of this era was the concept of the friendly and allied monarch, the indigenous ruler at the margins of Roman territory who functioned in close alliance with the Roman state, balancing the needs of his or her people with the global requirements of Roman policy. Previous treatments of Cleopatra Selene's mother and husband, Cleopatra VII and Juba II (who was also a husband of Glaphyra), as well as Salome's brother Herod the Great, all in their own way friendly and allied monarchs, have set the stage for this study of the queens. Needless to say, there have also been visits by the author, insofar as possible, to their territories and capitals.

Most of all, the author would like to thank Sarah Pomeroy and Ronnie Ancona not only for their editorial advice but for their faith in entrusting to him another volume of the Women in Antiquity series. As before, the author wrote the book in his study in Santa Fe, having conducted research at the Harvard College Library and the library of the University of California at Berkeley, and utilized the excellent interlibrary loan services of the Ohio State University library. Financial support was provided by the Emeritus Academy of the Ohio State University. Among the many who assisted in the completion of this work, the author would especially like to thank Sally-Ann Ashton, Stanley M. Burstein, Bridget Buxton, Carolin Hahnemann, Molly Ayn Jones-Lewis, Diana E. E. Kleiner, Kyra Nourse, Josiah W. Osgood, John Pollini, Letitia K. Roller, Eugenia Equini Schneider, Stefan Vranka and many others at Oxford University Press, and Wendy Watkins and the Center for Epigraphical and Paleographical Studies of the Ohio State University.

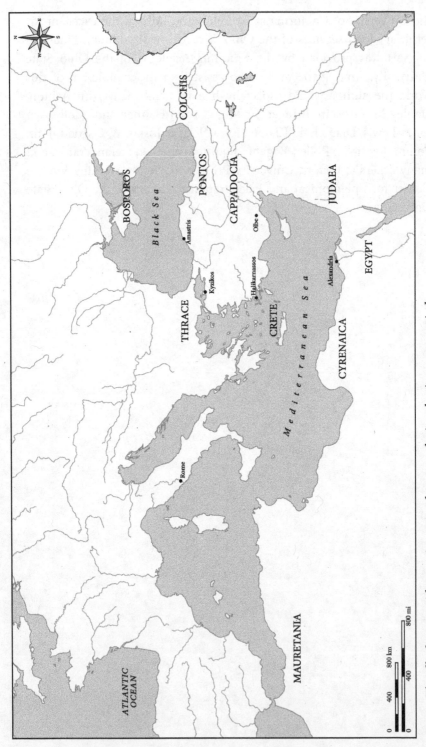

MAP 1. The allied states with prominent royal women during the Augustan period.

Genealogical Chart

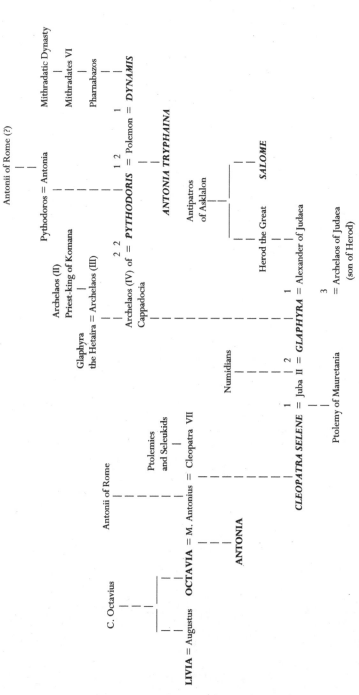

Although greatly simplified, this genealogical chart is designed to show the relationships between the royal women of the East and the leading women of Rome, as well as each other. For full stemmata of the personalities involved, see the various works by Richard D. Sullivan listed in the bibliography, and for the Herodians, see Duane W. Roller, *The Building Program of Herod the Great* (Berkeley, CA, 1998), 280–90. It should be noted that the two instances of the name "Antonia" on the chart do not designate the same woman. Names in bold italics designate royal women discussed in this volume; names merely in roman designate Roman women who had relationships with the royal women.

Introduction

On 10 August 30 BC, Cleopatra VII, queen of kings, queen of Egypt, Cyprus, and Libya, committed suicide, probably by ingesting poison. Her companion, until recently the triumvir of the Roman Republic, Marcus Antonius, had died ten days earlier, also by his own hand. Although Cleopatra's son Kaisarion maintained a brief theoretical rule of Egypt for a few days, he was soon eliminated, and the last of the kingdoms established by the successors of Alexander the Great came to an end after nearly three hundred years. Virtually all their territories were now under Roman control. Yet as Rome evolved from its ancient Republic to a new imperial system under Augustus, independent pockets of royal government survived, despite the Romans' antipathy to royalty; they had not been ruled by kings for hundreds of years.

The death of Cleopatra terminated nearly a century of civil violence within the Roman world, which had effectively begun when the tribune Tiberius Sempronius Gracchus was killed by a mob on the Capitol in 133 BC. The chaos and instability that continued for several generations brought about the rise and fall (usually by assassination) of powerful leaders such as Gnaeus Pompeius (Pompey the Great), Julius Caesar, and Antonius, and ended only in 30 BC.

In many ways the turning point of the final stage of the civil war was the death of Julius Caesar in 44 BC. Afterward, the surviving consul Antonius and Caesar's grand-nephew Gaius Octavianus (Octavian, later Augustus) emerged as the most powerful Romans, constituting themselves, along with Marcus Aemilius Lepidus, as triumvirs with a commission to restore the Republic and to eliminate the assassins of Caesar. The latter was effectively accomplished by the autumn of 42 BC at Philippi in Macedonia, with the death of the leaders against Caesar,

Marcus Brutus and Gaius Cassius. Antonius then remained in the East in order to stabilize matters. Octavian returned to Italy and the West.[1]

At this time the eastern Mediterranean was a patchwork of Roman territory, independent cities and districts, temple states, and allied monarchies. The concept of allied—often erroneously called "client"—monarchy had originated in the second century BC, when arrangements were made between dynasts on the perimeter of the Roman world and the Roman central government. The idea was that the monarchs, who were local and had a close relationship with their subjects, would rule their territories under Roman supervision, thereby providing local control and frontier security in return for political support and the introduction of Roman culture into their territories. Allied monarchies might evolve into Roman provinces, but this was a long and complex process that was never fully implemented until well after the time of Augustus.[2]

In the late 40s BC, when Antonius began to settle the affairs of the eastern Mediterranean, the local Roman presence was due to the fragmentation of the kingdoms that had come into existence after the death of Alexander the Great. Greece proper and Macedonia had become Roman territory in the second century BC. The Seleukid kingdom, which had ruled much of Asia Minor and the Levant, had been terminated by Pompey in the 60s BC, and its remnants were under either direct Roman control or that of various local entities. The Ptolemaic kingdom in Egypt still survived under reduced circumstances, yet its struggling young queen, Cleopatra VII, faced many difficulties.

As Antonius journeyed east from Philippi in late 42 BC and into the following year, he would have encountered various forms of rule. Western and southern Asia Minor were largely organized as Roman provinces, but most of the interior was under allied rulers, whose borders fluctuated depending on the status of the dynasties. Even Roman boundaries were not permanent: parts of Cilicia (on the Mediterranean at its northeastern extremity) would revert to the Ptolemies in the 30s BC and then to Archelaos of Cappadocia, who controlled a vast area of south central Asia Minor. The territories along the Black Sea coast were also in flux, with portions of the Roman province of Bithynia and Pontus, which had existed since the 60s BC, eventually transferred back to the local kingdom of Pontos, which also held the southeastern coasts of the sea. Farther around to the east and centered on the northern coast—in the area of the modern Sea of Azov—was the kingdom of Bosporos, a region that had been a Greek outpost since the fifth century BC and was still an independent kingdom in the Augustan era.

The Roman province of Syria, established in the 60s BC, was created out of the Seleukid heartland and radiated from Antioch, the old Seleukid capital. To the south was a complex area of local cities, dynasts, and chieftains that had evolved from the dying Seleukid Empire. On the coast were the ancient Phoenician cities such as Tyre and Sidon, which could at times be either independent or under Roman or Ptolemaic control. In the interior was the Hasmonean kingdom of Judaea, established about 100 BC; by the 30s BC it would be under the control of a vigorous young ruler, Herod the Great, placed on the throne by Antonius and Octavian. His difficult rule needed constant Roman support. Yet Cleopatra also coveted much of his territory and received parts of it as far north as Damascus, especially after 36 BC; these largely reverted to Herod after her death.

Farther south was a small area around the ancient city of Gaza that was controlled by the Nabataean Arabs (famous for their remote city of Petra), which served as a contact point between the traders of the Mediterranean and those of Arabia and interior southern Asia. Then there was Egypt, the historic center of the Ptolemaic Empire, which became Roman after the death of Cleopatra; at the same time, her external territories in the Levant, Asia Minor, and Cyprus came under Herodian, Cappadocian, or Roman control. The territory west of Egypt was Roman—although there was some dispute between Rome and Cleopatra about the status of the Cyrenaica (modern Libya) —and then far beyond, at the northwestern corner of Africa, were the twin kingdoms of eastern and western Mauretania, whose future was not to be settled until the 20s BC but whose current rulers were also very much involved in the affairs of the eastern Mediterranean.

This was the situation in 42 BC, yet twelve years after he had headed east from Philippi, Antonius was dead and Octavian had emerged as the sole ruler of the Roman Republic, taking the title Augustus in 27 BC. The civil war had come to an end, and the need for centralized rule under a single powerful yet benign personality had been generally realized. Augustus remained in control until his death in AD 14, transformed the Republic into an empire (although he would have objected to such terminology), and brought peace to a world so disrupted that no one alive had known anything but war. Part of his policy was to support the allied monarchs, and the rule by kings and queens along the Roman frontier increased during the Augustan years, following the groundwork laid by Antonius after 42 BC. Cleopatra was gone, but the Herodian, Cappadocian, Pontic, and Bosporan monarchies had survived, and soon a new allied kingdom would be established in Mauretania. Royal women would play an important role in this evolving Augustan world, and their interchange with the women of the Augustan family would become an important characteristic of the era.

Even in the Augustan period, the eastern Mediterranean remained fertile ground for dynastic rivalries and conspiracies, yet it was in this environment that the royal women who would be prominent in the Augustan world flourished: Cleopatra Selene, who went from Ptolemaic Egypt to Mauretania; Glaphyra of Cappadocia, who lived for a time in Judaea; Salome of Judaea; Dynamis of Bosporos on the Black Sea; and Pythodoris of Pontos, whose territory at its peak extended throughout much of central and northern Asia Minor.

The Sources

As is inevitable with women from antiquity, the sources for the queens of the Augustan period are scattered and limited. In ancient historical writing, women were often presented only in connection with the men in their lives, which becomes an especially pernicious problem when the women are independent. This can also be a failing of modern scholarship. This bias not only compounds the difficulty of any scholarly analysis, but diminishes the importance of women in Hellenistic and Roman society, where they were more prominent than they had been at any time since the Bronze Age. Even though the literature on the queens is the usual available for the Augustan period, their traces can be faint. The most important Greek writers are Strabo of Amaseia, who had a close yet undefined relationship with Pythodoris and provided a contemporary account of her, and Josephus, whose history of the Herodian family preserves most of what is known about Salome and Glaphyra. The early life of Cleopatra Selene was documented by Plutarch in his biography of her father, Antonius; evidence of her later years is more scattered. Dynamis is best represented by inscriptions, coins, and the late Roman historian Dio. Material culture plays an important role, especially in the case of Cleopatra Selene, with extensive art and coinage preserved from her royal seat, Kaisareia in Mauretania. Pythodoris's Sebaste in Pontos and Salome's Askalon have visible remains; the former and perhaps the latter also struck their own coinage. Portrait sculpture seems to exist only for Cleopatra Selene, yet inscriptions are an important category of evidence for her, as well as for Dynamis, Glaphyra, and Pythodoris.

Personal and Geographical Names

The handling of proper names from antiquity remains a complex and often insoluble process. The Roman Empire was truly multilingual, with Latin and Greek the primary languages, and Roman officials were expected to be fluent in both and would also write in both, using different forms of their own names depending on the language. Toponyms were also subject to variants in several languages—often the indigenous name used by the locals is not even known—and the modern spelling depends on the survival of sources and what language they were written in, and sometimes even forms developed in post-antique literature. Common vernacular forms in use today for both place and personal names have also passed through the Latinization of medieval and modern times, and thus what is now most familiar may have been unrecognizable to the bearer of the name or the inhabitants of a locality. The orthography is most difficult in the Roman East, where indigenous languages, Greek, and Latin all competed.

With that in mind, Greek place and personal names generally have been directly transliterated, except in some cases (such as Athens, Alexander, and Cleopatra) where common English forms exist. Latin names are generally in the style best known in English (such as Pompey, Octavian, and Rome), except that Marcus Antonius is retained rather than the Mark Antony of Renaissance drama. Names that originated in a third language (e.g., Hebrew or Egyptian) are presented in the most familiar English form (often the Greek or Latin version).

1

Queens and Royal Women

In Greek antiquity, women were always an essential part of any monarchical system, but their status and roles in society varied with the era. The use of "queen" (Greek *basileia* or *basilissa*) to designate a title or office was not consistent, and both ancient and modern authors have employed the word casually without being cautious about its legal specifications. In fact, the word "queen" is more appropriate to medieval or early modern contexts, and far fewer women in the Greek world were queens than one might imagine. The modern word does not reflect all the nuances of Greek terminology, but if one is going to translate *basileia* and *basilissa*, it is perhaps the best equivalent.[1]

The Origins of the Basileia

The first woman to be called a *basileia* in Greek literature was Penelope, the wife of Odysseus. To Homer, the word had a limited meaning, and it is astonishing to realize that most of the famous women of the Trojan War era were not addressed by this title, despite their royal lineage. Homer did not use *basileia* to speak of Clytaemnestra, Helen, or Hecuba. To be sure, they were generically called "queens" in later literature, especially in drama,[2] but this is anachronistic, and the word does not appear in the *Iliad*, suggesting that it may not even have existed in earliest times. In fact, in the first Greek documents, the Linear B tablets of the Late Bronze Age, the masculine form *basileus* (*pa-si-re-u*) referred to a feudal lord, but there is no evidence of any feminine form.[3] Yet by the time of Homer, the term *basileus* had evolved to indicate somewhat greater status. Nevertheless, *basileia* is not documented until Homer used it to refer to Penelope. The word occurs seventeen times in the *Odyssey*, almost always in reference to her. The only other women so addressed were Tyro, due to her relationship with Poseidon, and Arete and her daughter Nausikaa, perhaps because within the context of the story their status was uncertain and Odysseus was being respectful and cautious.[4]

This suggests that from earliest times the term *basileia*, translated today as "queen," was a limiting one, used primarily to describe a unique and special woman—Penelope—who was different from the other royal women in the epic tradition. Granted, Penelope, like so many others, was the wife of a king (*basileus*), but it seems that this would not have been enough to gain her the title of queen, for surely Clytaemnestra would also have been so addressed. Yet Penelope was unique in that she managed the palace at Ithaka and the state that it represented (not only Ithaka but several nearby islands) effectively for twenty years while her husband was absent, not seeking any companion for her labors.[5] Other royal wives left behind during the Trojan War, such as Clytaemnestra and Aigialeia, the wife of Diomedes, found relationships that would normalize their status and aid them in meeting the economic and political requirements of their administration, probably a greater need than any personal satisfaction. Clytaemnestra's liaison with her husband's closest male relative, Aigisthos, hints at the proper course of action for a royal woman when the husband is gone for a lengthy period and in all probability will not return. Yet Penelope was different: she sought no male relative or associate of her husband for assistance in managing Ithaka. Among her many suitors there certainly would have been reasonable candidates, presumably including members of her husband's family; their moral failings were probably irrelevant. Yet despite serious difficulty, Penelope remained free of them and was considered heroic for doing so, and thus earned the office of *basileia*, in addition to any title bestowed by her marriage.

Homer treated Penelope eulogistically, giving further force to the concept of "queen." Her first appearance in the *Odyssey*, when she comes down from her suite to the main room of the palace on Ithaka, attended by two maids and with her face veiled, is an impressive entrance that sets the tone for her character.[6] Although in some ways she is unresponsive to the surrounding chaos, this provides her with a dignity rare in the Homeric poems. Yet her passivity was not to be dismissed and in fact was a source of strength, as she was immune to the pressures not only of the suitors—who had been around for years—but of her father and brothers, who had their own dynastic and political agenda for declaring Odysseus dead and ensuring Penelope's remarriage.[7] For her part, Penelope was not without ambivalence about her position, something that she made clear to the disguised Odysseus.[8] But her strength lay in her ability to devise stratagems that allowed her not only to retain her position but to bring the unresolved situation on Ithaka to an end. First, there was the matter of the unraveling of the tapestry, a difficult step for a weaver to take—destroying her own art—which continued for three years, until the trick was exposed by one of the maids.[9] But her second maneuver was more effective: she was the one who proposed the contest of the bow.[10] Although placed in a context of submission to the suitors and departure from Ithaka to accompany her new husband to his home, Penelope probably realized that the engaging stranger who had arrived at the palace was in fact Odysseus, and there was now an opportunity to dispose of the suitors and to return Ithaka to normalcy. Significantly, it was Penelope—not her husband or son—who had the authority to implement the contest.

Just as Penelope made her entrance slightly more than three hundred lines into the *Odyssey*, her last appearance was slightly more than three hundred lines from the end of the poem. To be sure, the situation is peculiar: the setting is Hades and it is the dead Agamemnon who is speaking, someone who had his own issues with his wife, the antithesis of Penelope. Clytaemnestra had "contrived evil deeds," but Penelope, according to Agamemnon, was someone whose

> distinction of her excellence will never perish, and the
> immortals will create for those on the earth a beautiful
> song about discreet Penelope.[11]

The rare adjective that Homer used, "discreet" (Greek *echephron*), was almost entirely limited to Penelope, demonstrating his ability to craft specific terminology to describe her, just as those around her addressed her by another unusual word, *basileia*. Little did Homer realize the truth of the words spoken by Agamemnon, and Penelope's eternal renown. She established a pattern for the ideal queen of the heroic era, something well remembered in later times, which included an ability to manage the state on her own or, at the very least, in close partnership with her husband. She was the first queen in the Greek world, and her reputation created the prototype for the royal women of the Hellenistic and Roman periods.

By the sixth century BC, royalty was largely (yet temporarily) obsolete within the Greek world, as monarchy gave way to more broadly based forms of government, and in the following century its terminology was either anachronistic—referring to the heroic era—or essentially reserved for foreign states. But *basileia* retained its sense of an unusual royal woman of significant independence: of the three mentioned by Herodotos in his *Histories*, written in the fifth century BC, all were foreigners and from earlier eras.[12] Two seem to have been ruling alone (Nitokris of Babylon and Tomyris of the Massagetai), and the third, the wife of Kandaules of Lydia, has no preserved name but was clearly a woman of power and fortitude: her title and role as queen even transcended her own name. All three had had husbands but were presented by Herodotos as acting independently of them, either because they were no longer around or due to the nature of their relationship.

When Herodotos wrote, few Greek states had a monarchy, and the system and its associated royalty existed either among foreigners, at Sparta, or at the fringes of the Greek world, such as in Macedonia. Needless to say, the memory of monarchy was always part of the Greek self-conception, but in the fifth century BC royalty had little immediate relevance, and its terminology, such as the word *basileia*, faded from contemporary usage except to refer to a past or distant world. In fact, the idea of powerful women exercising authority became anathema to Greek political theorists. Aristotle in the fourth century BC developed the concept of *gynaikokratia*, or "rule by women," a situation in which there was too much power in the hands of women, resulting in political and economic decline, the very antithesis of the stability once exercised by royal women. Although the word may have originated in comedy—it is the title of at least two plays of Aristotle's time—he was totally serious in pointing out the pernicious effects of rule by women. The term may first have been applied to the Amazons, but it came to be essentially a pejorative word used to describe specific women who were seen to have exceeded the accepted limits of power, thus suborning men. Eventually the most notorious example would be Cleopatra VII.[13]

Despite the misogyny apparent in Greek political theory of the fourth century BC, the Greek world was beginning to change in a way that would create more favorable conditions for women of power, especially royal women. The impetus seems to have come not from within the Greek environment, but from the world to its east, the Persian Empire, where royal women had always had a certain authority, best demonstrated by Atossa, the wife of Dareios I and the mother of Xerxes, so vividly depicted in Aeschylus's *Persians*.

Northern Anatolia, which had been under Persian control since the sixth century BC but also had a strong Greek heritage, was an early region of prominent royal women. As always, the sources are scattered and one can obtain only glimpses of several women who achieved political prominence. This was the land of the Amazons, who were known to the Greek world as early as the time of Homer: they were warrior women from somewhere to the east, a strange mixture of myth and history. They were allegedly the inventors of horsemanship and were said to have swept west across northern Anatolia and into the Ionian Greek world, founding cities there.[14] In the time of Alexander the Great, they remained a potent cultural force: he was said to have had a relationship with the Amazon queen Thalestris.[15] Thus even in the Hellenistic period the memory of the Amazons was strong, and it is perhaps no coincidence that the territory associated with them produced an unusual number of prominent royal women in Classical and Hellenistic times.

When the Persians took over Anatolia in the sixth century BC, they divided it into a number of satrapies. The satraps were regional officials, usually members of the royal family or people favored by it. Needless to say, most of them were men. Yet an exception was Mania, who lived in the late fifth century BC and who has been ignored by many modern historians.[16] She was from the ancient city of Dardanos, at the mouth of the Hellespont. Her husband, Zenis, was the local satrap and controlled the coastal regions extending into the northern Troad, as well as some of the mountainous hinterland. He was under the supervision of Pharnabazos, the regional Persian official, who was stationed at Daskyleion, to the east. Yet Zenis acted as a virtually independent ruler, having amassed a large treasure that he kept hidden in fortresses on the slopes of Mt. Ida. When he died, Mania went to Daskyleion with a large retinue and presents, and requested that she be named successor to her husband, stressing the couple's loyalty. Pharnabazos, who was planning to appoint another man to the position, was convinced and confirmed her as satrap.

She created a military force of Greek mercenaries and expanded her territory to the south into the central and southern Troad, including the district of Troy itself; at her peak she controlled a region from the Hellespont to the Gulf of Adramyttion and into the interior uplands, perhaps the largest territory as yet ruled by a woman within the Mediterranean world. She accompanied her troops in battle, commanding her forces and providing tactical advice; it was said that she was never defeated. She also served as an adviser to Pharnabazos and joined him on campaigns to the interior of Anatolia, where there was increasing instability, since the western Persian Empire was beginning to deteriorate.

How long she maintained her position is unknown; the implication is that it was for quite some time. She had two children: a son, and a daughter who married a certain Meidias. By 399 BC he had become the focal point for opposition to rule by a woman, and he had both Mania and her son killed. This was not well received by either the locals or Pharnabazos, and even though Meidias assumed Mania's position, his rule was never stable. He attempted to reach out to the Spartans, who were already encroaching into Persian territory in the aftermath of the Peloponnesian War. Yet before long he lost both his territory and its hidden wealth to them, whereupon he vanished from the historical record. Nevertheless, his mother-in-law, Mania, remains a harbinger of the royal women of the Augustan period. She took advantage of increasing Persian weakness and became perhaps the first woman in antiquity actually to build on her inheritance and create her own state.

At the same time that Mania was ruling in the Troad, the city of Pergamon, just a short distance to the south, was under the control of a woman dynast, Hellas. In the year that Meidias was in the process of losing his own territories, the Greek adventurer and scholar Xenophon passed through the Troad (without, seemingly, any contact with Mania or Meidias) and ended up at Pergamon.[17] The city had long been ruled by the family of Gongylos of Eretria, who had been given the territory by Xerxes in return for services in the Persian War. When Xenophon arrived in 399 BC, Pergamon was under the control of Hellas, the wife of the most recent Gongylos (who was probably dead). She received Xenophon hospitably and suggested that he become involved in local guerrilla activity against the Persians, which he did. Yet Hellas's son, another Gongylos, soon opposed his mother and sent a force against the Greeks. A certain Prokles, a local ruler from a few miles southwest of Pergamon, did the same. Thus the conflict turned into a messy four-way struggle, representing local power dynamics more than any opposition against the Persians, and Xenophon and his men wisely and promptly withdrew to the south, leaving the chaos to the remaining forces.

This is all that is known about Hellas of Pergamon, but the situation seems a parallel to what was happening in the Troad: a woman rose to prominence upon the death of her husband and attempted to take advantage of the weakening Persian Empire, but met resistance from those around her and within her own family. Hellas's son Gongylos was not accommodated to her rule and opposed her authority. Yet the ultimate fate of the participants, unlike that of Mania and Meidias, is unknown.

The Hekatomnids in Karia

In the early fourth century BC, the Hekatomnid dynasty rose to power in Karia, becoming the most notable pre-Hellenistic state with prominent royal women. During its flourishing years, the capital of the dynasty was at Halikarnassos in southwestern Anatolia, an ancient city with a mixed Greek and indigenous population. The Hekatomnids attained cultural brilliance for less than a century, but at a level that looked ahead to many of the dynamics of Hellenistic royalty and the Roman imperial aristocracy. In fact, Halikarnassos had already produced the most famous royal woman of the early Classical period, Artemisia, who commanded a squadron at the Battle of Salamis in 480 BC and was part of the inner council of the Persian king Xerxes, persuading him, not without self-interest, to withdraw from the Greek world.[18] Herodotos, a compatriot and perhaps a relative, was effusive in his praise of her, possibly to the point of exaggeration, but nevertheless the brief notices of her career demonstrate a striking personality. She had become ruler of Halikarnassos after the death of her husband, Lygdamis. Her legal status is uncertain: Herodotos merely wrote that she "held his sovereignty." Knowledge of her career is limited to the few years of the Persian War era, but she was distinguished enough that the Spartans erected a statue of her in their agora. Later sources speak of her as "queen," which is probably anachronistic in this era of Persian power, but nevertheless she was the first major role model since the Trojan War for the royal women of the Hellenistic and Roman periods.[19]

Approximately a century later, Karia and Halikarnassos reached their peak under the Hekatomnids, who may have been descended from Artemisia.[20] Hekatomnos, from Mylasa, northeast of Halikarnassos, was the local Persian satrap, who contemplated declaring himself independent. He was unable to do this before his death, around 377 BC, but his five children, all of whom ruled, did adopt a posture separate from the deteriorating Persian Empire. The first were Mausolos and a second Artemisia, brother and sister and married to one another, the prototype for the later practice of sibling marriage among the Ptolemies.[21] Again, their legal status is not certain; although sources speak of him as king, this would have been unlikely as well as provocative, and he probably continued to call himself a satrap. Whatever title Artemisia had, if any, is unknown.

When Mausolos died in 353 BC, Artemisia became sole ruler. She may have inherited the title of satrap: Mania, half a century previously, provided a precedent for a woman satrap.[22] Artemisia commissioned her husband's tomb, the Mausoleion, which became one of the Seven Wonders of the World and produced the word "mausoleum."[23] Its dynastic portraits are among the earliest of that genre, and these and its impressive frieze sculpture—now visible in the British Museum— constitute a major innovation in Greek sculptural tradition. It was probably also the first important work of art in the Greek world sponsored by a woman.[24] Artemisia also won the grudging respect of her contemporary, the Athenian orator Demosthenes, and, like her famous predecessor of the same name, commanded a fleet in battle, when the Rhodians, unfortunately, believed that because a woman ruled, they could attack Halikarnassos with impunity. The result was that Rhodes itself ended up being captured by Artemisia.[25] She died two years after her husband, and the rule passed to their two siblings, Idrieus and Ada, also married to one another. As before, husband predeceased wife, but in time Ada was deposed, probably by the remaining child of Hekatomnos, Pixodaros, only to be restored when Alexander the Great passed through the region a few years later.[26] Yet the dynasty soon seems to have become extinct.

The short but brilliant Hekatomnid era foreshadowed many of the characteristics of royal women of the Hellenistic and Roman worlds. The younger Artemisia and Ada successively ruled jointly with their husbands and then alone, although while the husband was alive his position remained dominant. Nevertheless, the status of these women was more elevated than that of women at any time in the Greek world since the Trojan War: the ability of Alexander to restore Ada without major incident is solid documentation that the Karians had an unparalleled sympathy for women rulers. The public profile of the five Hekatomnid siblings looks forward to the role of Hellenistic royalty, with the construction of the Mausoleion (and other building projects) and the general patronage of the arts. To be sure, the contemporary rise of the Macedonians helped legitimize monarchy, especially through the personality and reputation of Alexander the Great, but they do not seem to have supported the same role for women as the Hekatomnids did. The only important Macedonian woman of the mid-fourth century BC was Olympias, the wife of Philip II and the mother of Alexander, a problematic example at best since she owed her prominence largely to a power vacuum existing after her son's death rather than to any recognized skills.[27] Of the successor kingdoms, only that of the Ptolemies—who were most like the Hekatomnids—consistently elevated the status of women, and it is among them that the concept of the royal woman as practiced in the era of Augustus came into existence.

The Basilissa

In the fourth century BC, a new word appeared in the Greek language, *basilissa*, a feminine variant of the word for "king" (*basileus*). It is generally translated today as "queen," but again inadequately, given the complex subtleties of Hellenistic royalty.[28] Like *gynaikokratia*, it may have had its origins in comedy, yet the earliest description of the term was by Xenophon, in his dialogue *Oikonomikos*, a treatise on estate management.[29] A certain Ischomachos told Socrates that his wife was the *basilissa* of the household, managing the servants like a commander inspecting his troops. This may have had vaguely comic overtones, and Ischomachos was hardly enlightened in his treatment of his wife, whom he compared to the queen bee, always staying in the hive. Yet his point of view suggests that *basilissa* could have originated in household terminology, but by the end of the fourth century BC it had evolved into a royal title.

In the last decade of that century, certain of the successors of Alexander began using the title "king" (*basileus*). The first was probably

Antigonos I Monopthalmos, in 306 or 305 BC, almost immediately followed by his son Demetrios Poliorketes.[30] Two other successors, Lysimachos and Ptolemy I, soon assumed it, and by the end of the century all the prominent leaders of the era who had been associated with Alexander were calling themselves kings. The circumstances under which Antigonos and Demetrios took the title suggest that its original purpose—beyond that of imitating Alexander and his father, Philip II— was commemorative and competitive: they had just defeated Ptolemy and, assisted by spontaneous acclamations on the part of their followers, immediately began calling themselves kings. Ptolemy's response was to assume the title himself. By the beginning of the third century BC, as the eastern Mediterranean resolved itself into three major kingdoms (Macedonian, Seleukid, and Ptolemaic), kingship was the normal form of government.

Yet the status of royal women also needed to be regularized. Rather than use the Homeric word *basileia*, royal women began calling themselves by the new term *basilissa*. Exactly how this word came to refer to a royal woman remains obscure. *Basilissa* as a royal title is first documented at the very beginning of 305 BC—at the time of the adoption of *basileus*—and, significantly, by Phila, the wife of Demetrios Poliorketes, who had just become the second successor of Alexander to call himself "king." She was the daughter of the longtime adviser to Philip II and Alexander, Antipatros, who was left in charge of Macedonia during the Eastern expedition. Phila had married Demetrios around 320 BC and remained his wife until her death at the end of the century.[31] Like Penelope, she was an exceptional person in difficult times, and it is fitting that she seems to have been the first Hellenistic royal woman to be called "queen," documented in two decrees of 305/4 BC, one from Samos and the other from Ephesos, which honor members of the entourage of *Basilissa* Phila.[32]

Another early user of the title *basilissa* was Amastris, the niece of Dareios III, the last king of Persia.[33] She was a transitional figure from the Persian to the Hellenistic era, who was captured by the forces of Alexander at Damascus in 333 BC and joined his expedition. She was married to several prominent successors of Alexander, including Lysimachos as well as Dionysios of Herakleia Pontika on the coast of the Black Sea. He died around 306 BC and she became ruler of the city, perhaps merely as regent for her sons. In time, however, she established her own city, Amastris (modern Amasra), about sixty miles east of Herakleia on the coast. This was a rare and perhaps the earliest example of a city founded by a woman. She seems to have made Amastris her royal residence and lived there for a decade or more, presumably leaving Herakleia to her sons. At Amastris she issued coins with the legend "*Basilissa* Amastris."[34] Significantly, these did not include her portrait, perhaps an indication that her title was tentative. Her fate was typical of royal women of the era: she was assassinated (through drowning) by her sons, perhaps around 284 BC. The sons were promptly executed by her former husband Lysimachos, who was the overall ruler of the region. Amastris may have been the first independent ruler to use the title *basilissa*. Within a few years Seleukid and Ptolemaic women also assumed the title, which became standard for royal women at the highest level throughout the Hellenistic period and into Roman times.

Royal Women in Early Hellenistic Egypt

When Ptolemy I assumed the title of king in 305 BC and began to rule from his new city of Alexandria, west of the Kanobic mouth of the Nile, he inaugurated a kingdom and dynasty that would last until the death of his direct descendant, Cleopatra VII, eight generations and 275 years later. At its territorial peak the Ptolemaic Empire included not only Egypt, with lands up the Nile as far as the First Cataract, but also the Cyrenaica (modern Libya) to the west, Cyprus, and much of the Levant and the Anatolian coast, including a number of the Greek islands. It would be the most stable and longest surviving of the Hellenistic kingdoms, and an early ally of the Roman presence in the eastern Mediterranean, which, ironically, would ultimately lead to its downfall. And it was within this kingdom that the concept of Hellenistic royal women and queens would reach its most developed form.[35]

The precedents for the role of Hellenistic queens were varied. Even though the term *basilissa* originated in estate management, this does not address the institution as it affected royalty in Hellenistic times. Since the Ptolemaic dynasty (and the other successor states) were Macedonian in origin, one might seek the royal use of the term there, but there are no meaningful examples. Alexander the Great was the primary model of Hellenistic kingship, yet the women around him were hardly viable candidates for queenship, and there is no evidence that the term *basilissa* or *basileia* existed in Macedonia at that time. Alexander's mother,

Olympias, owed her prestige, such as it was, to that of her husband and son, and her life after Alexander's death was turbulent and brief. Alexander's wife, Rhoxane, was a foreigner—from far-off Baktria—and although she gained a certain status for bearing his son, Alexander IV, she was never a major player in the few years that she survived after her husband's death, becoming little more than a pawn in the manipulations of the successors. Both Olympias and Rhoxane exemplified the inability of royal women to exercise significant power.

Better models were provided by Penelope, and also the women of Sparta, who at times had an independence rare in the traditional Greek world, with personal wealth and landownership.[36] Ironically, this elevated position of Spartan women—who owned 40 percent of the land—was believed by some Greeks to have contributed to the decline of that state.[37] Nevertheless, despite objections by Aristotle and others, Spartan women certainly held power and were probably an influence on later royal women. Yet the best prototypes came from the fringes of the late Persian Empire, especially the Hekatomnid dynasty of Karia, whose women embodied most of the characteristics of Hellenistic royalty and, moreover, in the case of Ada, had a direct connection with Alexander the Great.

During the 275 years of the Ptolemaic dynasty there was an extraordinary series of prominent royal women, from Berenike I to Cleopatra VII; these women came to epitomize the office, and their legacy survived—after the Ptolemaic state had ceased to exist—in queens such as Cleopatra Selene and Pythodoris. Ptolemaic queens had extensive personal wealth, endowed building programs, and had cities named after them. They used their resources to create armies and fleets, which they commanded in battle. Their wealth came largely from land and the income that it produced. They were educated and wrote scholarly treatises, were commemorated in literature and art, and participated in athletic contests. At times they were even addressed as "king." Like their Hekatomnid predecessors, they were often involved in and the product of sibling marriages.[38] They were important patrons of cults and became cultic figures themselves: the cult of Cleopatra VII, at least, lasted for hundreds of years after her death.[39] All these practices and attributes were also characteristics of the royal women of the Augustan period, with the exception of sibling marriage, which had essentially died out among royalty by the middle of the first century BC.[40]

The earliest Ptolemaic royal woman of note was Berenike I, a Macedonian who was the grand-niece of Antipatros, the adviser to

Philip II who controlled Macedonia while Alexander was in the east. After an early marriage to an obscure Philip, she came to Alexandria, probably around 320 BC, with her cousin Eurydike, Antipatros's daughter, who married Ptolemy I.[41] Before long Ptolemy and Berenike had established a relationship, and in time Berenike became Ptolemy's wife and the mother of Ptolemy II and Arsinoë II, as well as other children. She survived into the early 270s BC.

Berenike was a woman of unusual ability. Pyrrhos of Molossia and Epeiros, not yet famous for invading Italy, visited Egypt around 300 BC and was especially taken with Berenike, noticing her great influence at the royal court: he said that she was "the foremost in excellence and wisdom," terminology with a Homeric tone and remindful of Arete at the Phaiakian court. Pyrrhos married one of Berenike's daughters, Antigone, child of the obscure Philip.[42]

One of the more interesting aspects of Berenike's career was her sponsorship of chariot racing and a personal Olympic victory, probably in 284 BC. Male royalty had long been involved in Olympic racing, but Berenike seems to have been the first Macedonian woman to participate, even breeding her own horses. There had been a precedent at Sparta, where, in the fourth century BC, Kyniska, the daughter of King Archidamos II, had bred horses and had also won an Olympic victory.[43]

When Berenike died, or perhaps a short time before, she received cultic honors, according to the court poet Theokritos, who commemorated her as part of a festival in her honor sponsored by her daughter Arsinoë II, when the goddess Aphrodite deified her. At some time, a cultic building was constructed in Alexandria, the Berenikeion; it was in existence by 275/4 BC, since it was mentioned in the context of a festival procession that her son Ptolemy II held that year, and was perhaps one of the "temples fragrant with incense" that he built in honor of his parents. Nothing is known about the structure or its location.[44] By 270 BC, or perhaps as early as the time of the festival, Berenike and Ptolemy I were worshipped as the Savior Gods (*Theoi Sotera*), a role commemorated at Savior Harbor (perhaps modern Port Sudan) on the Red Sea.[45] In time, the cultic and divine aspects of queens would not only be attributed to them after their death: Cleopatra VII always appeared at state functions dressed as Isis.[46]

Further topographical honoring of Berenike was at Berenike Trogodytike, located at modern Medinet el-Haras, also on the Red Sea. It was the port for eastern trade and a flourishing cosmopolitan city that lasted into late Roman times.[47] Farther down the coast, at a location unknown today, was another Berenike.[48] Recognition of the queen was also reflected on the coinage of her children Ptolemy II and Arsinoë II, which showed their mother along with her husband, Ptolemy I, the first example of Ptolemaic coinage showing a king and queen as a joined pair.[49]

It is clear that Berenike I, although not Ptolemaic in origin, had many of the characteristics that would become commonplace among her female descendants: a strong personality, involvement in the operation of the royal court, participation in athletics, the founding of cities in her name, and deification and cultic worship. Much of her commemoration was not implemented by her or even her husband, but her children, indicative of her role as a transitional figure when the processes of Ptolemaic royalty were not yet fully formed. Within a few years of her death, however, she had attained the proper status of a Ptolemaic royal woman, and her daughter Arsinoë II carried this to its fulfillment.

Later Ptolemaic Queens

The descendants of Berenike I included all the remaining Ptolemaic kings, almost all the queens, and rulers in the Cyrenaica, Cyprus, and Mauretania. Most of the characteristics, offices, cults, and qualities of Hellenistic royal women were established by her. Her daughter Arsinoë II became the most important queen of the early years of the dynasty. She was the first Ptolemy to be involved in the institution of royal incest, which has received much comment in both ancient and modern times but was no longer a feature in the life of royal women by the Augustan period.[50] The son of her marriage, Ptolemy III, reached outside his immediate family for a spouse, marrying his cousin Berenike II (a great-niece of Berenike I), but not until she had disposed of an earlier candidate, Demetrios, the son of Demetrios Poliorketes, when he was caught in her mother's bed, a fine example of a future Ptolemaic queen taking her destiny into her own hands. Yet in the long run Berenike II could not withstand the growing intrigues of the Ptolemaic court and was assassinated in 221 BC as part of the accession struggles of her son Ptolemy IV.[51] Her most enduring legacy resulted from her dedication of a lock of her hair to Aphrodite upon her husband's safe return from the Third Syrian War in 243 BC. When the lock disappeared, two members of the court, the astronomer Konon and the poet Kallimachos, deftly reported that it had been removed to the heavens, where it is still visible as the Coma Berenices.[52]

So far, no Ptolemaic queen had ruled independently. Although Berenike I, Arsinoë II, and Berenike II were, in their own way, women of power and authority, they were always subordinate to their husbands or, at best, joint rulers, never holding any regal power apart from them. It was only from the second century BC that queens ruled alone or exercised a role superior to that of the males in their family. The change occurred after Cleopatra I married Ptolemy V in the winter of 194/3 BC. Ptolemy was the grandson of Berenike II, and Cleopatra the daughter of the Seleukid king Antiochos III; their marriage alliance brought to an end the Fifth Syrian War, which had been ongoing between the two kingdoms for several years.[53] Thus all successive Ptolemaic rulers would also be Seleukid descendants, and, as a harbinger of the future, the Romans were involved in the settlement.

Cleopatra I brought new blood into the Ptolemies, and also a new name, the most famous in Hellenistic royalty. "Berenike" and "Arsinoë" would continue to be names for Ptolemaic women, but neither had the distinction of "Cleopatra." "Berenike" seems to have been an indigenous Macedonian name, and "Arsinoë" had some obscure mythological authority (most notably as the nurse of Orestes). But the original Cleopatra was the wife of Meleagros, of Kalydonian Boar Hunt fame, mentioned by Homer. In a later era and perhaps more important, another Cleopatra was the sister of Alexander the Great. It was a name that would endure to the end of the Ptolemaic dynasty and beyond.[54]

From the time of Cleopatra I (ruled 193-176 BC), Ptolemaic queens began on occasion to exercise power alone or to be recognized as legally superior to their husbands or male children. There are no obvious precedents for these changes, although one could certainly look back to Penelope—who held sovereignty for many years in the absence of her husband—as well as the Hekatomnids. There were also examples of ruling women within indigenous Egyptian history, such as Hatshepsut in the early fifteenth century BC and Thuoris three centuries later, but their influence is problematic, since the Ptolemies (except for Cleopatra VII) were notorious for not learning the Egyptian language.[55] Yet it is most likely that the new authority of the queens was due to the turbulent times of the second century BC, with repeated wars against the Seleukids, loss of territory, the rise of Rome and its increased involvement in

Ptolemaic affairs, and intense rivalries within the dynasty itself, all of which allowed royal women to provide a greater continuity than their husbands, especially if the husband were dead and the heir-apparent still a child.[56] By the end of the dynasty, queens ruled without husbands.

The marriage of Cleopatra I and Ptolemy V produced three children, Ptolemy VI, Cleopatra II, and Ptolemy VIII.[57] In 180 BC Ptolemy V, who had presided over a steady loss of Ptolemaic territory, was attempting to reach out to the Greek world and was about to receive an embassy from the Achaian Federation when he was killed under mysterious circumstances.[58] The eldest child of the royal couple, Ptolemy VI, perhaps no more than six years of age, succeeded to the throne, yet his mother, Cleopatra I, not only was established as regent but assumed some of the royal titles as king. Papyri list her name before that of her son,[59] and she issued her own coins, which show her as Isis and have the legend "*Basilisses* Kleopatras" (of *Basilissa* Kleopatra); her son (Ptolemaiou *Basileos*) is named on the reverse but not pictured. These were minted in the Ptolemaic territories of Cyprus and the Cyrenaica as well as Egypt, so were distributed throughout the empire.[60]

It is possible that Cleopatra's status as the daughter of the greatest of Seleukid kings, Antiochos III, helped implement her enhanced role. She immediately embarked upon a change in Ptolemaic policy, ending preparations for yet another war between the two powers—one of her brothers, Seleukos IV, was the Seleukid king—and enacting a program of reconciliation. Yet in little more than three years—by the summer of 176 BC—she was dead, not even having reached the age of thirty. Her death seems to have been natural, if convenient, and the bright promise that she represented was lost as Egypt descended into chaos. Her son Ptolemy VI was only about ten years of age and fell under the influence of new regents from the palace household who had no royal status and reversed the late queen's policies.[61]

Titles similar to those held by Cleopatra I appear for her daughter, Cleopatra II, who married her brothers, first Ptolemy VI and then Ptolemy VIII.[62] The three siblings were always contending for power, and at times Cleopatra II was listed on papyri as sole ruler. In 131 BC she succeeded in driving Ptolemy VIII from Alexandria (Ptolemy VI had died in 145 BC) and seems to have ruled alone, under the title "Cleopatra the Mother-Loving Savior," until he returned a few years later. Eventually, Ptolemy VIII, still married to Cleopatra II, also married her daughter and his niece, Cleopatra III, who was also the daughter of Ptolemy VI: one can only speculate about the dynamics of a royal household in which mother and daughter were simultaneously married to the same man, who was also brother and uncle. Ptolemy VIII died in 116 BC and Cleopatra II a few months later, with the result that Cleopatra III became sole ruler, despite her two male children (the future Ptolemy IX and Ptolemy X). Virtual civil war within the dynasty continued, but Cleopatra III held the supreme royal power. One of her major accomplishments was to implement trade with India.[63]

There is no doubt that the unstable conditions of the last century of the Ptolemaic dynasty contributed to the ability of women to take power and become the dominant rulers, officially considered ahead of their spouses or sons. In the first century BC, Ptolemaic women began ruling alone with no partner: the earliest example is Cleopatra Berenike III, the daughter of Ptolemy IX and Cleopatra IV. She was sole ruler, probably in 81 or 80 BC, after both her father and her husband (Ptolemy X) had died. This lasted for a few months until her stepson Ptolemy XI became her husband and joint ruler, an arrangement implemented by the Romans in another example of their interference in Ptolemaic dynastic relationships. The arrangement did not please Ptolemy XI—he was now married to his stepmother, who was perhaps twenty years older than he was—and thus he murdered her within a month. Alexandrian popular opinion of this was far from favorable, and he was immediately abducted by a mob and killed in the local gymnasium.[64] The brief rule of Cleopatra Berenike III was an expedient forced by the chaotic politics of the era, but it did demonstrate that sole rule by a woman was possible, albeit under unusual circumstances, and that the people of Alexandria were perfectly accepting of this, and indeed would react violently at any attempt to destroy the arrangement.

Ptolemy XII, the son of Ptolemy IX and an unknown mother, became king after the violent events of 80 BC. Unlike Cleopatra Berenike III, he was not well liked in Egypt, and his questionable financial policies and closeness to the Romans brought about his flight to Rome in 58 BC.[65] Upon his departure, the throne was claimed by his sister-wife Cleopatra VI Tryphaina and their daughter Berenike IV, who may have held power jointly for a brief period, perhaps the earliest example of rule shared by two women. Cleopatra VI soon disappeared from the historical record, leaving the unmarried Berenike IV as sole ruler, with no connections to a male relative, the first Ptolemaic queen to rule under those circumstances for an extended period.[66]

Yet there was a sense that she needed a husband, and attempts were made to find one; after three failures, the successful candidate, put forth by the Romans, was a certain Archelaos (II), who was priest at Komana in Pontos (an office with royal privileges).[67] Nevertheless, he appeared only after Berenike had ruled alone for perhaps as long as two years. One could claim that this was actually a regency, since her father the king was still alive, living in Rome, but the fact remains that no Ptolemaic woman had ever held such an independent status.

Yet it was not to last, and with Roman support Ptolemy XII was restored in the spring of 55 BC. One of his first acts was to kill his daughter and her husband, which, ironically, was a demonstration of her power.[68] A member of the Roman expedition was twenty-eight-year-old Marcus Antonius (fig. 1), who met Berenike's fourteen-year-old sister, Cleopatra VII, for the first time and thus began his international career in the very city in which he would end it twenty-five years later.

In early 51 BC Ptolemy XII died. He left four children; only the eldest, Cleopatra VII, who had just turned eighteen, was an adult. The remaining three, Ptolemy XIII, Ptolemy XIV, and Arsinoë IV, were all eleven or younger.[69] It was natural that rule should devolve on Cleopatra, and by now there were enough precedents for a woman ruler that this was, in theory, no problem. Yet acceptance of her reign was not without difficulty—there was opposition within the royal court—and it was not until 47 BC, and with the personal assistance of Julius Caesar, that Cleopatra was able to claim sole rule, her brothers having been eliminated and her sister in exile.

The seventeen years during which Cleopatra VII was sole ruler of Egypt, the last of the Ptolemies to rule that territory, are well known and need not be recounted here. Suffice it to say that even though she presided over a dying empire and indeed brought it to its end, her brilliant reign was the culmination of all the characteristics of Hellenistic and Ptolemaic queenship that had been evolving since the days of the second Artemisia of Halikarnassos. Not only did she rule alone for longer than any previous queen in the Greek tradition, she was a well-educated linguist who spoke a dozen languages, a published author, and a naval commander. She was a skilled administrator and diplomat who strove valiantly to save her kingdom. Deeply concerned about who would rule after her, she chose her partners carefully in order to produce, by the standards of the era, the best possible heirs. She was an expert horsewoman and hunter, a patron of scholarship and

FIG. 1. Portrait of Marcus Antonius in green basalt. Kingston Lacey, Dorset.
Photo © National Trust/Simon Harris.

the arts, a royal builder, and a city founder. She continued the cultic responsibilities of her predecessors (especially devoted to Isis), was honored throughout the eastern Mediterranean and in Rome, and was the inspiration for petty dynasts on the fringes of her possessions. She brought the Ptolemaic territory to its largest extent in more than a century. Futile and failed attempts to save her kingdom from the Romans resulted in her suicide in 30 BC, but she remained a role model for centuries after her death. Her descendants, most notably her daughter, Cleopatra Selene, ruled elsewhere for two generations, and she was an inspiration to royal women for centuries after her death.

2

Cleopatra's Daughter

By the summer of 41 BC, having disposed of the primary assassins of Julius Caesar, Marcus Antonius had established his headquarters at Tarsos, at the northeast corner of the Mediterranean, an ancient Assyrian trading colony that had become a multicultural intellectual center. He met with various Roman officials and regional dynasts, but Cleopatra VII of Egypt ignored his many letters summoning her to appear.[1] Her position was fragile enough that she was reluctant to leave her kingdom, and, moreover, as a queen she was not impressed by the status of a mere Roman magistrate, even though the two had met previously in both Alexandria and Rome. But in time she decided that Antonius could be of use to her, realizing that the support of the most powerful Roman of the era would be valuable at home: the Romans had been providing military and political assistance to the Ptolemies since the days of her father.

In events that are well known not only from ancient history but through the versions popularized in later art and drama, Cleopatra sailed in her state boat up the Kydnos River to Tarsos. Whatever political issues she and the triumvir settled that summer, the relationship soon became personal, and Antonius was invited to Alexandria for a winter visit.[2] He stayed until the spring of 40 BC; by summer, when he had returned to Rome, Cleopatra had given birth to twins.

The Childhood of Cleopatra Selene

The twins are not mentioned in extant literature until three years later, when Cleopatra and Antonius met again.[3] At this

MAP 2. Mauretania at the time of the allied monarchy.

time—if not previously—they were given the names Cleopatra Selene and Alexander Helios, which reflect the dynastic thoughts of at least their mother. Antonius's motivations during the last decade of his life are often inscrutable, but Cleopatra had to think about the survival of her kingdom and royal line. The girl's name honored not only her mother but her Ptolemaic and Seleukid heritage: her ancestry included the Ptolemaic monarchs back to Ptolemy I, and she was also a direct descendant of the Seleukid princess Cleopatra I, who had married Ptolemy V in the early second century BC. The boy's name was more direct: it had been given in memory of Alexander himself. Moreover, no one would forget that Alexander the Great's sister was Cleopatra.

But the surnames of the children were more significant and symbolic. In naming them after the Sun and the Moon, Cleopatra VII gave them prophetic status that was a recognized part of contemporary thought in both Egypt and Rome, perhaps best expressed in Vergil's Fourth Eclogue, with its talk of a glorious new age inaugurated by the birth of a child.[4] By allegorically linking Rome and Egypt, as well as mythology and the present, and centering it all on Alexander the Great, she positioned the twins to begin the new golden age which would end the historic conflict between West and East that went back to the Trojan War.[5]

As is normally the case with women in antiquity, the life of Cleopatra Selene is difficult to fill out, and citations of her in the literature inevitably reflect her association with the men around her. This results in long gaps in the outline of her career, but nevertheless it is clear that she fulfilled the traditional role that one would expect from a women of Ptolemaic ancestry. Little did she know in her childhood that she would end up queen of one of the more remote territories of the Mediterranean, an important transitional figure between the Hellenistic royal world and that of the Romans.[6]

After Antonius acknowledged his paternity and approved her name (as well as that of her brother), Cleopatra Selene is not visible again in the sources until 34 BC, when she was a participant in what is today known as the Donations of Alexandria, a collective term for a series of processes in which Antonius, using his authority as triumvir of the Roman Republic, reorganized the eastern Mediterranean in favor of Cleopatra VII and her offspring. In addition to the twins, the queen had two other children: Kaisarion, the heir apparent, born in the summer of 47 BC and generally (if not universally) agreed to be the son of Julius Caesar, and Ptolemy Philadelphos, Antonius's third child with her, born in 36 BC, whose name reflected further dynastic aspirations.[7] The Donations of Alexandria took place between 36 and 34 BC, especially at a ceremony in the Gymnasion of Alexandria in the latter year. Accounts of the ceremony are confused and contradictory, and the chronology of the various territorial donations is not clear.[8] Yet according to Dio—and his statement was explicit—Cleopatra Selene received the Cyrenaica (essentially coastal modern Libya). He also implied that she might have obtained part or all of Crete. The Cyrenaica had regularly been Ptolemaic territory—or ruled by dynasts related to the Ptolemies—but the last king of the region, Ptolemy Apion, a son of Ptolemy VIII, had willed the territory to Rome in 96 BC,[9] and Cleopatra VII presumably believed that making her daughter queen was merely the normalization of an anomalous situation that had existed for the previous half century. In Rome, however, Antonius's fellow triumvir Octavian thought otherwise, and the Donations of Alexandria—publicized as giving away Roman territory to a foreign ruler and, moreover, to a woman—marked the beginning of the rapid decline of the fortunes of Cleopatra VII and Antonius.

Cleopatra Selene's relationship with Crete is only vaguely cited. The Ptolemies' interest in the island was limited to establishing a naval base at Itanos in the northeast corner, which existed from the 260s BC until abandoned by Ptolemy VIII shortly after 145 BC. The island as a whole became a Roman province in 67 BC.[10] Exactly what role Cleopatra Selene played in the organization of Crete after 34 BC is unexplained, and there is no evidence that it was anything beyond a legal fiction.

Although it is unlikely that six-year-old Cleopatra Selene had any involvement in the administration of her royal territories, there was some attempt to reestablish a Ptolemaic presence in the Cyrenaica. Coins depicting a crocodile—the visual symbol of Egypt—were minted at this time by a certain Crassus, whose exact identity is unknown but who was perhaps P. Canidius Crassus, an important member of the circle around Cleopatra VII and Antonius; he may have been the theoretical royal governor.[11] But it is probable that the existing Roman administration remained in place for the short time left to Cleopatra VII and the Ptolemaic dynasty. Nevertheless, the appropriation of the Cyrenaica was serious enough to Octavian that later he made special note of his recovery of the territory.[12] And it is probable that Cleopatra Selene believed for the rest of her life that she retained her royal title as queen of the region, even though it effectively ended with the Roman acquisition of Egypt in August 30 BC.

Little else is known about her fortunes before the collapse of Ptolemaic Egypt. She may have been too young to benefit from the royal tutors in Alexandria, the most distinguished being Nikolaos of Damascus, who would have a long later career as the ambassador to Rome of Herod the Great and who was a notable scholar, writing a universal history and other works whose fragments are a major source for the royal women of the Augustan world.[13] There is no evidence that Cleopatra Selene's parents survived long enough to consider marriage possibilities for her, which would have been a serious process for the queen of the Cyrenaica; her brother Alexander was betrothed to Iotape, the daughter of the king of Media and Lesser Armenia.[14] But all these arrangements, and presumably others not known, came to an end in the fatal summer of 30 BC.

The Removal to Rome

The events of that summer are familiar.[15] Almost a year after the defeat by the forces of Octavian at Actium on the west coast of Greece, and endless futile negotiations about the future of Cleopatra VII, Antonius, and the children, the queen committed suicide on 10 August

(Antonius had done so a few days earlier), handing over the kingdom to her eldest son, Kaisarion, who ruled as Ptolemy XV. Yet he was soon killed by Octavian's agents—as the only known son of Julius Caesar, he was too dangerous to be allowed to survive—and Egypt was annexed by the Romans, the event backdated to 1 August, the date of Antonius's death.[16] The three surviving children were sent to Rome, to the care of Octavia, the sister of Octavian, who was Antonius's former wife.[17] She had a long history of providing for unattached children, especially those of her late husband, as well as royal refugees, and her household was the natural place for Cleopatra Selene, Alexander Helios, and Ptolemy Philadelphos. Their destiny was as yet undetermined, and it may even be that there was some brief consideration of returning one or more of them to Egypt and a new but reduced Ptolemaic kingdom, which, needless to say, never happened.[18]

At this point Ptolemy Philadelphos vanished from the historical record: there is no reason to believe anything other than the six-year-old, whose life had been totally disrupted, died a natural death shortly after his arrival in Rome. Only the twins remained to appear in Octavian's triumph of August 29 BC, presented as a symbolic Sun and Moon, along with an effigy of their mother, who had committed suicide in part to avoid their fate.[19] The triumph is the last mention of Alexander Helios, and presumably he died shortly thereafter. Even as a refugee, he was the only surviving male Ptolemy, and his future and marriage would have needed to be promptly considered, but there is no evidence of any such efforts. Yet by this time there was no reason to have him killed, and like his younger brother, he probably succumbed to the rigors of his current life. By 25 BC, at the latest, Cleopatra Selene was the only survivor of the four children of Cleopatra VII.

She had turned eleven about the time that she appeared in Octavian's triumph, and was a unique personality. In addition to being the only survivor of the long Ptolemaic dynasty that went back to the first Ptolemy, the companion of Alexander the Great, she was also the only royal representative of the other great Hellenistic empire, that of the Seleukids, descended from another companion of Alexander, Seleukos I. Moreover, she was half Roman, one of several children of the late triumvir Antonius, who had been Octavian's brother-in-law. As a member of the Antonii family of Rome she could claim an ancestry back to the fifth century BC.[20] She was almost certainly a Roman citizen and may also have been descended from the indigenous Egyptian aristocracy through her maternal grandmother.[21] Thus she was a girl of complex status—a fine example of the multiculturalism of the late Hellenistic period—who had to be treated carefully and with respect as she approached the age of marriage. Moreover, Augustus—the title that Octavian assumed early in 27 BC—insisted that the various royal children within the household be educated and nurtured, and their marriage arrangements implemented, in the same manner as those in his own family. There were also traditional Roman obligations toward fatherless children.[22]

Children were an essential part of Augustan ideology, and Augustus was careful to lay plans for the future of the large number of children, domestic and foreign, within his household. This policy is best seen on the Ara Pacis in Rome, the commemorative altar dedicated in 9 BC that now stands on the bank of the Tiber, reconstructed near Augustus's mausoleum. To be sure, it is from more than a decade after Cleopatra Selene left Octavia's household, yet its mingling of children and adults demonstrates the hope for the future and the sense of family that was central to the Augustan world. Conspicuous on the altar are a number of children in foreign dress, showing the global reach of Augustus's thoughts and providing a visual record of the inclusiveness of the regime.[23]

Cleopatra Selene was too old to be represented on the altar as a child,[24] and her siblings were dead by the time of its construction, yet she and her twin brother, Alexander Helios, may appear on a trophy monument erected at Nikopolis, the victory city established by Octavian (with the help of his new ally, Herod the Great) at the site of his camp near Actium.[25] The monument was a large structure decorated with figured scenes, much in the style of the celebrated Pergamon Altar. It included Octavian and two young children in a chariot, presumably none other than Cleopatra Selene and Alexander Helios, a sculptural representation of their appearance in the triumph in Rome (fig. 2). There are no other reasonable candidates in the contemporary imperial family: imperial children of about the same age, such as Augustus's daughter Julia (ten years old) or his stepsons Tiberius and Drusus (twelve and nine), would hardly have had such a prominent role in the triumph, and, moreover, they were not twins. Thus it can be assumed that Cleopatra Selene and Alexander Helios rode with Octavian in the triumph, a wise move, since even though they were children of the destroyed and demeaned Cleopatra VII, they were also children of his late brother-in-law, Antonius, who still enjoyed great support and family connections in Rome. By having the children with him, Octavian could begin to

FIG. 2. Cleopatra Selene and Alexander Helios in chariot with Octavian in triumph of 27 BC; relief from Nikopolis in Epeiros.

Courtesy John Pollini.

emphasize his inclusive reconciliation policy that would characterize the new regime, demonstrated by the olive branch that he holds. Yet the scene shows the dual status of the twins: prisoners of war who had the honor of riding with Octavian, a suggestion of their bright future.[26]

Marriage and a Royal Position

As soon as any question of returning Cleopatra Selene to Egypt had been dismissed—the death of her brothers probably ended all thoughts in this direction—the question arose of a suitable marriage. She would reach the minimum proper age of twelve in the summer of 28 BC, and thus Augustus and Octavia had to pay immediate attention to the matter.[27] Following traditional Roman separation of tasks, Octavia would concern herself with the personal fulfillment of Cleopatra Selene's life, and Augustus would ensure her role in contemporary political needs.

For many years another royal refugee had been living in Rome, who was also in Octavia's household and was about eighteen years of age at the time of the triumph. This was the displaced heir to the Numidian kingdom, Juba II, who had arrived in the city in 46 BC as an infant when his father, Juba I, had committed suicide after having been defeated by Julius Caesar, at the time that the Roman civil war had spilled over into North Africa.[28] Numidia was the territory south and west of Carthage, and it had been provincialized upon the death of Juba I. Where his son lived during his first years in Rome is not known, but sometime before the arrival of Cleopatra Selene he had ended up with Octavia.[29] There was already an odd connection between the two refugees: Juba's ancestor, the Numidian king Massinissa (reigned 205-148 BC), and Cleopatra Selene's ancestor, Ptolemy VIII, had known one another, and Ptolemy, in his early years when he was king of the Cyrenaica, had visited Massinissa, an event that he discussed in his autobiography.[30] Both kings had Roman connections: Massinissa had reached almost mythic status as the ideal barbarian king, and Ptolemy VIII had come to Rome to court (unsuccessfully) the famous Roman matron Cornelia, the first known example of an attempt to make a marriage connection between the Ptolemies and the Roman aristocracy.[31] With such a family history—which Juba, at least, would have been familiar with, since he was trained as a historian—it is probable that when the two refugees met for the first time, there would have been an instant compatibility.

Cleopatra Selene and Juba were the most distinguished refugees in the Augustan household. When Augustus began to consider their future, both marriage and a royal position would have seemed an obvious choice. Neither could be returned to their ancestral territories, but there was a large unorganized district of Africa that needed a Roman presence. This was Mauretania, a sizable region that extended all the way from the western boundary of the Roman province of Africa at the Ampsaga River[32] to the Atlantic Ocean (essentially, modern Algeria and Morocco). It had been ruled by an indigenous dynasty since at least the third century BC, and there was also a Roman trading presence in its coastal cities that had developed after the fall of Carthage in 146 BC.[33] In the early first century BC, Mauretania had been split between two related (and contentious) rulers, Bogudes II in the east and Bocchus II in the west; the division was approximately along the modern Algerian–Moroccan border. Both kings became involved in the Roman civil war. Bocchus died naturally in 33 BC with no heir, and Bogudes abandoned his kingdom to join Cleopatra VII and Antonius; he was killed in Greece in early 31 BC.[34] Although the information is unclear, it seems that there was no official government for some years afterward in either part of Mauretania, since Roman attention lay elsewhere. It is possible that a number of settlements were established, yet the region was effectively ignored until the matter of Egypt was resolved and a solution presented itself.[35]

The solution, of course, was Cleopatra Selene and Juba. Both were potential monarchs without states to rule, and both were of North African origin. In 27 BC Augustus began to consider the status of the western Mediterranean, and late in the year he went for an extended stay at Tarraco (modern Tarragona) in Spain, where he could devote attention to the west as he had done with the east.[36] He remained there until early 24 BC, making a variety of decisions about the future Roman presence, including the matter of Mauretania. Juba was with Augustus in Tarraco, and it was decided that he and Cleopatra Selene would be established as joint rulers of a new allied kingdom of Mauretania that combined the old territories of Bocchus and Bogudes into one vast region that extended from the Ampsaga River to the Atlantic. With the acquisition of Egypt several years previously, this would mean that the Romans controlled, directly or indirectly, all of North Africa.

Juba returned to Rome in 25 BC to marry Cleopatra Selene. The date of the ceremony can only be assumed by the sequence of events, since there are no specifics in the sources.[37] Cleopatra Selene was now fifteen, above the minimum age for marriage (Juba was about twenty-two). It has been suggested that the event did not occur until 20 or 19 BC, when the first known dated joint coinage of the couple appears,[38] but this is from the sixth regnal year, which means that the monarchy was established by the end of 25 BC, and it seems improbable that the marriage was delayed for several years while Juba went to Mauretania alone, leaving the status of Cleopatra Selene unresolved. It would also mean that she was not married until about the age of twenty-one, especially late for a woman of the Augustan household. But nevertheless the date of the marriage—other than before 19 BC—cannot be definitively proved.[39]

Whenever it occurred, the marriage was an event of note in the imperial household, and the poet Krinagoras of Mytilene was commissioned to write about the occasion. He had a wide-ranging career, both as an ambassador from Mytilene to Rome and as a poet for the imperial family. He wrote on the death of Philostratos, who had been the tutor of Cleopatra VII, and thus may already have been known to Cleopatra Selene.[40] He commemorated her wedding as follows:

Great neighboring regions of the world, which the Nile,
swollen from black Ethiopia, divides, you have created

common kings for both through marriage, making one race of Egyptians and Libyans. Let the children of kings in turn hold from their fathers a strong rule over both lands.[41]

The epigram is geographically loose, using the Nile allegorically as a symbol of Africa (it hardly separated the ancestral homes of the couple) and speaking in a general sense about "children of kings" and "fathers," since Cleopatra Selene was only the granddaughter of a king, although she may have been sensitive to the fact that her mother had on occasion been addressed as "king." To be sure, the course of the Nile would be a major issue in the self-identity of the Mauretanian kingdom, based on a long-standing view that its source was in or near Mauretania, so both monarchs could have claim to the river, but any scholarly geographical analysis of this was yet to come.[42] "Libya," an anachronistic term in the Augustan era, had Homeric and epic value, and traditionally meant all of North Africa west of Egypt. The epigram subtly validated Cleopatra Selene's historic claim to the Cyrenaica and Juba's to Numidia, giving the couple theoretical control over all of North Africa except the small region around Carthage, a point of view best expressed poetically and a good example of how poets could say things that might be politically incorrect. It also demonstrated that Cleopatra Selene and Juba were joint rulers and equals or "common kings."

By the end of 25 BC, in all probability, the newly married royal couple was on their way to their kingdom. Cleopatra Selene, who most likely continued to think of herself as queen of the Cyrenaica (and even queen of Egypt)—however inappropriate such thoughts might be in the new reality of the Augustan world—now became queen of Mauretania, ruling as a woman of greater status than her husband. She was prepared not only to exercise these queenly roles as much as possible but to establish a virtual Ptolemaic government-in-exile in Mauretania.

Queen of Mauretania

Cleopatra Selene was queen of Mauretania for approximately twenty years, as joint ruler with her husband but with certain independent powers. Yet, inevitably, there are few details about her life at the royal court beyond what can be extrapolated from its material culture and the activities of her husband. The only things documented in the literature are her children and her death, and even for these the data are contradictory.

Cleopatra Selene would have realized that she was not the only eastern refugee who ended up far west of her original home. Centuries earlier Dido of Tyre had become queen of Carthage. She was the grandniece of another queen who had a difficult life, Jezebel, whose fate at Samaria is well known.[43] Cleopatra Selene may not have been particularly impressed by the account of Dido most familiar today—that put forth by Vergil and being written in these years—considering what the *Aeneid* said about her parents. But Vergil had been influenced by tales from their court, and transferred stories about lavish living in the last years of Cleopatra VII and Antonius to the world of Dido and Aeneas.[44] Yet the Mauretanian royal library had a Punic section,[45] and Cleopatra Selene might have had access to indigenous African versions of the Dido story, ones that were independent of her assumed involvement with Aeneas. Although the account of Dido had long since become totally hellenized and had been presented in a Greek version as early as the fourth century BC,[46] there are parallels between Dido and Cleopatra Selene. Both were from the eastern Mediterranean and had to leave because of local civil strife, finding a new home and greater status in Africa as queen in a remote area. Moreover, both had issues with the Roman world. There may even have been dramatic versions of the Dido story available: the most complete extant historical account, by Pompeius Trogus, roughly contemporary with Cleopatra Selene, shows hints of messenger's speeches. In addition, Juba was an expert on the theater, writing a *Theatrical History*, and one would expect that he had access to a large number of plays.[47] At the very least Cleopatra Selene may have been familiar with the non-Vergilian versions of Dido's story and may have seen her own career as a parallel.

The queen and Juba arrived in Mauretania at the end of 25 BC, taking up residence at a place called Iol, on the coast (modern Cherchel in Algeria). It was originally a Carthaginian outpost that had been developed as a Mauretanian royal city in the second century BC.[48] Its location probably had much to do with the presence of an island immediately offshore (the modern Corniche des Dahra) that provided a certain amount of shelter on a coast otherwise lacking it; except for this, the site of Iol is hardly propitious, with virtually no coastal plain and mountains rising high behind the city. Iol was probably in decline when the new monarchs arrived, and they chose to live there presumably because it lay roughly midway along the lengthy Mediterranean coast of Mauretania. In the emerging fashion of the era, Iol was renamed Kaisareia, or Caesarea, honoring Augustus; cities with such names were founded by allied monarchs during much of the last quarter of the first century BC. Mauretanian Caesarea may have been the first: the Caesarea of Herod the Great came three years later, and Archelaos (IV) of Cappadocia, the father of Glaphyra, founded his at about the same time. Today Caesarea in Mauretania is a rich archaeological site with numerous remains, including a theater, amphitheater, city walls, harbor, and evidence of the street grid and forum. The royal palace does not survive, but its location near the waterfront is apparent (fig. 3).

Decayed Iol was rebuilt lavishly, with all kinds of marble used in constructing the royal city, including Italian, Greek, and African.[49] How much Cleopatra Selene participated in this architectural transformation is not known—the city did include a temple to Isis, her mother's alter ego—but her efforts are most apparent in the artistic program of the kingdom. As the exiled queen of Egypt, she took care to commemorate her heritage. She would have felt devoted to her mother's legacy: at the time that she became queen, the demonization of Cleopatra VII was being vigorously asserted in contemporary Latin literature, and Cleopatra Selene would have taken no comfort in reading that her mother was merely the cowardly Egyptian mate of Antonius or that

FIG. 3. General view of Iol-Caesarea (modern Cherchel in Algeria).
Courtesy Duane W. Roller.

her death caused great rejoicing.[50] As her only living descendant, she had not only the chance but the obligation to set the record straight by commemorating her mother at her new capital, especially through portrait sculpture.[51]

It may seem that she took a personal risk in promoting her mother's heritage so vigorously, given the official opinion in Rome, but this suggests that the attitude toward Cleopatra VII was far more nuanced than is generally believed today, and the official point of view—mostly vividly represented in Augustan poetry—was essentially government propaganda. Moreover, Cleopatra Selene was a daughter of Antonius, whose other living descendants were still quite active in the political life of Rome. Her status—as well as the memory of her mother—is well shown on her coinage; a series of autonomous issues (without the name of her husband) having the legend "Kleopatra *basilissa*" demonstrates royal privileges separate from his. Some of these coins have the Nile crocodile, a reminder not only of Egypt but also of the coins issued in the 30s BC when she was named queen of the Cyrenaica (fig. 4). Juba also had his autonomous coins, indicating that the two monarchs acted independently of one another in certain undefined ways. There was also joint coinage, but even here the distinction between the two is apparent, since Juba's legend is always in Latin while Cleopatra Selene's is in

FIG. 4. Cleopatra Selene silver crocodile coin. British Museum RPK, p. 218.1.JubII. Photo © The Trustees of the British Museum.

Greek—emphasizing the bilingual nature of the court—and the two monarchs appear on opposite sides of the coins, never together. [52] In at least one case, Cleopatra is identified merely as "Selene," a memory of the role that she was destined to play before the collapse of the Ptolemaic dynasty. Most significantly, she also issued coins with the legend "queen Cleopatra, daughter of Cleopatra," strong evidence of her devotion to her mother's memory.[53]

Cleopatra Selene's emphasis on her Ptolemaic heritage was also apparent in the sculptural program at Caesarea. In addition to the expected portraiture of herself and her mother, there was an elaborate display of historical Egyptian sculpture, from as far back as the time of Tuthmosis I (reigned ca. 1504-1492 BC).[54] There was also a statue of the Egyptian god Ammon, and he and Isis appeared on the obverse and reverse of the joint coinage, suggesting divine roles for the monarchs.[55]

Perhaps the most interesting sculpture at Caesarea is a statue of the Egyptian priest Petubastes IV, who died (according to the inscription) 31 July 30 BC at the age of sixteen (fig. 5).[56] He was perhaps a cousin of Cleopatra Selene and, as a member of the priestly aristocracy, would have been the last indigenous claimant to the Egyptian throne. There is little doubt that he and Cleopatra Selene knew each other in Alexandria, and the setting up of his statue in Caesarea is the most tangible evidence of her memory of that last summer in Egypt. As much as possible, she sought both to establish herself as the last Ptolemaic queen and to create a new Alexandria at Caesarea, bringing Egyptian material culture from more than fifteen hundred miles away.

Probably the most celebrated work of art that may represent Cleopatra Selene is a silver dish from Boscoreale, near Pompeii in Italy, which shows a woman surrounded by symbols of Africa (fig. 6). She resembles a portrait of Cleopatra VII or Cleopatra Selene from Mauretanian Caesarea, and the image is probably of the latter. It may have been commissioned after her death. The dish is a complex piece of symbolism that positions Cleopatra Selene within the dynastic needs of the Augustan regime, yet at the same time subtly notes that it owes its existence to the destruction of her parents. Attributes of Herakles are prominent on the dish—in particular a lion and a club—coupled with symbols of abundance and Egypt, linking Cleopatra Selene's ancestry (she was a descendant of Herakles), her original home, and the prosperous world of Mauretania and Augustan Rome. Moreover, her husband

FIG. 5. Petubastes IV, from Cherchel. Cherchel Museum S75.
Courtesy Duane W. Roller and Agence Nationale d'Archéologie, Algiers.

was also a descendant of Herakles. The hero had first carried civilization to the western extremities of the known world—Mauretania—and now his descendants brought the power and prosperity of Rome to these farthest lands.[57]

When Cleopatra Selene arrived at her new capital, she presumably had a royal entourage, both from Alexandria and from Rome. The appearance of the name "Antonius" among members of the royal household, such as Aischinos Antonianus,[58] demonstrates some connection to her father or his family, and thus despite the emphasis on her Ptolemaic heritage, the queen also remembered her father: one of her childhood playmates in Octavia's home would have been Antonius's daughter the younger Antonia, the future mother of the emperor Claudius.

FIG. 6. Gilded silver dish from Boscoreale, perhaps representing Cleopatra Selene. Louvre Bj 1969.

Courtesy Musée du Louvre. Photo © Lessing Images.

Two of the freedmen connected to the Antonii were persons of particular note. Gnaios was a famous gem cutter who had worked for the triumvir and who came to the Mauretanian court, carving a portrait of the queen as well as mythological figures and possibly also supervising the art of the Mauretanian coinage.[59] An epigram that refers to a ring cameo of Methe belonging to a Queen Cleopatra may also reflect the gems at the Mauretanian court, but its authorship and date remain uncertain.[60]

More famous was Antonius Euphorbos, the royal physician. He was the brother of Augustus's physician, Antonius Musa, and was presumably also a freedman of the triumvir who became attached to Cleopatra Selene.[61] He was remembered for discovering a plant on an expedition to the Atlas Mountains whose juice cured snake bites and improved vision. Juba named it *euphorbion*—its exact identity is not known—and wrote a pamphlet about it. *Euphorbion* became widely known and was discussed by the medical authors Dioskourides and Galen.[62] Cleopatra Selene's freedman Euphorbos is the best known surviving legacy of her role as queen of Mauretania, since he was the namesake for the extensive botanical family Euphobiaceae and the genus *Euphorbia*, or spurge.

The name "Cleopatra" also appears among freedwomen of the court; whether these refer to the queen or her mother cannot be determined.[63] Nevertheless, Cleopatra Selene's management of the royal household meant reliance on people sent from Rome and Alexandria who had been attached to her parents.

Any pretense that Caesarea was the new Alexandria would fail without some effort at creating a significant scholarly presence. Caesarea had a library and attracted a number of intellectual personalities. The library included not only Greek and Roman literature but indigenous North African material, the remnants of Carthaginian and Numidian scholarship.[64] Most of the known scholars at the court are obscure—at least in terms of the surviving mainstream of Greco-Roman literature—but none was as important as Juba himself, one of the most notable historians and ethnographers of the Augustan period. Nearly a dozen works of his are known, all fragmentary, with recent evidence also revealing that he wrote an autobiography, a genre that followed his wife's royal ancestors as well as Nikolaos of Damascus and even Augustus himself.[65] The fragmentary treatises include a Roman cultural history, a linguistic analysis, works on painting and the theater, a discussion of the expedition of Hanno (the Carthaginian who around 500 BC went along the coast of West Africa into the tropics), and the pamphlet on *euphorbion*. His major works, which most show the influence of Cleopatra Selene and which survive in the largest number of fragments, are two complementary treatises, *Libyka* and *On Arabia*. These collectively examined the entire southern extent of the known world, from the Atlantic coast to India, and made a major contribution to the Augustan conception of the breadth of Roman control.

Juba's treatises have been discussed in detail elsewhere.[66] Cleopatra Selene probably stimulated Juba's interest in the Nile and Egypt: the course of the river was discussed thoroughly in *Libyka* on the assumption that it originated in Mauretania, an early point of view that was surprisingly persistent and lasted into the nineteenth century.[67] By writing about the course of the Nile and tracing it from Mauretania to Egypt, Juba fulfilled the promise suggested in Krinagoras's wedding epigram. Juba made extensive use of Ptolemaic sources, including the works of his wife's ancestors, the Ptolemaic kings.[68] His extensive research on the Red Sea region reflects access to information supplied by Ptolemaic explorers, both on the sea and along the upper Nile, especially those from the third century BC at the time of Ptolemy II.[69] Copies of these obscure reports may have been brought to Caesarea as part of Cleopatra Selene's inheritance, or Juba may have spent time in the Alexandria library, since it is probable that the queen had contacts in that city who may have eased his access to little-known material. Yet unlike that of other scholars discussing the Nile, Juba's perspective on the river was unique because he described it downstream, from the couple's new home back to Cleopatra Selene's birthplace at its mouth.[70]

The king continued his research after his wife's death with his final ethnography, *On Arabia*, which discusses much of the Red Sea as well as Arabia and the routes to India. There is no doubt that his marriage to a Ptolemy and the couple's desire to validate their rule of Mauretania and connect it to the Ptolemaic heritage—geographically, historically, and culturally—was an inspiration to Juba's pattern of scholarship. When he completed *On Arabia*, probably in the first decade of the first century AD, the entire southern limits of the known world had been brought into the Augustan horizon, a global conception based on the research and exploration originally commissioned by Cleopatra Selene's ancestors.

The Royal Children

Cleopatra Selene is not mentioned in literary sources after her marriage except in regard to her son and her death. Her son was Ptolemy, generally called today Ptolemy of Mauretania.[71] His birthdate is not certain; the earliest documentation of the Mauretanian heir apparent is in AD 5, on coins that show him as an adolescent, suggesting one of around 10 BC, which fits with the other sparse data known about his life.[72] This would be about fifteen years after his parents married, which raises the possibility that he was not their first child, and it has been ingeniously suggested that a boy on the frieze of the Ara Pacis is an otherwise unknown son of Cleopatra Selene, perhaps about seven years of age in 13 BC, when the altar was dedicated, and that he was brought to Rome by his mother, who may be the figure just to the right.[73] It is probable that Cleopatra Selene and Juba visited Rome on occasion; this was a common practice among allied monarchs (both Cleopatra Selene's mother and Juba's father had spent time in the city), and they would have been able to visit their adoptive family.

If the mother and child on the Ara Pacis are Cleopatra Selene and her son, he was born about 20 BC and perhaps named Juba, but did not survive long enough to be considered an heir to the throne, and rule devolved onto his younger brother, Ptolemy, who became king upon the death of Juba in AD 23 or 24.[74] His mother had already died.[75] Ptolemy succeeded to the throne and lasted until summoned to Rome by his cousin, the emperor Gaius Caligula, because the king had been acting with increasing independence, issuing gold coins and assuming triumphal regalia.[76] The emperor was erratic and never sympathetic to his relatives, and Ptolemy was in all likelihood flaunting his superiority as the descendant of many kings who had achieved military renown (unlike Caligula), a status validated even by the late emperor Tiberius.[77] The result was that he was executed while at the Roman imperial court, perhaps in late AD 40 or early the following year. After some difficulty the Mauretanian kingdom was provincialized, and the Ptolemaic dynasty was truly at an end.[78]

Cleopatra Selene and Juba also had a daughter, according to an inscription from Athens.[79] Juba was known in the city, as was Ptolemy of Mauretania, and it is reasonable that a daughter would also have been there. Unfortunately, no name is preserved, but the most likely one would be Cleopatra. Another Athenian inscription, citing a king's daughter from Libya (the old epic term for Africa), could be either this daughter or even Cleopatra VII, who may have visited the city in the 50s BC when her father was in exile.[80]

More enigmatic is a statement by Tacitus referring to a granddaughter of Cleopatra VII and Antonius named Drusilla, who married Felix, a freedman of the emperor Claudius and governor of Judaea in the AD 50s.[81] It has long been assumed that Drusilla was an otherwise unknown child of Cleopatra Selene and Juba, but there are both chronological and onomastic problems, and the word used by Tacitus to describe her status, *neptis*, is ambiguous. There are several possibilities. *Neptis* may have to be emended to *proneptis* (great-granddaughter instead of granddaughter), which would solve the chronological issues (it is hard to image a daughter of the Mauretanian monarchs being of marriageable age in the AD 50s). The name "Drusilla" is unlikely but not impossible for the context of Juba and Cleopatra Selene: it would refer to the wife of Augustus, Livia Drusilla. *Neptis* can also be used more generally, to mean any female descendant, and Drusilla may have been the daughter of Ptolemy of Mauretania, but no explanation is totally satisfactory, and the evidence is scattered and contradictory. On balance it seems that Drusilla was a descendant, not a daughter, of Cleopatra Selene.[82]

The Eclipse of the Moon

Near the end of the first century BC, Krinagoras of Mytilene wrote another epigram for Cleopatra Selene:

> The moon herself grew dark, rising at sunset, covering her
> suffering in the night, because she saw her graceful namesake,
> Selene, without breath, descending to Hades. With her she
> had the beauty of her light in common, and mingled her own
> darkness with her death.[83]

The name "Selene" is not otherwise known among prominent women from the Augustan period, so there is no doubt that the poem is a eulogy on the death of the queen. The epigram is not dated, but it refers to a contemporary lunar eclipse. Assuming that Krinagoras was not writing totally allegorically—which seems pointless—it is possible to relate the epigram to known eclipses and thus suggest a date. There were total ("darkness") lunar eclipses in 9, 8, 5, and 1 BC.[84] The one that fits the best, for a variety of reasons, is that of 23 March 5 BC; the others are also possible. It cannot be any later, because in 2 BC or early the following year Juba accompanied Gaius Caesar, the grandson of Augustus, to Arabia, presumably as an expert on that part of the world (portions of his treatise *On Arabia* resulted from these travels). The expedition lasted until AD 4,[85] but Juba may not have remained the entire time, and there is nothing about it that actually affects the status of Cleopatra Selene, yet while he was in the East he married Glaphyra, the daughter of King Archelaos (IV) of Cappadocia—another adviser to Gaius—an event that took place before AD 5 and probably several years earlier. This is unequivocal proof that Cleopatra Selene had died by this time, certainly no later than the eclipse of 1 BC and probably in 5 BC, before Juba set forth to the East. Polygamy, although a feature of the ancestors of both monarchs, was hardly possible for them, having been raised in a Roman household. Yet there was no stigma attached to remarriage after the death of a spouse.[86]

The one fact that seems to bring into question Cleopatra Selene's date of death is a hoard of coins from Alkasar near Tangier from around AD 17 that includes joint coinage of the king and queen, as well as autonomous coins of her alone.[87] It is easy to assume they prove that she was still alive in the second decade of the first century AD, some years after Juba's marriage to Glaphyra (whom he had divorced by AD 5). Yet the coins themselves are not securely dated (other than before AD 17), and modern explanations suggesting polygamy or that Juba and Cleopatra Selene got back together after his adventures in the East are highly improbable.[88] It is better to assume that the coins commemorate an important event within the royal family, perhaps the raising of Ptolemy of Mauretania to joint rule with his father. Posthumous coinage did exist within Juba's ancestral tradition, including some in honor of Massinissa.[89]

The best evidence is that Cleopatra Selene died—"descending to Hades"—in the last decade of the first century BC. She was buried in a mausoleum that is still visible near Tipasa, about twenty-five miles east of Caesarea, one of the major ancient monuments in this part of Algeria (fig. 7).[90] Known erroneously in early modern times as the Tomb of the Christian Woman, it is an impressive round monumentalized tumulus more than 100 feet high and nearly 200 feet in diameter, with an

FIG. 7. Mauretanian Royal Mausoleum.
Courtesy Duane W. Roller.

Ionic facade surmounted by a stepped cone. In AD 23 or 24 Juba was also buried there. The exact date of its construction is unknown: it may have been built by a member of the indigenous Mauretanian dynasty, perhaps Bocchus II (ruled ca. 64-33 BC), or, more likely, by Juba and Cleopatra Selene themselves. The monument is a local form derived from royal tombs of the Hellenistic era—similar types exist in Numidia—but is most remindful of the Mausoleum of Augustus in Rome, constructed in 27 BC shortly before the royal couple left for Mauretania. Its combination of North African and Roman architectural elements well demonstrates the cross-currents of the world of Cleopatra Selene and Juba.

The Legacy

Cleopatra Selene was the most important royal woman of the early Augustan period. Her ancestry from both the Ptolemies and a distinguished Roman family was an early example of the blending of east and west that was to characterize the Roman imperial world. Despite the self-destruction of her parents—who had also attempted, in their own way, to bring east and west together—Cleopatra Selene could point to them as representing a lineage that typified the best of Hellenistic monarchy and Roman aristocracy. Her vigorous promotion of her mother's legacy stood in sharp contrast to the negative image being disseminated in contemporary Augustan poetry. In theory, she could claim rule of almost all of North Africa and presumably was greatly respected throughout her actual territories. Her promotion of art and scholarship provided a transition between Hellenistic monarchy and Rome. Her legacy remained visible in Mauretanian Caesarea, where the personal names "Cleopatra" and "Selene" (as well as "Ptolemy") were still used in the second century AD.[91]

She was also an important player in the establishment of the role of aristocratic women in the Augustan world, especially in the case of her half-sister and childhood playmate, the younger Antonia, who would come to exercise a dominant role in Rome—within the strictures of the Roman system—much as Cleopatra Selene did in Mauretania. If the queen maintained a household in Rome after her accession, as seems probable,[92] she would have continued to bring ideas about Hellenistic monarchy into the Roman environment, thus assisting in the elevation of women throughout the Augustan world.[93]

3

Glaphyra of Cappadocia

The Dynasty of Cappadocia

Cappadocia (Greek Kappadokia, based on the indigenous toponym Katpatuka) is the interior territory of southeastern Asia Minor, a region totally within modern Turkey. It is a fertile upland with various crops and cattle among its products, as well as various minerals, a district of early peoples and cultures, with its original connections more to the east and southeast.[1] Assyrian traders had moved into the region by early in the second millennium BC, establishing an outpost at Kanesh (modern Kültepe). Later Cappadocia came under the control of various foreign powers, such as the Phrygians, Medes, and Persians. Greeks became aware of the region when they began to engage the Persians in the late sixth century BC.[2] During Hellenistic times, the local dynasty extended its power to the Black Sea and the Mediterranean.

When Alexander the Great passed through in 333 BC, the Persian satrap, Ariarathes (I), did not submit to his rule and established an in-dependent dynasty that lasted into the first century BC—although often under nominal control of the major Hellenistic states—with all of its eight kings named Ariarathes. After the death of the last, around 96 BC, the Romans began to intervene in the territory, and there were various rulers until the triumvir Antonius arrived with his commission to settle the affairs of the eastern Mediterranean after the death of Julius Caesar. The current king was Ariarathes IX (also designated X, depending on how various claimants are counted, and not related to his homony-mous predecessors), who had been in power since 42 BC but does not seem to have been particularly effective. Antonius began the process of removing him and by 36 BC had placed his own candidate on the throne, one Archelaos (IV), unrelated to his predecessors.[3]

Antonius clearly wanted a break from the earlier dynastic history of Cappadocia, and perhaps from persons named Ariarathes, one of whom, probably the fifth, of the preceding century—indulging in what Strabo called "childish amusements"—had caused a major ecological disaster when a dam that he had built to create a private pleasure lake broke, resulting in the devastation by flooding of extensive parts of Cappadocia, including villages, and requiring Roman intervention.[4] By choosing Archelaos (IV), who had a distinguished background, Antonius could move away from the past. Archelaos's lineage could be traced back through three ancestors, all named Archelaos. The earliest, Archelaos (I), was a commander of Mithradates VI of Pontos, who was involved in the invasion of mainland Greece in 89 BC and who later defected to the Romans.[5] His son, Archelaos (II), was appointed by Pompey the Great to the priesthood of Komana in Pontos; this was no minor office, but one with royal rank and control of a cult city with more than six thousand temple servants.[6] This Archelaos had even greater ambitions and in 56 BC ended up as the husband of Berenike IV (the sister of Cleopatra VII), although both husband and wife were killed the following year when the sisters' father, Ptolemy XII, was restored. Ironically, the one who ensured a proper royal burial for Archelaos and Berenike was the future triumvir, Antonius.[7]

Archelaos's son, yet another Archelaos (III), then received the priesthood at Komana, but overextended his privileges and was removed from office by Julius Caesar in 47 BC. He was the father of the king of Cappadocia installed by Antonius.[8] This history may explain why the latest Archelaos (IV) was chosen to be king: the family had, for the most part, distinguished itself, its members had regularly supported Rome, and the triumvir had known the new king's grandfather, although, to be sure, under strange circumstances.

But there may be another reason that Archelaos was awarded his kingship, for Antonius was said to have made the appointment because of his fondness for the king's mother, Glaphyra.[9] The evidence is unclear: the sequence of events in Appian's narrative provides a date of 41 BC—just before Antonius met Cleopatra VII at Tarsos—and the person he favored was named Sisenes, not Archelaos. This may be a personal name to distinguish this Archelaos from his three homonymous ancestors, or Sisenes may have been an unsuccessful contemporary claimant to the throne.[10] What is curious is that their mothers had the same name, Glaphyra. This suggests that Archelaos and Sisenes may have been brothers and their identities have become confused, or that they were even the same person.

There are two dates (41 and 36 BC) for the accession of Archelaos, which probably result from the uncertain conditions in Cappadocia due to the deposing of the preceding dynasty and the general instability of the era. Archelaos may have been designated in 41 BC, but perhaps it took five years for him actually to obtain the throne, especially if there were competition from within his own family.[11] What remains unquestioned is that Antonius had some sort of relationship with his mother, something well known by 40 BC, since Octavian wrote a scurrilous epigram suggesting that Antonius's wife, Fulvia, would respond to the situation between her husband and Glaphyra by entering into a relationship with Octavian. Why Fulvia would want to do this is by no means clear, and the epigram says more about her (and indeed Octavian) than about Antonius, but it was still current a century later when Martial quoted it.[12] Fulvia's negative qualities may have been exaggerated in the literary tradition, much like those of Cleopatra VII: both were women of power demonized in later writings. Yet the epigram demonstrates that whatever happened between Glaphyra and Antonius, she wielded enough power to be a threat to the triumvir's wife, which suggests that the matter was not merely one of slander originating in Rome.[13] At the time Octavian may have been more worried about Fulvia than Antonius, since she was in Italy and had extensive political ambitions.[14] But she suddenly died in the summer of 40 BC, and so her rivalry with Glaphyra became moot.[15] Presumably the epigram was written before that date, indicating that Antonius's relationship with Glaphyra began after he arrived in Asia Minor in the spring of 41 BC and began to determine the fate of the Cappadocian monarchy. Dio called Glaphyra a hetaira (essentially a paid companion), perhaps suggesting nothing more than that she was not the legal wife of Archelaos (III), but the sources are explicit in recording that she was the mother of the new king.[16]

Glaphyra the hetaira was important enough to have been honored by Magnesia, a free city on the lower Meander River, located within the Roman province of Asia. The date is unknown but was probably after her son became king. On the inscription that mentions her, she has the title *basilissa*, probably more honorific than implying any sense of ruling power.[17] It also had her father's name, but only the initial "O" is preserved. In addition to Archelaos, she may have had another male child, whose name is unknown; one wonders if he was the mysterious Sisenes, since the only notice of him refers to the difficulty that he caused King Archelaos.[18] No dates for Glaphyra's career are known beyond her attractiveness to Antonius in 41 BC, but the brief comments demonstrate the upward mobility of women—especially those attached to royalty—in the late Hellenistic period.[19] A final honor to Glaphyra came when her son, Archelaos (IV), named his daughter after her.

Thus Archelaos (IV) was appointed to the throne of Cappadocia by 41 BC. It is unlikely that Antonius's relationship with his mother caused the appointment, but it demonstrated his familiarity with the family. Archelaos remained on the throne until AD 18, becoming a scholar and the most senior of the allied kings, one of the last survivors of the era of Antonius.[20] He expanded his kingdom from the core territory of Cappadocia as far as he was able—the Romans almost surrounded him—in time receiving parts of Cilicia that had originally belonged to Cleopatra VII. Eventually he established his primary royal seat at the town of Elaioussa (modern Ayaş on the Turkish coast of the Mediterranean), a location well positioned to receive traffic between the Levant and points west (fig. 8). After 27 BC, he renamed the city Sebaste, from the Greek

FIG. 8. Elaioussa-Sebaste.
Courtesy Sapienza University Italian Archaeological Mission.

name for Augustus.[21] He also reached out through marriage alliances to the other allied monarchs: Herod in Judaea, Juba in Mauretania, and Pythodoris in Pontos. His wife and the mother of his children is not known by name, but she claimed Persian and Armenian royal descent. She had two known children: Archelaos (V), who was king of a portion of Rough Cilicia from AD 19 to 36 (Cappadocia was provincialized upon his father's death), and the second Glaphyra, who became a central personality in the dynastic connections of the Augustan era.[22]

The Younger Glaphyra

Glaphyra was born in the 30s BC, perhaps shortly after her father came to the throne. She was named after her grandmother; the name means "elegant" or "refined" and may be Thessalian in origin, from the town of Glaphyrai, which was known to Homer but which has not been located.[23] Glaphyra's birthdate is assumed from the time of her first marriage, to Alexander of Judaea, the second eldest of the numerous sons of Herod the Great, who was born around 36 BC. He and his younger brother Aristoboulos were sent to Rome for their education when they reached adolescence.[24] They returned from the city a few years later, with Herod going in person to retrieve them. The date is not certain but must fall between 19 and 16 BC, perhaps at the time of the *ludi saeculares* of June 17 BC, when the king might have wanted to be in Rome. After they arrived back in Judaea, the sons were married: Aristoboulos to his cousin Berenike (I of Judaea) and Alexander to Glaphyra.[25]

But Glaphyra soon found herself unpopular at the Herodian court. She flaunted her noble descent—Persian and Armenian—and claimed that she was the highest-ranking woman in the Herodian family, allegedly acting in an especially disagreeable way toward her brother-in-law's wife, Berenike. Hostility may have been inevitable, since she was the first member of the court from outside the southern Levant. Moreover, her father's tendency to involve himself in Herodian politics caused further difficulties. Herod was well aware that Archelaos had strong connections in Rome and thus found him of use, but this meant that he was drawn into the intrigues at the Herodian court, which reflected on his daughter.[26] Soon Glaphyra incurred the wrath of Berenike's mother and Herod's sister, Salome, an unwise enemy to make. Moreover, rumors began to spread that Herod himself was showing undue interest in her: in time these were traced to Salome. She denied everything, but was in no way sympathetic toward Glaphyra.[27] The situation demonstrates not only the continually poisonous atmosphere of the Herodian court, but the power of Salome, who claimed, with some accuracy, that she was the ultimate object of this slander.

Reports of the hostility toward Glaphyra soon reached Archelaos at Elaioussa-Sebaste. He and Herod had long enjoyed a good if wary relationship—both had been made kings at about the same time by Antonius—and Herod realized that Archelaos was an important ally. Yet in time, perhaps around 13 BC, the situation had reached the point that Glaphyra's husband, Alexander, was accused of conspiracy against his father. Archelaos, quite naturally worried about the future of his daughter, came to Judaea to arbitrate. For a time he was able to stabilize matters, pointing out that the connection between the two families was essential, yet he also threatened to dissolve the marriage and, moreover, reported everything to Augustus. But the only immediate result was that Herod accused Archelaos of being part of the conspiracy against him, along with Alexander and his brother Aristoboulos, and to some extent Glaphyra. Archelaos offered to provide sanctuary for the sons in his own kingdom, but it was to no avail, and around 8 BC they were executed by Herod.[28]

How much Glaphyra was involved in this remains unknown. But Herod may have wanted to salvage some sort of relationship with Archelaos, so he sent her back to Elaioussa-Sebaste, along with a sum equal to her dowry.[29] Her marriage to Alexander of Judaea had lasted perhaps ten years and produced two sons, a younger Alexander and Tigranes (V), both of whom probably went to Elaioussa-Sebaste with their mother. When the kingship of Armenia fell vacant around AD 6, Tigranes was placed on the throne as a distant relative (through his mother) of Armenian royalty. At an uncertain date he was removed from office by the Romans and seems to have lived in Rome thereafter, until he was involved in a plot whose details are not known, perhaps connected with contemporary succession struggles in Armenia. He died or was executed in the last years of the emperor Tiberius. As far as is known, he had no children.[30]

The younger Alexander is obscure, but his son, Tigranes (VI), was appointed king of Armenia by Nero around AD 60. Yet he was deposed two years later, vanishing from the historical record.[31] His descendants survived for at least four more generations, into the second century AD, becoming outstanding examples of the blending of Hellenistic royalty with the Roman aristocracy. Most notable was yet another Alexander, Glaphyra's great-grandson, who was king of Cilicia for many years and then came to Rome and was consul, perhaps around AD 100.[32]

Glaphyra's Second Marriage

Thus around 7 BC Glaphyra found herself back at the court of her father, remaining there for several years. In early 1 BC the recently widowed Juba II of Mauretania came to the eastern Mediterranean, as part of the advisory team for Augustus's grandson Gaius Caesar on his expedition to Arabia.[33] Glaphyra's father, Archelaos, was also a consultant. Whether Juba passed through Elaioussa-Sebaste on his way east is not known, but eventually, after his services to the expedition were no longer required, he ended up at Archelaos's court. The two kings would have had much in common: both were scholars (Archelaos wrote an *Alexander History* and works on cults and agriculture),[34] and both ruled extensive kingdoms. Cleopatra VII and Herod the Great were gone, so Juba and Archelaos were the most powerful allied monarchs. Archelaos was perhaps ten to fifteen years older than Juba and may have given good counsel to the latter, who had never known his father. Before long, Juba and Glaphyra married: both kings seem to have seen this as a linkage between West and East, indicative of grandiose ambitions that in time would cause trouble for both dynasties. The marriage probably took place before the summer of AD 1, since at some time the royal couple was honored by the Athenians, and they may have been in mainland Greece for the Olympic Games that summer, which the allied monarchs often attended and were even involved with: both Archelaos and Herod were benefactors of the festival. The inscription commemorating Juba and Glaphyra was carved on a base, so there was a portrait statue of them—now lost—on the Akropolis of Athens.[35]

It is probable that Archelaos, having failed to create a marriage alliance with the Herodians—whose importance had declined with the death of Herod in 4 BC and the refusal of Augustus to allow any of his surviving sons to have a kingship—now turned his ambitions toward Mauretania, given that Juba had recently become available as a son-in-law with the death of Cleopatra Selene, around 5 BC.[36] The arrangement allowed Glaphyra to assume the title of queen for the only time in her career. But this marriage was not to last, and there is no evidence that she went to Mauretania to assume her queenly role. It had ended before AD 6 with a divorce, not with death, since both monarchs survived the separation.[37] The most probable explanation for the termination of the marriage is that Augustus refused to validate the agreement because it created a dangerously large power base across the entire Roman Empire; Archelaos's own recent marriage to the widowed Pythodoris of Pontos, who herself ruled a vast territory, may also have given Augustus reason for concern. The connections with Juba and Pythodoris meant that in theory Archelaos's sphere of influence now extended from the Black Sea to the Atlantic, something that the Romans certainly would have questioned.[38]

The Return to the Herodians

Glaphyra was now once widowed and once divorced. Before long, another son of Herod the Great, Archelaos (probably named after Glaphyra's father), appeared at Elaioussa-Sebaste, perhaps in AD 4 or 5. This Archelaos was currently ethnarch of Judaea, Samaria, and Idumaea, having been awarded that title and territory by Augustus upon the death of his father in 4 BC.[39] Glaphyra was his former sister-in-law, whom he would have already known. Allegedly Archelaos fell for her while at her father's court, and they were married and returned to Judaea. This must have occurred before AD 6, because in that year (the tenth of his reign) Archelaos was deposed by Augustus and sent to reside at Vienna in Gaul.[40] He was removed because of serious difficulties between him and the aristocracies of Judaea and Samaria, and it certainly did not help his reputation that his marriage to Glaphyra violated Jewish law, since it was improper to marry the widow of one's brother unless the earlier marriage had been childless.[41]

But when Archelaos was deposed, Glaphyra had already died. According to Josephus, shortly after she arrived in Judaea for the second time, she had a dream in which her first husband, Alexander, reproached her for both her second and third marriages—especially the latter—and a few days later she was dead.[42] Dreams are a common feature in Josephus's narratives, and he was somewhat concerned that his readers might not take them seriously, but he believed that they were important when they involved royalty and because they demonstrated divine concern for human affairs.[43] Yet even if a literary fiction, the dream shows the inevitable misgivings Glaphyra surely had about returning to an environment that had caused her so much difficulty a decade previously, although she was probably not particularly sensitive to the nuances of Jewish law. Her death occurred before her husband went into exile, in AD 6, as there is no suggestion that she accompanied him. She was probably around forty years of age.

The Legacy of Glaphyra

Although at first glance Glaphyra seems merely to have been a pawn of her father and husbands, and there is some truth to this, nevertheless her career demonstrates the power that royal women wielded in the Augustan period. Her astute and cagy father used every possible means to expand his kingdom, and with only two children, his options were limited. As his only daughter, Glaphyra became an important part of his ambitions, yet her dynastic marriages were less than successful: those with the Herodians bordered on disaster, and the only one that might have worked was with Juba, but it was so powerful an alliance that it was vetoed by Augustus. Archelaos's own attempt to enhance the Cappadocian kingdom was reflected in his marriage to Pythodoris of Pontos, also an example of his vigorous efforts to improve to his own advantage the interconnectivity of the eastern dynastic network. Yet Glaphyra's personality remains shadowy: she received the title of queen only during her brief marriage to Juba and never seems to have visited her new territories. There are no extant portraits of her or coins bearing her name, and no activities are known beyond her marriages and other family relationships.

She was, to some extent, a victim of the pernicious internecine squabbles of the Herodians. Yet the Herodian women's envy and jealousy of her—even if somewhat self-inflicted—demonstrates that she was a person of power and authority. Except for the inscription from Athens, knowledge of her comes solely from the writings of Josephus, and she is a prime example of how faint the record of women of importance can be. Yet ironically her descendants survived for a longer span of time than those of the Ptolemies, the Seleukids, or Augustus or, in fact, most other eastern dynasties. What her relationship was to the Roman aristocracy remains an enigma: all her husbands and her father were well known in Rome, and she was important enough to be honored by the Athenians and to be a challenge to Augustus. Yet except for the visit to Athens, there is no evidence for her outside her father's kingdom or Judaea. Her father continued to pursue his ambitions for more than a decade after she died, until he again overreached and was called to account by Tiberius in AD 17, dying while in Rome, which resulted in the provincialization of his kingdom.[44] Juba returned to Mauretania after the divorce, spending his final years finishing *On Arabia* and writing his autobiography, as well as gradually transferring power to his son Ptolemy. Glaphyra was an important player in the lives of her father and all her husbands.

4

Salome of Judaea

The Background

In the second century BC, deteriorating and increasingly repressive conditions in the Levantine regions of the Seleukid Empire—between Syria and Egypt—led to the rise of an indigenous liberation movement under the Hasmoneans, named after a little-known Hasmon.[1] He was the ancestor of a priestly family whose first prominent member was a certain Mattathias, father of the famous Judas Maccabeus (died 167 BC), who led the revolt against the Seleukids. By the end of the century, the descendants of Mattathias were calling themselves kings: the first to do so, in 104 BC, was probably his great-grandson Aristoboulos I, whose brother, Alexander Jannaios (ruled 103-76 BC), certainly held the title.[2] The borders of their territory varied, depending on their relations with the Seleukids and Ptolemies, but at its greatest extent in the early first century BC the Hasmonean kingdom extended from north of the Sea of Galilee to the Egyptian frontier and east into the desert beyond the Jordan, although there were various independent cities along the coast.[3] The Hasmoneans continued in power until the second half of the first century BC. Around 37 BC a Hasmonean princess, Mariamme, married Herod, of Idumaean ancestry and later to be known by the epithet "the Great." He had just been named king by Antonius and Octavian in place of the weak Hasmonean candidates. With the death in 35 BC of Mariamme's brother, Aristoboulos, the last Hasmonean claimant to the throne, who mysteriously drowned in one of the palace pools at Jericho, the Hasmonean dynasty evolved into a Herodian one.[4]

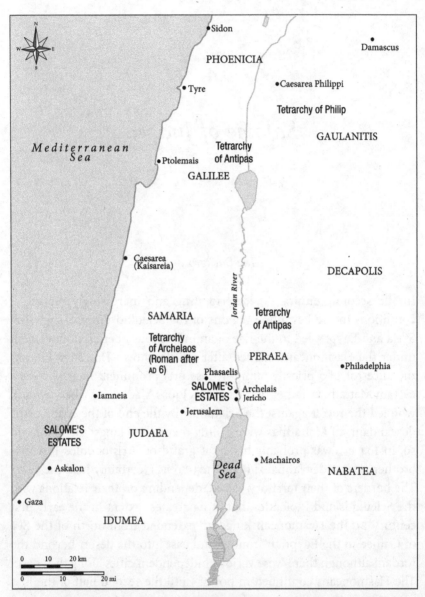

MAP 3. The southern Levant after the death of Herod the Great, showing the estates of Salome.

Idumaea (biblical Edom) was the territory at the southern edge of the Hasmonean kingdom, between the coast and the Dead Sea. The Herodians probably came from Marisa, about twenty miles inland at modern Tel Sandahanna, today a prominent mound with extensive

FIG. 9. View of ancient Marisa.
Shutterstock 630021467.

remains (fig. 9).[5] In the late second century BC, the Idumaeans were forcibly converted to Judaism; the Herodians, at least, were also Hellenized
and eventually Romanized, creating multiple allegiances that could be
problematic.[6] A wealthy citizen of Marisa, Antipatros, rose to prominence in the early first century BC, and his fortunes and those of his
family eventually drifted toward nearby Askalon, a famous independent
coastal city that had long been a major port and trading center control-
ling a fertile hinterland (fig. 10). Remains from Neolithic through medieval times have been found at the site: the city flourished even more
after Herod the Great favored his home region.[7]

Around 80 BC Antipatros strengthened his position by marrying
the Nabataean princess Kypros.[8] Information about her is vague, but
she was probably related to the new Nabataean king, Aretas IV, who
had just come to the throne. Within a decade Antipatros had won
the favor of the ruling Hasmoneans and had become commander
(*strategos*) of Idumaea.[9] He soon became involved in Roman affairs,
eventually assisting Julius Caesar in 48 BC with the war in Alexandria
that confirmed the reign of Cleopatra VII, and as a result he was given
Roman citizenship (which devolved onto his descendants). He generally supported the Roman cause, but by 42 BC he had been assassinated,

FIG. 10. View of ancient Askalon. Shutterstock 248945809.

a victim of the turbulent politics of the era.[10] His widow, Kypros, is last known when her son Herod placed her and other members of the family in the fortress of Masada before he went to Rhodes to meet Octavian after the Battle of Actium, in order to explain his previous support of Antonius.[10] Herod honored both his parents architecturally: the fortress of Kypros lies in the hills a few miles west-southwest of Jericho at modern Tell el-`Aqaba, and Antipatris (modern Ras el-`Ain) was a city at the interior edge of the coastal plain northwest of Jerusalem.[11]

Kypros and Antipatros had five children: Phasael (77-40 BC), Herod (73-4 BC), Joseph (70-38 BC), Pheroras (65-7 BC), and Salome (57 BC-AD 10). Their names reflect the multicultural environment into which they were born: one Nabataean (Phasael), two Greek (Herod and Pheroras), and two Jewish (Joseph and Salome).

Salome and Joseph

Salome was probably named after Alexandra Salome, who had died in 67 BC and had been the Hasmonean queen when Antipatros of Askalon achieved prominence. Any birthdate before the 50s BC for the younger Salome seems unlikely because she was in young adulthood when the

Herodian court took refuge at Masada due to the Parthian invasion of 41 BC: a close reading of Josephus's text implies that she already had a child. Although not mentioned by name in the narrative of these events, those going to Masada included Herod's sister, and Salome was the only one.[12] Moreover, she was still of marriageable age as late as around 20 BC.

Salome's first husband and the putative father of the unnamed child at Masada was her uncle Joseph, a typical example of the uncle–niece marriage common in the eastern Mediterranean. Little is known about his early career: he may have succeeded his brother Antipatros as commander of Idumaea.[13] Joseph was the last survivor of his generation and thus had a certain amount of prestige within the evolving Herodian family. He and Salome seem to have had only one child, the daughter who accompanied her mother to Masada in 41 BC. Her name is not known.[14]

Salome's marriage to Joseph had thus presumably taken place by 42 BC and increased her status, putting her on the path to becoming one of the most powerful women at the Herodian court. Two years later Herod was named king by Antonius and Octavian. Yet the court was already a pit of intrigue, with the tensions between the deposed Hasmoneans and the ascendant Herodians reaching the danger point: the marriage of Herod to the Hasmonean Mariamme in 37 BC, instead of creating a peaceful alliance, only increased the potential for disaster.[15] After the last Hasmonean claimant, Mariamme's brother, Aristoboulos III, drowned at Jericho in 35 BC, their mother, Alexandra, the matriarch of the Hasmonean family, devoted the rest of her life to exacting revenge. Alexandra appealed to Cleopatra VII in Egypt, who had her own reasons for causing trouble for Herod, since she wanted much of his territory. This meant that Herod was now in the unenviable position of having both his mother-in-law and his greatest political and military rival allied against him. Cleopatra persuaded Antonius to investigate Herod's activities, and thus in 34 BC he was summoned to the triumvir's headquarters at Laodikeia in Syria.[16]

When Herod went to Syria, he left his uncle Joseph in charge of the affairs of the kingdom. This was an obvious move, since Joseph was the most experienced and senior member of the family. Herod had no idea what would happen at Laodikeia, and he left instructions with Joseph to eliminate Mariamme should he not return; the reasons for this are not totally clear (beyond an early manifestation of Herod's infamous erratic behavior). Yet it was rumored that Antonius and Mariamme were interested in one another—she allegedly sent him her portrait[17]—and Herod was clearly worried about a Hasmonean–Roman alliance should he be detained or eliminated in Syria.

Before long a rumor spread that in fact Herod had been put to death by Antonius. Alexandra, seeing her chance, convinced Joseph to remove himself and the royal women, including his wife Salome, her mother Kypros, and Mariamme, from Jerusalem and to seek refuge with the Roman legion that was stationed outside the city. Alexandra's exact motive for this is not obvious, but it is probable she thought that putting Herod's uncle and sister in Roman hands would help her own position, as well as that of her daughter, Mariamme, and cause a movement away from the Herodians back toward the Hasmoneans, since the king was presumed dead.

But then a letter arrived from Herod stating that all was well, and moreover Antonius had absolved him of all charges, confirmed his position, and even rebuked Cleopatra. Alexandra's plans suddenly fell through. When Herod returned to Judaea, he learned everything from Salome and their mother, Kypros. In addition, Salome, perhaps seeing her chance to gain the ascendancy, accused her husband Joseph of having an affair with Mariamme. The ease with which charges were made about Mariamme's faithfulness is suggestive, and the truth of the matter will never be known, but Herod, who was genuinely fond of her, was alternately angry and forgiving—perhaps another early sign of the mental instability that would plague him for the rest of his life—and eventually decided to exonerate his wife. More serious was the suggestion that Joseph and Alexandra were conspiring against Herod—unlikely since the two were generally at odds—and thus Joseph was summarily executed and Alexandra arrested. Salome was clearly Herod's informant for much of this, whether or not it was true.

Her ambitions essentially ended Alexandra's plans for a Hasmonean restoration. In a quick and decisive move, Salome had eliminated an elderly husband for whom she probably never had much affection and whose usefulness was nearing its end, and had as well neutralized the most prominent Hasmonean woman. Although Mariamme was spared, her influence was waning, and she would be Salome's next target. She also had demonstrated her role as a confidante to her brother Herod and, despite issues between them for the next thirty years, she would be the only family member to remain largely on good terms with him as long as he lived.

Soon the widowed Salome married an Idumaean aristocrat with a priestly background, Kostobaros.[18] He first appeared in the service of Herod at the time of the latter's assumption of the kingship, when he became commander of Idumaea and Gaza. He almost immediately began to object to Herod's rule, largely on religious grounds—resenting the forced conversion of the Idumaeans to Judaism—and probably also because of an issue of national identity. But these feelings were presumably little known outside his immediate circle when he married Salome not long after the execution of her husband Joseph, in 34 BC.

Before his marriage, Kostobaros had seen a potential ally in Cleopatra VII, whose territorial ambitions were at their peak. This was around the time of the Donations of Alexandria, when she was attempting to expand her possessions into the Levant. In fact, he may have lost territory to her as part of the Donations.[19] Despite this, Kostobaros reached out to the queen, suggesting that she should control Idumaea, believing that placing her and Herod in competition would be to his own advantage, perhaps with himself emerging as the ruler of an independent Idumaea. Cleopatra did ask Antonius for Idumaea, but the request was denied. At the same time Alexandra, the Hasmonean matriarch, saw these actions as her chance for renewed power and began to support Cleopatra's ambitions: all this led to the complex intrigues that resulted in Herod's summons to Antonius in Syria in 34 BC and the eventual death of Salome's first husband, Joseph. Moreover, there was a shadowy Idumaean nationalist and populist group, called the Sons of Baba (seemingly pro-Hasmonean and anti-Herodian), which Kostobaros was cultivating and protecting.[20]

After Herod's return from Syria, the death of Joseph, and Salome's marriage to Kostobaros, animosity between Salome and Mariamme reached a dangerous level. They were rivals for the leadership of the women at court, and Salome claimed that Mariamme was abusive and adulterous: there were already issues of improper dealings between her and Antonius, an easy charge, perhaps, given Antonius's fondness for royal women. There was a peculiar incident involving Salome, Mariamme, Herod, and a love potion, which Herod believed was really an attempt by either his sister or his wife to poison him. Then Salome suggested to Herod that Mariamme, as one of the few surviving Hasmoneans, had an extensive popular following. As this family squabble unfolded, greater things were happening: in 31 BC Cleopatra and Antonius were defeated at Actium, and early the following year Herod was ordered by Octavian to come to Rhodes in order to explain his previous support of Antonius. Needless to say, Herod successfully absolved himself and became a follower of Octavian, but the situation within the Herodian family had become even more perilous. By 29 BC he had been persuaded of Mariamme's treachery and had her executed. Few doubted that Salome's enmity had played a major role in these events.[21]

This left only one potential rival for Salome, Mariamme's mother, Alexandra, who had turned against her daughter in her last days, perhaps for reasons of self-preservation. Tensions between the Idumaean side of the family (represented by Herod and his siblings) and the Hasmonean (Mariamme and her half-Hasmonean children) were a constant feature of the dynastic politics of the era, even as those who were full Hasmoneans died off. All the male members of the dynasty were dead by 30 BC, often helped on their way by the Idumaeans.[22] Yet despite this, the repercussions from the death of Mariamme and the heightened potential for a pro-Hasmonean uprising gave Alexandra a final chance to seize power. In 28 BC, when Herod was stranded in Samaria due to a major illness, she attempted to take control of Jerusalem, but the plot was exposed and she was promptly executed.[23]

Thus Salome had not only engineered the elimination of her rivals at court but essentially brought the Hasmonean dynasty to extinction, with the exception of the half-Hasmonean children of Herod and Mariamme. The nature of Salome's relationship with her husband Kostobaros at this time is uncertain: the implication is that she was in the palace in Jerusalem while he was posted to Idumaea, probably residing at Askalon. He was still plotting revolution, but from a substantially weakened position due to the demise of his two major supporters, Alexandra and Cleopatra VII. As the world settled into the new Augustan regime and an unprecedented period of peace, Salome dominated the women of the Herodian court and, to some extent, her brother the king. Even though she and Kostobaros spent much of their time apart, she probably had informants in his entourage and eventually learned about his intrigues.[24] In particular, there was the matter of the Sons of Baba, whom Kostobaros had harbored for a number of years: his ability to do this for so long, and without Herod's knowledge of it, may suggest that the Sons were not particularly powerful or a great threat. Nevertheless, Salome informed the king about the activities of her husband, who denied everything. But Herod tracked down the Sons of Baba and eliminated them: this was said to be the last extinction of the Hasmonean line, although how the group was related to it is uncertain. In fact, there was also a Hasmonean woman still alive, a niece of Alexandra, who married Herod's son Antipatros. Her name is unknown, she hardly appears in the historical record, and she was never a political threat; any Hasmonean aspirations ended with the Sons of Baba.[25] Salome, realizing that any further connection with Kostobaros was unwise, filed for divorce, an action technically in violation of Jewish law (as the husband, not the wife, had to initiate proceedings), but Greek and Roman divorce customs had penetrated Judaea, and under certain circumstances Salome's actions would have been considered legal.[26]

But the matter of divorce soon became moot as Herod had Kostobaros executed, probably in 26 BC, leaving Salome a widow again.[27] The marriage, which had lasted for about seven years, had produced several children. The most prominent was Berenike (I), who, as already noted, would be a player in the matter of Glaphyra.[28] She married Aristoboulos, a son of Herod and Mariamme, and became the ancestor of many Herodian descendants, including the future royal line represented by the kings Agrippa I and II.[29]

Salome had at least two other children. The better known was another Antipatros, who became greatly involved in the succession struggle after the death of Herod but who vanished from the record thereafter; the assumption that he was Kostobaros's offspring is based on a reference to an unnamed son of the couple. Salome also had a second daughter. These were her last known children, yet with the death of her second husband she was probably only in her early thirties and still a good marriage prospect.[30]

The Arrival of Syllaios

Around 20 BC, the chief minister of the Nabataeans, Syllaios, came to the Herodians. He was the dominant personality at the Nabataean court—the king, Obodas, was weak—holding the title "the brother of the king," a legal formulation demonstrating his power.[31] In 25-24 BC Syllaios had served as guide for the prefect of Egypt, Aelius Gallus, who made a reconnaissance into Arabia: the problems that the expedition encountered did not reflect on him, despite attempts by Gallus's friends to make the charge.[32] Syllaios was a man of great ambition, the effective ruler of Nabataea, and one suspects that his plans included a major role in the new environment of the Levant in the years after the death of Cleopatra VII. His service to Gallus presumably came with the expectation of Roman support and enhancement of his position, but this never happened.

In addition, he was particularly concerned about Herod's increased status, especially with his acquisition of much of Cleopatra's Levantine territories. Moreover, Augustus gave Herod districts to the northeast of his traditional kingdom—roughly the modern Golan—that seemed to encroach on regions historically Nabataean.[33] Syllaios realized that some arrangement with the Herodians was necessary, and so in time he made an official visit to Herod. At a dinner party he and Salome were immediately attracted to one another, according to reports; whether this was Syllaios's original intention cannot be determined. Yet it was said that the activities of the couple bordered on the indiscreet. Regardless of their feelings, Syllaios certainly had a larger agenda on his mind—if he came to rule an enhanced Nabataean kingdom, Salome would be a suitable queen—and she presumably was favorably disposed to the prospect of a new marriage to an attractive and handsome young man of power.[34] A few months later, on the occasion of another visit to the Herodian court, Syllaios formally asked Herod to be allowed to marry Salome.

The exact date of this request is difficult to determine. Salome had been married until about 26 BC, and Syllaios was occupied with Gallus's expedition into 24 BC, so his visits to the Herodians were probably no earlier than that year. The territorial donations to Herod in the Golan began at that time and were completed in 20 BC—a period when Syllaios might have felt particularly threatened by Herodian expansionism—and this is probably when he would have believed a marriage alliance with them might be useful.[35] It had to be before 12 BC, because at that time a group of chieftains from Trachonitis (the region south of Damascus) fled to Syllaios after an unsuccessful revolt against Herod, having taken advantage of Herod's journey to Rome in that year, and Josephus noted that this was after the time of the marriage proposal. But there is no suggestion that it was at any time close to that date, and thus it was probably around 20 BC, perhaps shortly after Augustus was in Syria at the beginning of the year.[36]

Salome may have gone so far as to sign a wedding contract, but soon Herod forbade any marriage. The official reason was that Syllaios refused to convert to Judaism, but this was merely an excuse—there was no such issue when Glaphyra of Cappadocia married into the Herodian family twice some years later—and the real reason was that Herod realized Syllaios was dangerous. Rumors that Salome was giving him sensitive information added to the problem. She took the unusual step of writing Augustus's wife, Livia, for advice. It is clear that Salome wanted the marriage and had a personal feeling for Syllaios, but unfortunately Livia advised against it.[37]

This is the first demonstration of a relationship between Livia and the Herodian family. Livia had married Octavian in 38 BC and had become the most powerful woman in the new Roman imperial family.[38] There is no precise knowledge of when Livia and Salome might first have had personal contact, yet the most probable time is when Augustus and Livia were in Syria, in 20 BC: if Salome had just met her when the issue of Syllaios came to a peak, there might have been a reason for seeking her advice.[39] But Livia was astute enough to realize the dangers (both to the Herodians and the new Roman regime) of a connection with the overly ambitious Nabataean. Nevertheless, this initiated a long period of close relations between the two women that would last until Salome's death thirty years later. In fact, the correspondence between them was so important to Herodian ambitions and policy that in time forged letters were appearing. Livia contributed lavishly to the festivities for the dedication of Herod's Caesarea in 10 BC and may have helped endow the athletic and music contests that were to be commemorated there every five years. She was also generously remembered in the wills of both Herod and Salome.[40]

But Livia would not support the marriage, and Syllaios returned to Nabataea and devoted most of the rest of his life to causing difficulty for the Herodian family, such as harboring the rebels from Trachonitis. Herod and the Nabataean remained at odds for more than a decade, each trying to destabilize the other's regime. When a succession struggle erupted in Nabataea in 9 BC and Syllaios was disappointed in his hope of being named king, he retaliated in frustration against the Nabataean aristocracy and even attempted to have Herod killed. Herod reported this to Rome, and Syllaios went there to plead his own case. Yet Augustus felt that he had been a problem long enough and had him executed, probably around 7 BC.[41]

All this was in the future when Salome and Syllaios were denied the right to marry. With his dismissal, presumably in late 20 BC, there was still the question of a husband for Salome, and Herod arranged a marriage to one of his close associates, Alexas, who came from a family long connected with the Herodians.[42] He was an important member of the king's entourage, perhaps his military chief of staff, and his family would be major landowners in Judaea for some time. Salome had little choice other than to accept the marriage, since she had been somewhat discredited by the Syllaios affair, and, moreover, this time Livia endorsed it. Yet of all three of her husbands he is the most obscure, although he played a prominent role at the time of Herod's death. He remains a shadowy figure, and in an unusual reversal of the normal parameters of ancient historiography, he is essentially known only because of his marriage to Salome. There were no recorded children from this relationship.

The Final Turbulent Years at the Court of Herod the Great

Despite the elimination of her rivals, after her new marriage Salome became involved in the heightened tensions of the last years of her brother's reign, but the twists and turns of these intrigues, alliances, and broken alliances can be both difficult to follow and relatively uninteresting. The sons of Herod and Mariamme, Alexander and Aristoboulos, were reaching their maturity, and as the first to have been born after Herod became king, were seen as heirs apparent. Both began to be at serious odds with their aunt. As previously noted, the arrival at court, perhaps around 17 BC, of Glaphyra of Cappadocia, who became Alexander's wife and was an outsider who flaunted her social superiority, began to cause major difficulties.[43] At about the same time, Aristoboulos married Salome's daughter Berenike (I), and the mother did her best to create dissension between her daughter and Glaphyra.

Salome sought an ally in her brother Pheroras, but eventually they turned against each other, with Pheroras upbraiding his sister for her alleged secret marriage contract with Syllaios.[44] Pheroras had been close to Kostobaros, and the reason for his animosity toward Salome may have been that she had revealed her former husband's plans to Herod, leading to his execution. Pheroras also reported to Herod that Salome had said that the king was too friendly with Glaphyra. Glaphyra's husband Alexander wrote an extensive treatise (four books) claiming that he had been slandered by both his aunt Salome and his uncle Pheroras, who were plotting to eliminate Herod. Moreover, he said that Salome had forced herself into his bedroom one night.[45] Then the issue of Syllaios erupted again, several years after his departure but while he was still a problem for the kingdom, and Salome was charged not only with continuing to make improper contact with the Nabataean but also with having revealed state secrets. To complicate things, some letters appeared that Salome allegedly had written Livia and that made violent attacks on Herod, dating from the time of the relationship with Syllaios.[46] Although there was certainly legitimate correspondence between the two women, these letters turned out to be forgeries of Antipatros, Herod's eldest son, who had spent most of his life away from the court—he had been born before Herod became king and thus was not considered for the succession—but who had been recalled around 14 BC and was enjoying Herod's favor.[47]

Salome nearly met her death at this time, but a warning from her nephew and son-in-law Aristoboulos allowed her to prepare an eloquent and dramatic defense before her brother the king, and she was pardoned. In fact, Herod then arrested both Alexander and Aristoboulos and, on the advice of Augustus, eventually put them on trial at Berytos.[48] The trial became a great event, with Roman officials, Herod, Salome, and Pheroras in attendance, and the sons were convicted and executed. Alexander's widow, Glaphyra, was sent back to her father in Cappadocia. Salome's daughter Berenike, the widow of Aristoboulos, had a brief and unsuccessful marriage to one of Herod's brothers-in-law, Theudion, and then moved to Rome with her children and was welcomed by Augustus, flourishing in the circle that developed later around Antonia, the daughter of the triumvir Antonius. She died between AD 29 and 37.[49] Pheroras withdrew to his own estates in Peraia, east of the Jordan, vowing never to return to the Herodian court as long as the king was alive, and died shortly thereafter. Rumors were common that Herod had poisoned him, but it is more probable that he was the victim of a plot within his own household.[50]

By this time Herod had only a few years to live, and the recent events showed that he had become dangerously unstable. With the deaths of Alexander and Aristoboulos, the heir apparent was their elder brother Antipatros. Yet he was already implicated in the palace intrigues, since he had written the forged letters from Salome to Livia. His aunt closely watched him and reported his activities to her brother, with the result that Antipatros was arrested and executed in 4 BC only days before the king's own death.[51]

The Death of Herod

At the time of the death of Antipatros, Herod was at Jericho, residing in the palace whose remains are prominent today. One of his last acts was to alter his will in light of recent events, favoring Salome and naming one of his remaining sons, Archelaos, king. He also ordered that the leading men of Judaea were to be locked up in the hippodrome at Jericho, which is also still visible. Then he summoned Salome and her husband Alexas. Josephus reported his final words to his sister:

> I know that the Judaeans will celebrate my death with
> a festival, but I can have the mourning of others and
> a magnificent funeral if you assist me and agree to
> these instructions. You are aware of these men [in the
> hippodrome]: as soon as I expire, immediately have them
> surrounded by soldiers and killed, so that all Judaea and
> every household will involuntarily weep for me.[52]

Although speeches in ancient texts are always problematic, there is a good chance that these are close to Herod's words, if not an actual transcription: the account is straightforward, without any rhetorical flourishes, and Josephus relied on the contemporary report of Nikolaos of Damascus, who was almost certainly in Jericho at the time and would play a major role in subsequent events.[53]

When Herod died, Salome was for the moment the effective ruler of the kingdom. She immediately went to the hippodrome, before the king's death had been announced, and released the prisoners, telling them that Herod had changed his mind and they were free to return home. Her action was remembered for generations as the greatest of public services.[54] She then called a public assembly and had Herod's will and final letter read. In the letter Herod thanked the soldiers for their loyalty and urged them to support his son Archelaos as his successor. The will, the last of several that he had written, named Archelaos king and created tetrarchies out of the northern and eastern parts of the kingdom for his two other sons, Antipas and Philip. There were various bequests, including ones to Augustus and Livia, but Salome was the major beneficiary, receiving five hundred thousand pieces of silver and the territories of Iamneia, Azotos, and Phasaelis.[55] These estates were described as toparchies (*toparchiai*), a Hellenistic Greek word referring to a local district, which was perhaps originally applied to Egypt but which came to be common in the southern Levant.[56] As ruler of a toparchy, or toparchies, Salome was *despotis* (mistress), a term seemingly originally from Greek tragedy and applied to aristocratic women of authority.[57] Thus she was more estate manager than royal ruler.

Agriculture was an important part of the economy of contemporary Judaea, in fact the major source of income for the Herodian family. Royal estates, such as those Salome acquired, were everywhere, and land taxes were exceedingly high. Farming was more efficient than it had been in Hasmonean times, with better irrigation and a greater diversity of crops, as well as the benefits of the global economy of the Roman world.[58] The territorial bequests gave Salome a revenue of sixty talents annually. Iamneia was slightly inland, about twenty miles northeast of Askalon, with a port city to its northwest. It was a Philistine town—this stretch of coast was the heartland of the ancient Philistine territory— that had come under Idumaean control and eventually was part of Herod's kingdom. Iamneia was a regional market center, but little is known about the site, since it is essentially unexcavated.

A few miles to the southwest of Iamneia was Azotos, biblical Ashdod, also slightly inland with a port city. Important since the Late Bronze Age, it was also a Philistine settlement but had a long history of adopting an independent profile; it was prominent enough to be one of the few cities in the southern Levant known to the Greek world by the fifth century BC. Extensive excavations, although focused on earlier periods, have revealed some of the Herodian city.[59] The territories of Azotos and Iamneia were adjoining, and to the south of Azotos was Askalon, part of which Augustus added to Salome's inheritance. Exactly what portion of it she obtained is not certain—her possessions may have been limited to the royal estates—but thus she controlled a district from north of Gaza (probably at the modern Nahal Shikma) to beyond Iamneia (at the Nahal Sorek, just south of Tel Aviv), or about thirty miles of coast, as well as the interior of the coastal plain, probably as far as the beginning of the Judaean hills, a fertile and productive region of perhaps five hundred to seven hundred square miles, although the city of Askalon itself probably remained independent. Salome's husband Alexas may have already owned property in this region, whether hereditary or given to him by his brother-in-law Herod.[60]

Separate from this was the third district of the bequest, Phasaelis. This was a town about fifteen miles north of Jericho on the west side of the Jordan valley. It was a new foundation, built by Herod probably in the early 30s BC in honor of his brother Phasael, who had died under mysterious circumstances late in 41 BC or early in the following year.[61] Phasaelis was designed to develop the agricultural potential of an unpopulated area, and by the time Salome obtained it thirty-five years later, it was a rich agricultural colony, with date plantations that still flourish. The site is at modern Fasa'yil, which preserves the ancient name, and although there are extensive visible remains, it has not been excavated.

The Succession Struggle

Shortly after Herod's death, the survivors mounted a notable expedition to Rome.[62] The participants included Salome and her children Antipatros and Berenike, Herod's sons Archelaos (the heir apparent) and Antipas, Nikolaos of Damascus, and other prominent members of the court. The third son, Philip, remained in Judaea to manage the royal interests.[63] Since the account of the events, extant in Josephus's two treatises, relies on the eyewitness report of Nikolaos, who was Salome's opponent regarding the future of Herod's kingdom, some of the negative information about her that pervades the narrative may originate from the historian's personal animosity.[64]

Salome, using a variant will, had promised to support Antipas for the kingship, who was supposedly to receive only a tetrarchy. Upon arrival at Rome, she presented Augustus with an indictment of Archelaos, which future events would prove to be a perceptive analysis of his character. Augustus convened a council of his intimates and family members and asked the various plaintiffs to state their cases. The most eloquent was Salome's son Antipatros, who spoke at length against Archelaos. This was refuted by Nikolaos. There was also a party that promoted the abolishment of the monarchy and the attachment of Herod's kingdom to the Roman province of Syria.

After several days of deliberation, Augustus upheld most of Herod's will, except that he rejected any claims to kingship. He gave Archelaos the territories willed by Herod, but granted him only the title of ethnarch, a term common in the Levant for a regional ruler. Antipas and Philip were confirmed in their tetrarchies. But going beyond Herod's bequests, he also gave Salome the estates at Askalon. This was an astute move on his part, because it gave her a primary residence outside of Archelaos's territory, since Askalon had remained independent and had never been part of Herod's kingdom, despite its role in the history of the family. Archelaos was already gaining a reputation for violence and cruelty, which became fully apparent when he took up residence in his ethnarchy and initiated a purge of his opponents.[65] His turbulent reign lasted fewer than ten years, until mounting complaints to Rome resulted in his dismissal, with Augustus banishing him to Vienna in Gaul and confiscating his property.[66] Had Salome returned to Archelaos's tetrarchy, her safety would have been problematic.

In fact, she may have remained in Rome for a while after Augustus's judgment. She was respected by the imperial family and was a friend of Livia. Moreover, her daughter Berenike had similar close relationships; Augustus honored both women.[67] Some years later the emperor Tiberius had a slave named Idumaeus, who may have been a bequest from Salome to the emperor's mother, Livia.[68] Eventually Salome returned to her estates at Askalon; local coins that seem to display a portrait of Augustus may represent her assumption of power.[69] Herod had devoted great efforts to rebuilding the city that was essentially the ancestral seat of his family—probably Salome's birthplace—but her royal residences are not known archaeologically.

The Final Years

Salome probably remained in Askalon for the rest of her life. She may soon have been widowed again: her husband Alexas is not mentioned after his involvement in the events surrounding Herod's death. Her last years were probably the only quiet time she had ever experienced. Significantly, she does not seem to have been involved in the ruling affairs of any of her three nephews and was wise enough never to enter their territories again. She played no known role when her nemesis Glaphyra returned to the court as Archelaos's wife. Salome was more than fifty when Herod died and would no longer be useful as a marriage prospect, even if widowed again.

In AD 6, when Archelaos was banished, she was granted the district of Archelais, another date-producing region. This city had been founded by Archelaos and lay at modern Khirbet el-Beiyudat, between Jericho and Phasaelis; thus the acquisition expanded Salome's territory in the Jordan valley to the south. No remains of the Herodian period are visible.⁷⁰ Archelaos had enlarged the date plantations, which were already world famous (and remain so today); somewhat earlier Horace had written of "Herodis palmetis pinguibus" ("the rich palm groves of Herod").⁷¹ These orchards were well known for an exceptionally large variety of date (about four inches long) called the nikolas, a name bestowed by Augustus in honor of Nikolaos of Damascus; the emperor was particularly fond of the dates and received regular shipments.⁷² Salome's acquisition of this productive region would have added substantially to her revenue and created a large estate north of Jericho that was one of the most agriculturally prosperous in the southern Levant.

Nothing further is known about her last years. She died sometime between the dismissal of her nephew in AD 6 and the death of Augustus in AD 14.⁷³ When Archelaos was sent to Gaul, the Romans gained control of the ethnarchy—although obviously Salome's new estates were not included—and created a small sub-province under the control of the governor of Syria.⁷⁴ The local Roman administrator had the title of prefect, an office first held by a certain Coponius, followed by Marcus Ambibulus, during whose tenure Salome died. Neither is documented in any other context, and it is not known when the office changed hands other than within the eight-year span of AD 6-14. Presumably Salome died around AD 10. She was perhaps nearly seventy and by far the last survivor of her generation. She left her estates to Livia, although the royal residence at Askalon is not mentioned in the bequest and may have reverted to local control, since the city remained an independent entity within the empire.⁷⁵ Livia sent her own estate manager with the title of procurator, a certain C. Herennius Capito, a career military officer who served for many years; he was still in office when Livia died in AD 29 and the estates passed to her son, the emperor Tiberius, remaining imperial property thereafter.⁷⁶

As with so many women in antiquity, Salome's character is difficult to assess. With one exception, everything that is known comes from the writings of Josephus, relying on Nikolaos of Damascus, who had his own issues with her. Moreover, she suffers from some of the same prejudices and source problems as her contemporary Cleopatra VII—whom she surely knew—and is most remembered for her perceived negative qualities, in this case vindictiveness and hostility toward her relatives. Also like Cleopatra, she was said to have been sexually promiscuous and interested in activities inappropriate to a woman. Salome never exercised any legal power other than as mistress of her toparchies in her last years, but nevertheless she was highly influential within the Herodian dynasty as one of the major advisers to her brother. Her activities often seem violent, which is probably an accurate assessment given the vicious atmosphere at the Herodian court. She had few role models: her mother, Kypros, despite being a Nabataean princess, never had much authority and, despite her long life, remains shadowy. There were Hasmonean women of power, although given Salome's hostility to that dynasty it is problematic how influential they were. Herod's mother-in-law Alexandra was more a rival than a mentor. Alexandra's grandmother Alexandra Salome, the wife of King Alexander Jannaios, was Salome's namesake and the only independent queen in the Hasmonean line, ruling for nine years from 76 BC after the death of her husband, yet not without opposition and amid the inevitable accusations of improper activities for a woman.[77] She might have provided a model: Salome was born a few years after her death and may have been able to profit from any received memories of her career.

Nevertheless, Salome never had a chance to be queen and exercise royal power. It is perhaps curious that at the time of her brother's death there were no proposals that she be made queen of Judaea, but clearly this had not occurred to Herod (or had been rejected by him), and Salome did not have the advantage of having been married to or descended from a king. This might have changed if she had married Syllaios, but in fact her role was limited to mediation—however drastically—within the cantankerous Herodian household, more in the tradition of a Roman matron, which in the last analysis was a concept that may have had the greatest influence on her. Especially after her mother and the younger Alexandra died, she was undisputed mistress of the family, but still had to contend with Herod's wives (he was married nine times, although not all were in residence at once), his numerous children, and their spouses.

The strongest alliance that Salome made was with Livia, which not only provided her access to the imperial family and all that it represented politically and culturally in the Augustan era, but also gave her an understanding of the concept of the Roman matron; her role and that of Livia within their own families often seem to parallel one another, for better or worse.[78] These contacts in Rome would not only bring stability to the last decades of Salome's life as well as to the Herodian family (even though forced attrition also played a role), but prove beneficial to her descendants. It is most significant that the only mention of her outside the accounts of Josephus, by her contemporary Strabo, refers to the respect that she had within the imperial family.[79] Yet an odd twist to her reputation is the early Christian allegation, preserved in the *Acts of the Pagan Martyrs* (also called the *Acta Alexandrinorum*), that the emperor Claudius was her son. There may have been many strange tales about his birth, given his physical disabilities, and Salome had close connections with Claudius's actual mother, Antonia.[80]

Whether a physician named Salome was the same person as the sister of Herod is not known, although it has been suggested. She is recorded in only a single reference by Galen, the medical writer of the second century AD, who reported on a pain reliever allegedly associated with a certain Salome. Whether this was the mistress of Askalon is purely speculative, and the name may merely be in honor of her (or someone else), in the manner of the nikolas date.[81]

5

Dynamis of Bosporos

The Bosporan Kingdom

Greeks began to explore the remote coasts of the Black Sea in early times. The story of Jason and the Argonauts, although disputed as to detail, provides the first hints of Greek seamanship in this region, perhaps a search for precious metals.[1] From the eighth century BC, Greek settlements began to encircle the sea. Of particular interest was its northern edge, where a fifty-mile-long strait led to an interior body of water. The strait was called the Bosporos, which has been suggested to mean "Cow Ford" from the wanderings of Io in her bovine form, but is probably an indigenous name.[2] To avoid confusion with the better-known Bosporos at the other end of the Black Sea (the route to the Aegean), the northern Bosporos was often called the Kimmerian Bosporos, after the local inhabitants.

The Kimmerian Bosporos (modern Strait of Kerch) is from four to twenty miles wide and has long been considered the boundary between Europe and Asia. It leads to the Maiotis (the modern Sea of Azov), which is the outlet of one of the major rivers of the Black Sea drainage, the Tanais (modern Don), flowing twelve hundred miles from a source near modern Tula in Russia. The Tanais was an excellent trade route into the interior, and by the seventh century BC Greeks had established the trading post of Pantikapaion (at modern Kerch) on the European side of the Bosporos near its northern end (fig. 11). This region was connected with Colchis—a son of Jason's father-in-law, Aietes, was the traditional founder of Pantikapaion—and whether or not this was the case, these tales may have helped bring Greeks into the region.[3] Pantikapaion was

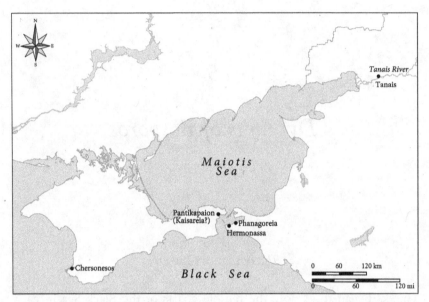

MAP 4. The Bosporan kingdom.

FIG. 11. Pantikapaion.

Shutterstock 365774894.

a primitive outpost at first—a remote Greek settlement—but eventually grew into the most important city of the region, especially after a local ruler, Archaianax, rose to power around 480 BC.[4] Archaeological evidence shows the evolution of Pantikapaion from a village of dugouts to a typical Greek city, with a prominent temple of Apollo, metal and pottery workshops, and a circuit wall of more than two miles around an akropolis.[5] Its territory extended to the mouth of the Tanais, nearly two hundred miles away, and its economy was based on the grain trade with the Greek heartland, especially Athens: by the fourth century BC, the region was the Athenians' primary supplier.[6] At approximately the same time, the rulers of Pantikapaion began to call themselves kings of Bosporos. The Bosporan sphere of influence extended south and east along the coast of the Black Sea toward Colchis; on occasion, as an economic strategy the rulers of Bosporos helped implement the piracy that was endemic in this region, although this probably came to an end by Roman times.[7]

The kingdom was ruled under a variety of dynasts until 109 BC, when Paraisades V was unable to restrain barbarian incursions and yielded his realm to the Pontic ruler Mithradates VI (whose lands were centered on the south shore of the sea). Bosporos was thus incorporated into his vast territories.[8] Mithradates ruled much of the Black Sea littoral for the next half century; his lengthy wars with Rome are well known. After his death in 63 BC, the Bosporan portions reverted to an independent kingdom under the rule of his son Pharnakes II, who reconstituted a powerful Bosporan state under close Roman supervision.[9] This kingdom lasted until late Roman times.

Bosporos was an alien and remote part of the Greco-Roman cultural sphere. Although no farther north than central France, it was perceived as being at the edge of the inhabitable world, near the endless northern forests and the unknown interior of Asia. The Bosporan cities were the northernmost Greek settlements, and both the Greek and local reactions to the cold were a matter of curiosity: ice could break bronze vessels, animals were different from those familiar in the Mediterranean world, and the Bosporos Strait was frozen several months out of the year. There was even a battle on the ice during the reign of Mithradates VI. The grapevine—the ultimate determining factor of Greek civilization—grew only with difficulty.[10] It could take two weeks to sail to Alexandria, even with a favorable wind, a long journey for the Mediterranean world, and

Greek geographers were astonished at how much the climate changed over this distance.[11]

With the death of Mithradates VI, his kingdom passed to the Romans, who provincialized parts of it and established allied rulers in others. Bosporos was made a separate entity and its territory somewhat reduced. The Roman candidate for rule was his son Pharnakes II, whom Mithradates had designated as his successor but who had betrayed his father in his last days. Taking the title Great King, Pharnakes reasserted Bosporan control as far as the mouth of the Tanais and even made attempts to reconquer cities on the southern shore of the Black Sea that had been part of his father's realm. And about the time he became king of Bosporos, or slightly before, his daughter, Dynamis, was born.[12]

With Pharnakes's expansionism, the Romans began to reconsider their support and may have reached out to a certain Asandros, whom the king had left in charge of Bosporos proper when he moved south.[13] With or without Roman encouragement, Asandros revolted against Pharnakes in 47 BC. By now the Romans realized that Pharnakes was more threat than ally, and Julius Caesar, returning from Egypt and Cleopatra VII, engaged Pharnakes at Zela in Pontos; this was the battle that Caesar described in his famous three-word dispatch: "I came, I saw, I conquered."[14] Pharnakes's ambitions were at an end: he fled back to Bosporos and was soon killed by Asandros.[15] His greatest legacy was his only known child, Dynamis, born around 63 BC to an unknown mother, perhaps an indigenous woman. Pharnakes must have had high hopes for his daughter: her name (Power) was taken from a word as old as Homer—used regularly to describe the bodily strength of the heroes of the *Iliad*—but virtually unknown as a personal name before her time.[16]

Asandros, now in charge of Bosporos and holding the title "archon,"[17] was ignored by Caesar, who had his own candidate for the kingship, a certain Mithradates of Pergamon. He claimed to be a son of Mithradates VI of Pontos, but was actually a member of the aristocracy of Pergamon, the renowned Greek city in northwestern Asia Minor. He had spent time in Rome and had cultivated the leading people of the era, becoming a close friend of Caesar as early as 59 BC. A decade later he had assisted him in Alexandria in the struggle that put Cleopatra VII securely on the throne, and was with him at Zela. Caesar chose him for the kingship of Bosporos because he was a well-known personality who would uphold Roman interests better than the revolutionary and obscure Asandros.[18] But Mithradates had no status or support in the Bosporos and was promptly killed. Asandros then consolidated his territory, moving cautiously and refusing to call himself king until the Romans allowed it; the change appears on his coinage from his fourth year as ruler, probably 43 BC.[19] But most astutely, he married Dynamis, the daughter of Pharnakes and granddaughter of Mithradates VI, thereby positioning himself within one of the most celebrated dynasties of the late Hellenistic East. The date of the marriage is unknown—presumably around 46 BC—and Asandros and Dynamis ruled Bosporos for many years.

Dynamis provides a prime example of the near invisibility of women in antiquity. She was an important personality in the affairs of Bosporos and the Roman world, with a career that extended from the era of Julius Caesar to the last years of Augustus, yet she was mentioned by only a single extant ancient author, Dio, writing in the early third century AD. That a Roman history written two hundred years after Dynamis's death should be the sole source to mention her is strong proof of the frustrating vagaries of ancient historiography and text survival. Unfortunately, Dio rarely mentioned his sources, often relying on "I have heard" rather than making any actual citation, and there is no obvious suggestion as to how he obtained his material.[20]

Dynamis and Asandros were joint monarchs of Bosporos until the latter's death around 17 BC, and then Dynamis ruled the territory alone as queen for another twenty years, an independent reign for a woman of the era equivalent in length to that of Cleopatra VII and exceeded only by that of Pythodoris of Pontos. Yet she is ephemeral today, and her life must be reconstructed, insofar as possible, from physical evidence more than literature. Since the literary notice of Dynamis is so scant, it is worth quoting Dio's account in full, which presents the situation from around 15 BC and includes personalities of that era who will be discussed later:

A certain Scribonius, who said that he was a grandson of Mithradates [VI] and who received the kingdom from Augustus after Asandros had died, took as his wife Dynamis, to whom the rule had been transferred. She was actually the daughter of Pharnakes [II] and the granddaughter of

Mithradates. When Agrippa learned about this he sent Polemon [I] against him, who ruled the part of Pontos next to Cappadocia. But he found that Scribonius was no longer living, since the Bosporans, when they learned about the expedition, had already killed him. Yet they resisted Polemon through fear that he might be given the rule over them, and thus he attacked them. He was initially victorious, but was not able to prevail against them until Agrippa came to Sinope in order to make war against them. Then they laid down their weapons and were given over to Polemon. The woman Dynamis lived with him, but of course not without the approval of Augustus.

This complex passage demonstrates the inadequacy of extant litera-ture in providing anything close to a thorough historical record. Other details about Dynamis's life must be filled in from information about her husbands, as well as data from coins and inscriptions, which fortunately augment the scant literary information.

Presumably Dynamis married Asandros shortly after he disposed of Mithradates of Pergamon in 47 BC; whether she was the "daughter of Pharnakes" offered to Caesar before the battle at Zela—more as bribe than alliance—cannot be determined.[21] Dynamis's birthdate can only be assumed from the fact that she was of marriageable age around 47 BC, and thus it was no later than the late 60s BC, making her an exact contemporary of Augustus. Asandros was not young: according to the treatise *Makrobioi* (*Long Lives*), attributed to Lucian of Samosata of the second century AD, he lived to the age of ninety-three and committed suicide after the usurpation of Scribonius around 17 BC.[22] This would mean that he had been born about 110 BC and was about sixty when he married Dynamis. He presumably had long been a retainer in the family of Mithradates VI and his son Pharnakes II, and he was senior enough to have been entrusted—unwisely, as it turned out—with the administration of Bosporos when Pharnakes's ambitions turned toward the south.

Asandros, archon and then king, was the first Bosporan monarch to take the title *Philoromaios* (Friend of the Romans) and to have a relation-ship with Rome.[23] But Dynamis was co-ruler, perhaps from the very be-ginning: she brought far more status to the marriage than her husband. An inscription from Pantikapaion, the Bosporan capital, records how a certain naval commander, Pantaleon, made a dedication to Poseidon and Aphrodite in honor of "Asandros, the Great King, King of Kings, and Queen Dynamis." Presumably he did this after a naval victory, but there are no further details about either the engagement or Pantaleon.[24] Nevertheless, the inscription demonstrates that Dynamis and Asandros shared power, even if her titles were not as effusive as his, and the astuteness of the king in linking himself to the most distinguished family of the region is apparent and would serve him well during his reign.

Asandros was more cautious than his late father-in-law, Pharnakes, and did not allow his ambition to spread into territory south of the Black Sea or that claimed by the Romans, even if they had been the lands of his wife's ancestors. Yet he asserted his control as far as the lower Tanais estuary, and in the region known as the Chersonesos (the modern Crimea) he built a wall about forty-five miles long to protect the peninsula from barbarian incursions.[25] Remains of the construction are visible today near modern Perekop.

Presumably the kingdom of Dynamis and Asandros continued to base its prosperity on grain exports to the Greek heartland. Although from a much earlier era, the comments of the Athenian orator Demosthenes in the fourth century BC were probably still largely valid: at that time the Athenians imported more grain from Bosporos than from all other regions combined, and remission of customs duties for Bosporan merchants eased the process.[26] By the first century BC, the Bosporan grain exports were not as important as previously but were still a major commodity. Other products sent from Bosporos to the Mediterranean included hides, fish, and hemp.[27]

Little is known about the thirty years in which Dynamis and Asandros shared power, a demonstration that there were no serious threats to stability during that period, essentially from the era of the assassination of Julius Caesar to the second decade of Augustus. From their capital at Pantikapaion, the royal couple controlled a region that extended to the lower Tanais, where a homonymous city had been founded as a Bosporan outpost in the third century BC; Greek merchants had penetrated the region long before. The city of Tanais stood at the western end of a complex network of trade routes into the interior of Central Asia that would eventually evolve into the Silk Road to China.[28] Bosporos controlled the southern side of the Sea of Azov, west across the Bosporos strait into the Crimea, and also some settlements to the west and east along the northern Black Sea coast. Yet the territory lay at the fringe of the Mediterranean cultural sphere, and barbarian incursions from the north were a constant threat, as the Chersonesos wall demonstrated. But all the evidence points to the fact that the kingdom was essentially at peace, and the Romans, so involved in the destinies of the Eastern dynasties, saw no need to intervene.

Dynamis and Asandros may have had at least one child, Aspourgos, who ruled Bosporos after the death of his mother, around AD 10, and remained in power until AD 39. His parentage is not totally certain, but an inscription from Pantikapaion calls him "son of King Asandrochos," who can hardly be anyone other than Asandros. His succession immediately after his mother's death is further evidence of this, although it has been improbably suggested that he was an indigenous chieftain who took control after Dynamis's death or that he was even Dynamis's last husband.[29]

Scribonius and Polemon

The peaceful era of the Bosporan kingdom came to an end around 17 BC. The approximate date is based on the movements of Marcus Vipsanius Agrippa, discussed later in the chapter. The exact chronology is unknown, but about that time a certain Scribonius seized power, evidently with a fair amount of local support, his claim perhaps strengthened by an assertion that he had Roman endorsement and was a grandson of Mithradates VI.[30] "Scribonius" is a Roman plebian name, known from as early as the second century BC, but it is unlikely that the usurper was in fact a renegade Roman or Italian who had established himself in Bosporos; he was more probably a local who had adopted a Roman name, perhaps even a member of the royal entourage. King Asandros, now ninety-three years of age, may have been losing control, and Scribonius was popular enough that a number of Bosporans, seemingly including members of the military, defected to him. Asandros, after an attempt to retain power, committed suicide. Scribonius asserted that he had received approval for his actions from Augustus, but this seems improbable, given the long period of peace that had now been disrupted and the Roman intervention that took place after Asandros's death. Scribonius also allegedly married Dynamis, now about fifty years of age, perhaps taking her hostage or claiming her as a right of conquest rather than intending to establish a permanent relationship. There is no evidence that

Dynamis was a participant in Scribonius's plans: gold coinage suggests that she maintained her own profile, and a close reading of Dio's text implies that she ruled alone, at least for a while, after Asandros's death.

If it is true, however, that Dynamis accepted marriage to Scribonius (and the limited evidence makes such an interpretation speculative), it may show that he had some reasonable claim to power or credibility as a future ruler—perhaps his assertion of regal descent was legitimate—or Dynamis may not have had much choice given the turbulence of the era. Yet Scribonius did not last long, because the Romans moved to normalize the situation, hardly acting with favor toward the usurpation of the kingdom of their longtime stable ally.

Word of the problems in Bosporos soon reached the Roman authorities. It was essential to keep the peace there, as the kingdom was important both as a grain supplier and as a bulwark against the northern barbarians.[31] The nearest senior official was Augustus's prime adviser, Agrippa, who had been on an extended tour of the East and was with Herod the Great in Jerusalem in late 15 BC, which is probably where he heard about the revolt in Bosporos.[32] After wintering in Mytilene, he headed toward the Black Sea, eventually joined by Herod. But it seems that they went no farther than Sinope, an ancient Greek city on the south shore of the sea, historically the most important seaport of the region and at this time part of the allied kingdom of Pontos. Agrippa dispatched the king of Pontos, Polemon I, to Bosporos in order to settle the matter, although it is not certain whether he was sent before or after Agrippa and Herod arrived at Sinope.

Polemon had been king of Pontos since 37 BC, when he had been placed on the throne by Antonius. He was now near the end of his career, having ruled Pontos—essentially north central Asia Minor, the heartland of the old Mithradatic Empire—for nearly a quarter of a century. His career and the fate of his kingdom are examined more thoroughly in the discussion of his last wife, Pythodoris.[33] He was sent north by Agrippa, presumably with a broad commission to arrange matters in Bosporos, a reasonable decision, given the historical ties between that region and Pontos. Agrippa did not go north himself—his presence at Sinope was enough to stop the revolt—and returned overland to Ionia.

When Polemon arrived in Bosporos, he found that the locals had already taken care of the problem of Scribonius by eliminating him. But they were not particularly welcoming toward Polemon, and a battle was fought, although it is by no means clear exactly whom he was engaging.

He presumably reported his difficulties back to Agrippa, who may have planned at this time to intervene himself—the sequence of events in Dio's narrative is unclear—but the final result is unequivocal: local resistance came to an end and Polemon became king of Bosporos. He and Dynamis entered into some kind of relationship: the word used by Dio, *synoikesen*, to describe this arrangement effectively means "to live together" (the earliest documentation of the term is a reference to Clytaemnestra's decision about whether to live with her son, Orestes). In a loose sense the word can mean "marriage," but it is better to take it literally and assume that Dynamis and Polemon worked together to stabilize the situation in Bosporos, probably living under the same roof.[34] Whatever personal relationship they had is hardly relevant. In fact, Polemon soon married Pythodoris of Nysa, or was already married to her, and while polygamy is not out of the question, it is unlikely, and thus it is more probable that Dynamis and Polemon had some sort of professional association of convenience, not a formal marriage.[35] Moreover, Pythodoris inherited some of Polemon's Bosporan territories after his death, which further suggests that the arrangement with Dynamis was more informal.[36] The matter defies precise explanation.[37]

Yet it must be remembered that Dynamis had far more status in Bosporos—in fact, anywhere in Asia Minor—than Polemon. He was not of royal background, but she was a descendant of a long line of royalty and a granddaughter of the great Mithradates VI. In the tense situation that had developed with the revolt of Scribonius and the death of Asandros, Dynamis, who had been queen for thirty years, was the sole source of continuity. Even though Mithradates had been defeated by the Romans half a century previously, his memory and reputation were still strong, and Dynamis could exploit this to her advantage and receive local support as she, Polemon, and the Romans normalized the situation in the kingdom. Much as the descendants of the defeated triumvir Antonius did in Rome, those of Mithradates retained power and prestige in Bosporos and Pontos.[38]

But Polemon faced problems in Bosporos: the people of Tanais revolted and thus the city was sacked, and a local tribe, the Aspourgianians, were enough of a nuisance that they were attacked. The result of this foray was the death of Polemon himself.[39] It is not certain when this happened; it was obviously after 14 BC and may have been as late as 8 BC, when coins began to appear that seem to have been struck by Dynamis alone.[40] Exactly what happened in the years after 14

BC remains problematic. If Polemon survived as late as 8 BC, it is unlikely that he spent all those years in Bosporos—he had a kingdom and
wife in Asia Minor—but may have returned on a regular basis to assist
Dynamis, eventually meeting his death. He had legal title to Bosporos—
this had been validated by Augustus—but it was really Dynamis who
was in control.

The Sole Ruler of Bosporos

The remaining years of Dynamis's life cannot be reconstructed in any
coherent narrative, but coins and inscriptions give some hints. Her last
gold coins are dated to AD 7/8.[41] By AD 10 a certain Aspourgos was on
the throne, whose identity is something of a mystery. To be sure, there
was a regional ethnic group called the Aspourgianians, who had been
responsible for the death of Polemon, and it is quite possible that King
Aspourgos was a representative of these peoples, somehow gaining the
throne about twenty years later.[42] Yet it seems unlikely that the Romans
would have allowed an indigenous leader to seize control and, moreover, to remain in power for nearly thirty years, after which (around
AD 38) rule reverted to the established dynasty, represented by Polemon
II, presumably the grandson of Polemon I.[43] Moreover, Aspourgos did
have Roman endorsement, and even went to Rome in AD 14 or 15 to seek
confirmation of his rule.[44] It is best to assume that he was a member
of the intermingled families of Pontos and Bosporos, presumably a
son of Dynamis and Asandros. On the inscription from Pantikapaion,
Aspourgos is titled "Great King" and *Philoromaios*, indicative of some
sort of Roman approval.[45] When he came to the throne, Dynamis, if
still alive, would have been in her seventies, hardly a good marriage
prospect, even if merely for the sake of convenience, and it is better to
assume that he was her son.

Yet his name, which seems to reflect a local ethnic group, gives one
pause, and since the Aspourgianians were a known power in the region, who in fact had eliminated the previous king, Asandros may have
adopted their name for political reasons, just as a grandson of Herod
the Great was called Tigranes, the common Armenian royal name—
despite little connection to the Armenian ruling line—eventually becoming King Tigranes V of Armenia.[46] Such convenient names may

even have been adopted only after accession to power, with Tigranes and Aspourgos not the actual birth names of the future kings. What seems most plausible, however, is that the name "Aspourgos" reflects the military aspirations of the Bosporan regime, much as "Germanicus" and "Britannicus" became personal names in the Roman imperial family.

In summation, it is best to assume that after the death of Scribonius in 14 BC, Dynamis effectively ruled alone for a number of years, but with the temporary assistance of Polemon I as a close colleague (whose primary interests were in his own kingdom of Pontos). Dynamis may have lived until around AD 10 or died somewhat earlier. Her assumed son Aspourgos became king, and ruled for thirty years with Roman approval.

The bulk of the evidence for Dynamis's career in her last quarter century comes from inscriptions and coins. An inscription from Hermonassa, near modern Taman, describes how *Basilissa* Dynamis, *Philoromaios*, honored Augustus. There is also another from Pantikapaion with essentially the same text; the former is somewhat more effusive because it describes Augustus as "ruler of all the lands and seas."[47] This was a poetic formula that also appeared (in a slightly different form) at Philai, on the border of Egypt and Aithiopia, suggesting that it was standard terminology for a dedication honoring Augustus at the extremities of the known world and an assertion of the broad extent of Roman power. It reflected contemporary thought in Augustan literature; in fact, the Philai inscription is in the form of a Greek epigram, written by a certain Catilius.[48]

More interesting, perhaps, is another inscription, from Phanagoreia, where Queen Dynamis, *Philoromaios*, honored "Livia the wife of Augustus" for her good deeds.[49] It is unfortunate that it cannot be dated beyond the obvious, when Dynamis was sole ruler of Bosporos and thus presumably after around 8 BC. But, like Salome of Judaea, Dynamis had a special relationship with the Roman imperial family and, in particular, Livia. Livia's connection with Bosporos was probably similar to her connection with Judaea, but that with Bosporos lacks the detail of Josephus's account of Judaea and the Herodians, and there is no evidence as to whether, if ever, Dynamis and Livia met. But presumably Livia offered advice and indirectly assisted in maintaining the stability and prosperity of the kingdom in the years after the matter of Scribonius. She may have encouraged Augustus to support Dynamis's relationship with Polemon I, since it is known that she involved herself in the personal lives of the Herodians. The dedication to Livia is from a base, so there was a public statue of her—probably without her husband—in Phanagoreia. Phanagoreia (near modern Taman) was the second most important town in the core region of the Bosporos, lying at the head of a deep gulf on the Asian side of the strait. It was one of the original Greek cities in the region, founded in the sixth century BC as an outpost of the Ionian city of Teos, and thus was far older than Pantikapaion, the Bosporan capital. The city was incorporated into the Bosporan kingdom at an early date but retained a certain semi-independent status. It may also have been Dynamis's birthplace.[50] Phanagoreia was literally at the ends of the inhabited earth, and although outside actual Roman territory, it still gave credence to the statement that Augustus was ruler of all the lands and seas.

There may even have been a cult of Livia in Bosporos, represented by a glass portrait of her discovered at the site of Nymphaion, just south of Pantikapaion (fig.12). Although it probably dates from the mid-first century AD, after the death of both Dynamis and Livia, it is testimony to the unique position that Augustus's wife held in the region, and her cult may have been established by the queen.[51]

Allied monarchs had to balance carefully their obligations to Rome and to their subjects, resulting in policies that might be contradictory or even impossible to reconcile. The Romans could see the monarch as not sufficiently pro-Roman, while the locals might believe that he or she was a Roman puppet who did not have their best interests in mind.[52] Sometimes these tensions could be fatal to the ruler, as Ptolemy of Mauretania learned.[53] Dynamis was capable enough to follow successfully the narrow path of twin loyalties. She could publicly express her devotion to the Roman imperial family and the regime that it represented, erecting a statue to Livia (and, presumably, one to Augustus, probably at Pantikapaion). Yet for local consumption she stressed her other connections, best shown by an inscription from Phanagoreia which relates that Queen Dynamis, *Philoromaios*, was descended from the Great King Pharnakes (II)—her father—and the King of Kings Mithradates (VI) Eupator Dionysos, listing her grandfather's titles and thus leaving no doubt as to his importance.[54] Mithradates had been dead seventy years or more when this inscription appeared, but it is obvious that his name still resonated among the descendants of his former subjects; he had died, in fact, at Pantikapaion, the Bosporan capital.

FIG. 12. Miniature glass portrait of Livia, from Nymphaion in Bosporos. The State Hermitage Museum, St. Petersburg, NF.83.235.

Yet the text also demonstrates the ambivalence of the situation. It made no mention of any Romans, and there was only a wise but cautious use of Dynamis's title, *Philoromaios*; anything less might have bordered on subversion. Moreover, the inscription was erected by the people of Agrippia, which presumably was the name that Phanagoreia had adopted after Agrippa intervened in the Bosporan succession or after his death in 12 BC. Thus the text shows the complex priorities of those regions under indirect Roman control but with their own traditions; it was produced in an ancient Bosporan city that had officially taken the name of a Roman magistrate (a name that lasted only as long as it was politically correct to retain it) and honored its queen and her distinguished descent—including that from the greatest local opponent Rome had ever seen—while also acknowledging her as a Friend of the Romans. Another inscription from Pantikapaion records that a certain Myron son of Myron and his wife, Kyriaina, honored Queen Dynamis (again cited as a Friend of the Romans and also naming both her father and grandfather) by making a dedication to Aphrodite on her behalf, presumably evidence for a local cult or temple to the goddess.[55]

Dynamis's long survival—through the twists and turns of the later stages of the Roman civil war and almost the entire era of Augustus—demonstrates her excellent understanding of the political nuances of her era. She also had locals in her entourage, which would create a more stable political situation: one of these, a certain Mathianes, the son of Zadaros, had his tombstone erected by the queen. The sculpted relief on the monument shows a Sarmatian horseman, suggesting that Mathianes had been recruited from that tribe of horse nomads whose territory lay northeast of the Black Sea.[56] Dynamis also reached out to other Greek cities in the region: her envoy was sent to Chersonesos in Tauris (near modern Sebastopol in the Crimea) and concluded a treaty. She was also honored by the city of Tanais, at the northeastern extremity of her kingdom.[57]

Coinage also gives some insight into Dynamis's policy. She was probably responsible for renaming Phanagoreia as Agrippia, commemorated not only on the inscription discussed earlier, but on coinage that shows a veiled female head, perhaps Livia or the queen herself. There are similar coins with the name "Kaisareia," showing that another town bore this name, perhaps Pantikapaion.[58] In these renamings Dynamis was following the standard policy of the allied monarchs: localities named Kaisareia (or Caesarea) appeared during the Augustan period throughout the kingdoms, but unlike most of the others, the Bosporos city did not retain its new name. Using "Agrippa" toponymically is rare, but Herod had renamed the Levantine coastal city of Anthedon (modern Teda, north of Gaza) Agrippias. The date of these changes is unknown; toponyms honoring Agrippa may have been in vogue shortly after his death in 12 BC, with Bosporan Kaisareia perhaps somewhat earlier.[59]

Coins with the portraits of Agrippa or Augustus bear a monogram that may indicate they were struck by Dynamis, between 8 BC and AD 7, but the symbol is not interpreted with certainty.[60] The only unquestioned portrait of Dynamis is on a gold stater dated to Bosporos Year 281 (17/16 BC), when, it seems, she was able to issue coins autonomously, in the period near or after the death of Asandros or during the Scribonius incident. This coin shows a draped bust facing right, with the hair in a thick roll, and with a diadem.[61] Another gold stater dates from 21/20 BC, when her husband, Asandros, was unquestionably still alive.[62]

The iconography of the queen may be further represented in a bronze bust of a mature woman wearing a Phrygian cap, discovered in 1898 at Novorossiysk, on the Black Sea coast southeast of the Kimmerian Bosporos (fig. 13). This has long been identified as Dynamis and is still generally so published, but the attribution has been called into serious question recently, and the person depicted, although certainly a Bosporan queen, cannot be identified with absolute certainty.[63]

Dynamis is one of the more elusive of the royal women of the Augustan era. During her long life—she and Augustus had almost exactly the same lifespan—she was devoted to her kingdom of Bosporos. But so little is known about her that one can only speculate about much of her career, and, predictably, her first fifty years are hardly documented beyond her marriage to Asandros. Yet her life after Asandros's death becomes particularly difficult to untangle, with speculation building

FIG. 13. Bronze bust of a Bosporan queen, from Shirokaya Balka. The State Hermitage Museum, St. Petersburg, PAN.1726.

upon speculation. She had some relationship with the usurper Scribonius, who did not last long, and then with Polemon I of Pontos when he came to rule the Bosporos. If she had merely a working agreement with Polemon, her later career becomes somewhat easier to understand. But if she and Polemon married, then it is necessary to explain her status when Polemon married Pythodoris, sometime before 8 BC. To be sure, the role of marriage in personal relationships can be overemphasized — the most notorious example is the relationship between Cleopatra VII and Antonius—but an official marriage would mean either polygamy or some sort of termination, either through death or divorce. There is no evidence for any of these alternatives, and one is left without resolution. If Dynamis had died by 8 BC, there would be an unexplained gap in the Bosporan royal chronology before the reign of Aspourgos is documented, twenty years later. He did not go to Rome to meet with Augustus until around AD 14, so it seems that this would be close to his date of accession.

Further confusing matters is that Pythodoris had some legal status in Bosporos after Polemon's death, when the situation of Dynamis remains enigmatic, and it is impossible to reconcile the territorial possessions or chronology of the two queens. If Dynamis and Polemon were never legally married, and it can be assumed that Pythodoris gave up her claims to Bosporan lands (which may have been minimal) shortly after Polemon's death (concentrating her efforts on her home territory of Pontos, where she ruled for many years), Bosporos would have reverted to Dynamis, who lasted until succeeded by Aspourgos, probably but not certainly her son. Yet no explanation seems to fit all the facts, scant as they are.

What seems most definitive is that around 8 BC Dynamis was left to rule Bosporos alone for the last twenty years of her life. Her only known child was probably Aspourgos, but even here the record is clouded, and there is no explicit statement that he was her son; the assumption is based merely on the continuation of historic dynastic names in the generations that followed. The vagueness of the data has even led to the suggestion that Aspourgos was the last husband of the queen—based on a possible connection between him and the Aspourgianians[64]—but it seems difficult to credit the idea that Dynamis, who had regularly sought the advice of the imperial family throughout her career, would, at almost seventy years of age, secretly marry a barbarian chieftain and allow the Mithradatic–Bosporan dynasty that she had worked so hard to sustain to pass to unrelated descendants. Moreover, it is equally unlikely that any of this would have happened without objection from Rome or the other allied monarchs. There were certainly many descendants of the Mithradatic line who could have taken the throne and who might have been preferred by the Romans.

Yet the limited and contradictory evidence does not hide the fact that Dynamis was a woman of power. Her ability to strike gold coinage was a privilege not normally extended to allied royalty; this would be one of the circumstances that led Ptolemy of Mauretania to his fate.[65] In fact, Bosporos was the only allied kingdom known to do this legally. Dynamis's father, Pharnakes, also had the privilege of issuing gold coinage, at least for a period in the late 50s BC, and this right passed down to his successor Asandros and then to Dynamis. Gold coinage may have been subsidized by the Romans as a way of keeping the kingdom prosperous, but it seems that the coins did not circulate outside of Bosporos.[66]

Living as she did at the edges of the Greco-Roman world, Dynamis was perhaps more isolated than most of her regal colleagues. There is no firm record of personal contact with members of the imperial family or of travels to other kingdoms or to the Roman provinces, but this may be due to the deficiency of the record. It has been suggested that a royal woman with a boy on the south frieze of the Ara Pacis in Rome, just to the right of and behind Marcus Agrippa, is Dynamis, which would mean a trip to the city around 13 BC (fig.14). The Ara Pacis is very much a monument to Agrippa's extended time in the East, which included settling the matter of the Bosporan succession, and there might have been a reason to place the queen next to him. There is no doubt that the boy is the woman's child—her hand is on his head—and this would mean that the queen, about fifty years of age, had a son about ten or younger. This is not impossible, but it is one of the reasons recent opinion has moved away from identifying the figure as Dynamis, although she is obviously a foreign royal woman of importance. Identification of the people on the Ara Pacis remains eternally problematic.[67]

Dynamis upheld Greco-Roman values—as well as the memory of her famous grandfather Mithradates VI—in a place so remote that it was considered by many to be barely inhabitable.[68] In the last analysis, her career demonstrates not only the power of royal women in the Augustan world, but the deficiencies of extant ancient literature insofar as the historical record is concerned. Yet her name, unknown before her time, was in subsequent years used with greater frequency in the Greek world and even as far as Italy.[69]

FIG. 14. Ara Pacis in Rome, perhaps showing Dynamis.
Courtesy Duane W. Roller.

As a final note, she could trace her ancestors back to the fifth century BC and the time of Mithradates I "the Founder," who established the Pontic kingdom. Her descendants are known with certainty into the third century AD, and perhaps longer, since the same royal names appear into the following century.[70] The kingdom itself lasted until it was destroyed by the Huns in the fourth century AD. Thus the combined Mithradatic–Bosporan dynasty is known for nearly eight hundred years, perhaps the longest such span in antiquity.

6

Pythodoris of Pontos

The most important royal woman of the later Augustan era was Pythodoris, who, for more than half a century, ruled much of central and northern Asia Minor and the eastern Black Sea littoral. She survived well into the period of Tiberius and became the ancestor of a line of royal women that extended past the middle of the first century AD. Like all women in antiquity, she remains shadowy, but due to the eulogistic comments of the geographer and historian Strabo of Amaseia, her career is better documented than that of many of her ruling colleagues.[1]

Nysa

The city of Nysa lies on the north side of the Meander River in southwestern Asia Minor, in a striking location on either side of a ravine at modern Sultanhisar, where many remains are still visible. It was not an ancient foundation, owing its establishment to one of the Seleukid kings of the early third century BC.[2] Nevertheless, it was located in a region of ancient prominence: just to its west was a famous healing sanctuary and entrance to the underworld, a shrine of probably prehistoric origins.[3] By late Hellenistic times, Nysa had become an important intellectual center: Strabo was educated here in the late 50s BC. The city was situated in a region of great cultural diversity, lying at the border of two of the major districts of ancient Anatolia, Lydia and Karia. Karia had once been ruled by the dynamic Hekatomnid family,[4] and Lydia had been the home of the fabulously wealthy Croesus. Ethnic and linguistic remnants of both peoples survived into the Augustan period. Greeks had been in the region since shortly after the fall of Troy, and the Romans arrived by the second century BC, with the territory becoming Roman in 129 BC. It was also an area of great abundance, situated in the fertile Meander plain and on one of the major east–west routes of the ancient world, which began at the Aegean and went across southern Anatolia, and eventually as far as Mesopotamia: conquerors, traders, and merchants had used it since prehistoric times. In the late Hellenistic period, Nysa was especially prosperous, as the agricultural riches and east–west trade came together to make it one of the wealthier towns of its era. It is no accident that with such a cultural heritage and continuing prominence, Nysa was populated by affluent families who contributed significantly to the dynamics of the late Hellenistic and Augustan eras.

In 88 BC a wealthy local, Chairemon—perhaps even the richest citizen of Nysa—provided the Roman army (in the field against Mithradates VI) with 60,000 *modii* of wheat flour, something that his son recorded on an inscription.[5] This was hardly an insubstantial sum—possibly 15,000 bushels—enough to supply a legion for an extended period of time.[6] Needless to say, his role as supplier to the Romans was not looked upon favorably by Mithradates, and a price of 40 talents alive or 20 dead was put on his head. Chairemon had to leave Nysa and went to Rhodes, and then sought sanctuary at the Ephesian Temple of Artemis, whereupon he vanished from the historical record, perhaps eliminated by agents of the king.

Nevertheless, Chairemon demonstrates the potential of private citizens in late Hellenistic times to become exceedingly prosperous, acquiring "the wealth of royalty"—a phrase eventually applied to Chairemon's son—and in time even becoming royalty themselves, as happened to Chairemon's granddaughter Pythodoris, a break with the ancient tradition that a royal position had to be inherited.[7]

The Family of Pythodoris

At her peak Pythodoris ruled a territory extending from the Mediterranean coast to the north shores of the Black Sea, rivaling in extent that of Cleopatra VII a generation earlier; in fact, the two successively controlled some of the same regions of southern Asia Minor. But unlike Cleopatra, Pythodoris did not have a royal background; there is no evidence that her family members were anything other than private citizens, yet wealth and prominence became a path to a royal position in late Hellenistic and Augustan times.

Her grandfather Chairemon had two sons, her father Pythodoros, and Pythion.[8] Both figured in the Mithradatic difficulties of their father and fled with him to Rhodes. Pythion is hardly known, but eventually Pythodoros ended up in Tralleis, an ancient city about twenty miles west of Nysa, also in the Meander valley, and likewise sharing in the abundance of the region. The family would have owned land around the city and probably also in Nysa: agricultural estates were presumably a source of its wealth. Tralleis was allegedly an early Greek foundation, located on a tableland (where remains are still visible) at the modern town of Aydın.[9] The family's difficulties with Mithradates do not seem to have diminished its prosperity: by the 40s BC Pythodoros had personal assets of more than 4,000 talents, perhaps 12,000,000 Roman *denarii*, making him one of the richest men in the eastern Mediterranean.[10] He also became an *asiarch*, one of the Roman representatives in provincial cities, especially where there was no Roman official in residence. Part of their role was to administer Roman cults, but they also served as liaisons between the locals and the Roman government. Pythodoros's children— Pythodoris is the only one known by name—inherited the property, which their father was able to turn over to them undiminished, probably at some time in the early Augustan period.

Pythodoros was a survivor in difficult times. Assuming that he was at least an adolescent when he had to flee Nysa with his father and brother, he was probably born in the early 90s BC. After successfully avoiding the wrath of Mithradates and perhaps erecting the inscription that honored his father, by 59 BC he had become one of the most distinguished citizens of the region and a supporter of Pompey the Great, who was at the peak of his power, since he had defeated Mithradates VI and had spent much of the 60s BC dissolving the moribund Seleukid Empire and reorganizing the eastern Mediterranean to Roman advantage. Reliance on wealthy locals was a cornerstone of Roman policy, and Pythodoros became a prime example of this.[11]

Unfortunately for him, his support of Pompey meant that when the latter was killed in 48 BC, the victor in the civil war, Julius Caesar, confiscated 2,000 talents of Pythodoros's wealth, probably in land. Yet his resources were great enough that upon Caesar's death in 44 BC he was able to buy it back. His importance was such that he may have been received in Rome, if he was the Pythodoros who was supported by the future Augustan intimate M. Valerius Messalla Corvinus.[12] Nothing more is known about his career other than the crucial fact of his marriage, although it is probable that Antonius gave him Roman citizenship, which would have been inherited by his daughter.[13]

The Mysterious Antonia

At some uncertain time Pythodoros married Antonia, who would become the mother of Pythodoris. The suggested dates for this marriage—as well as for the subsequent birth of their daughter—vary from the early 50s to the 30s BC. An earlier date would mean that Pythodoros, old enough to be a threat to Mithradates VI in 88 BC, was in his forties when he married, which is certainly reasonable.[14] Yet it would give his daughter an unusually long life span, since she would have been around eighty when Strabo wrote about her in the early AD 20s. It would also mean that she had three children in her forties. None of this is impossible but seems unlikely: Strabo's account, in particular, hardly describes someone in extreme old age. On the other hand, if the marriage between Pythodoros and Antonia did not take place until the 30s BC, he was around sixty, with no evidence of any earlier relationship. Yet the chronology that provides a later birth for the future queen seems more likely. There may even be a missing generation in the descent from Chairemon, the opponent of Mithradates, to Pythodoris, perhaps a second Chairemon or Pythodoros, which would solve some of the chronological problems, but this is purely speculative.[15]

The identity of Pythodoris's mother, Antonia, remains a matter of great controversy, and it is of more than idle curiosity because it is an important factor in the ancestry and social position of her daughter. Antonia is known only through an inscription from Smyrna that commemorates her grandson Zenon:

> The people honored Zenon, son of Queen Pythodoris the
> Mother Loving, and of King Polemon, and maternal grandson
> of the benefactress Antonia.[16]

This important document reveals that Antonia was a woman of status, not only because she was married to Pythodoros but because of the honor given to her by her daughter—who took the surname Philometor

(Mother Loving)—as well as her own role as benefactress. These are not empty titles, but important aspects of Hellenistic royalty, indicating a person of particular distinction. "Philometor" seems to have first been used by Ptolemy VI of Egypt, whose mother was the Seleukid princess Cleopatra I, who was responsible for joining the two great dynasties of the Hellenistic world.[17] *Euergetes* (benefactor) was an ancient term that identified people of particular note within the royal system, generally those of high status.[18] Although there was perhaps a certain honorific quality to the titles, they were not used casually and both demonstrate that Antonia was a person of importance; one can perhaps contrast the mother of Cleopatra VII, who is not recorded in any extant source.

The question remains, however, as to who this Antonia was. Nothing is known about her ancestry. The obvious suggestion (possible only if Pythodoris was born later, not earlier) is that she was a daughter of the triumvir Marcus Antonius. Yet it must be emphasized that there is no actual proof of this beyond her name, and there are serious difficulties with the attribution, most notably that such a distinguished connection for Pythodoris is not mentioned in any surviving source. In particular, Strabo, not only well informed about the career of Antonius in Asia Minor but an intimate of Pythodoris and the primary literary source for her career, failed to mention any such ancestry.[19] Descent from Antonius, despite the problematic nature of his later career, was still of importance in the Augustan period and beyond, and during the years that Pythodoris was queen of Pontos, Antonius's undisputed grandson Germanicus pointed to his descent as having enhanced his career.[20] Thus it is odd that no mention seems to have been made of a similar relationship between Pythodoris and Antonius, and recent opinion has moved away from belief in such an association.

Nevertheless, it remains remotely possible that Antonia was indeed the daughter of the triumvir.[21] During his active career he had at least ten children by five different women. He was born in 83 BC, and thus would have had children of marriageable age from the 40s BC. If Antonia were a daughter of the triumvir, she is not documented as such, especially in the catalogue of Antonius's children provided by Plutarch.[22] Yet this account is not complete, because it fails to mention that at an early date Antonius had children by a certain Fadia, daughter of the freedman Q. Fadius, although there was probably no marriage. But an illegitimate child who was a freedman's granddaughter would hardly be a good match for the wealthy and famous Pythodoros, and such a possibility can easily be dismissed; Cicero—promoting his own agenda, to be sure—pointed out the unsuitable nature of the relationship between Antonius and Fadia.[23]

Antonius's first marriage was to the daughter of his uncle Gaius Antonius Hybrida, consul in 63 BC along with Cicero.[24] This probably occurred in the late 60s BC, and any daughter born to the couple would have been named Antonia and would have been of the proper age to be the mother of Pythodoris. Antonius might have been seeking to enhance his status by a connection with one of the most important local families in the province of Asia, a technique that he was well known to have used, given his relationships with Cleopatra VII and the elder Glaphyra. Moreover, there is one documented case where Antonius attempted to marry one of his children into an important Eastern family: in 34 BC his son Alexander Helios became engaged to Iotape, the princess of Media Atropatene.[25] Needless to say, this arrangement was never fulfilled and was nullified within a few years with the collapse of Antonius's own aspirations.[26] Yet it is clear that in the 40s and 30s BC he was seeking alliances throughout the eastern Mediterranean, and it is quite plausible that he married one of his daughters to the influential Pythodoros, whose position was such that he was compared to royalty.

Yet this remains improbable. It is equally unlikely that Antonia was a freedwoman or a member of a local family that took the Antonius name because of some favor done to them by the triumvir, for she would hardly have had the necessary status. But Antonia could have been the daughter of another member of the triumvir's family, which was politically active and important in the mid-first century BC. Marcus Antonius and his two brothers, Gaius and Lucius, were men of power and authority, as Cicero noted in 50 BC. Gaius was praetor in 44 BC; Lucius was quaestor in Asia in 50-49 BC, where he might have come into contact with Pythodoros.[27] Since all female children in the family would have been named Antonia, there is the definite possibility that the mother of Pythodoris was the daughter of an Antonius other than the triumvir. Yet he was by far the most important member of the family, and descent from him would have provided the greatest possible enhancement of Pythodoris's reputation.[28]

But any connection between a daughter of the triumvir and Pythodoros must remain speculative: there is no proof of one, or even of a daughter to be a party to a marriage. Most important, the failure of Pythodoris, her children, and her chronicler Strabo to mention such a relationship, although not free of the dangers of negative evidence, argues against its having existed. The best that can be said is that Antonia the mother of Pythodoris was a person of importance who had some unproven connection with the Roman family of the Antonii.

Pythodoris and Strabo

Because of Strabo, Pythodoris, while still elusive, is less shadowy than many Augustan queens.[29] Strabo cited her eight times, which may seem scant but is an unusually extensive literary documentation for a ruling woman. Although he still fell into the trap of tending to define her by her father, husbands, and sons, his account of her reign, scattered through the Anatolian portion of his *Geography*, is particularly full; it discusses various elements of her rule, territories, and personal life, serving as a strong and unusual statement asserting the power of women.[30]

The exact nature of Strabo's relationship with the queen will never be known and indeed can easily be overemphasized. Their families may have come into contact while both were living in the region of Nysa, as early as the 50s BC. Pythodoris was not yet born, but her father was at the peak of his career, and Strabo was in school there.[31] Strabo's family, like that of Pythodoris, was part of the wealthy Anatolian elite of the late Hellenistic period, and although Strabo himself had moved to Rome by the time the future queen was born, in the small world of aristocratic Nysa and Tralleis it is probable that the two families crossed paths. Many years later, in the AD 20s, when Strabo was finishing his *Geography*, in all probability he returned to his native Pontos, which Pythodoris had been ruling for two decades.[32] By this time geographer and queen were hardly of the same social class, but they were both deeply involved in the destiny of Pontos, each affecting it in his or her own way. Strabo was probably independently wealthy and did not need Pythodoris as a patron in the traditional sense—it is relevant that the *Geography* was not dedicated to anyone—but they may have been in contact. Moreover, it is possible that they first came to know each other in Rome—Pythodoris probably accompanied her second husband, Archelaos, to the city when he was summoned there by Tiberius in AD 17—and then queen and scholar renewed contact when Strabo moved to Pontos a few years later.[33]

Nevertheless, regardless of any personal interaction, Strabo's notices of the queen are highly eulogistic and demonstrate his great respect for her and her policies. There is no continuous biography, but a carefully written series of comments that illuminate the position of a royal woman of the Augustan era (and the early years of Tiberius) and her relationship to her subjects and territories.

It is significant that Strabo's first mention of Pythodoris connects the geographer and queen in a territorial and historical sense.[34] Strabo had been describing the land of Colchis—the southeastern corner of the Black Sea, in modern Georgia—famed to all as the location of the Golden Fleece and Jason's quest for it. He then related that his great-uncle Moaphernes had been governor of the territory under Mithradates VI but that in Strabo's day it was part of the kingdom of Pythodoris, whom he styled "queen of the Colchians." She also controlled Trapezous and Pharnakeia (modern Trabzon and Giresun in Turkey), two cities on the southeastern shore of the Black Sea, as well as "the barbarians living above them." The chronological context is after the death of Pythodoris's first husband, Polemon I, in 8 or 7 BC, when she became sole ruler of Pontos, and obviously before Strabo's own death in the AD 20s, perhaps earlier in this period rather than later. To be sure, the notice is more revealing of Strabo's own worldview, but nevertheless is also informative about the broad reach of the queen early in her reign. Her central territories of Pontos were not even mentioned at this point, but, significantly, Pythodoris (and Strabo) were succinctly placed within the sweep of history: from Jason and the Argonauts to the world of Mithradates to Strabo himself and the queen.

Strabo's next comment about her is more biographical but again is focused on her territories.[35] Having established that she ruled Colchis, the coast to its west, and the hinterland, Strabo mentions by name two of the barbarian ethnic groups subject to her: the Tibarenians and the Chaldaians, inland mountain peoples west of the regions previously cited. Thus Strabo's account has moved to the west. But there are also personal details: her ancestry, further mention of her first husband, Polemon I, and the matter of his death among the Aspourgianians,[36] and their three children, with their current status. Moreover, Archelaos of Cappadocia, the father of Glaphyra, who has already played a significant role in the *Geography*[37] but has not yet been connected with Pythodoris, was revealed to have been her second husband, with the important statement that "she remained with him to the end," suggesting that she was with him when he died in Rome in AD 18. Nevertheless, as a widow, she "now" rules all the places that Strabo has already mentioned, as well as others yet to be cited. This is a significant biographical datum about the queen's career, since it falls in the narrow six-year span between the death of Archelaos and the completion of the *Geography* by AD 24. It also links Pythodoris to another Eastern dynasty, that of Cappadocia, thus greatly extending her world.

Strabo, who began his account of the queen by connecting her with territory administered by his great-uncle, next moved to the heartland of her realm, Pontos itself, his own ancestral home, which he described in eulogistic terms. It was abundant in grapes and olives, the two agricultural commodities that defined civilization to a Greek. Moreover, it was a sacred land with many fabled cult centers, especially Pontic Komana, where another ancestor of Strabo's had been royal priest. Pythodoris established her capital at Kabeira (modern Niksar), a city that was once a royal seat of Mithradates VI and had been rebuilt after his death by Pompey; Pythodoris called it Sebaste, following the contemporary practice of allied royalty in naming cities after Augustus, here using the Greek form of his name, Sebastos. She also gave the name of Sebastopolis to the city of Dioskourias in Colchis (modern Sukhumi in Georgia), at the eastern end of the Black Sea and well known as one of the most remote Greek cities. It had been founded in the fifth century BC and was at the end of a trade route to the Caspian Sea and beyond. Sebastopolis was far beyond Roman territory, but naming it after Augustus showed the global reach of both queen and emperor.[38]

West of Komana was the ancient city of Zela, another of her possessions, allegedly founded by the legendary Assyrian queen Semiramis, who was revered as an archetypal ruler and a great builder. Thus Strabo, who had already linked Pythodoris with Jason and the Argonauts, now connected her with the greatest of ancient queens, as well as the greatest of Pontic kings, Mithradates VI, and, needless to say, the current regime in Rome. Although there is clearly flattery in this account, Strabo had little to gain from it: his own ancestry was hardly lacking in distinction, and he had no reason to expect anything from Pythodoris in return for his eulogistic portrait. Nevertheless, it is a fine account of the benefits of local rule that was connected to the Augustan regime but was also outside Roman territory.

The final comment on the queen takes the reader full circle, to her origins.[39] In his description of Tralleis, Strabo reminded his readers of Pythodoris's father, pointing out that his "wealth of royalty" set into motion the path that actually allowed her to become royalty despite a lack of any royal ancestry.

Although Strabo provided the bulk of information about Pythodoris, and her biography can be filled out with the evidence from other sources about her husbands and children, a few inscriptions and extensive coinage are further direct evidence for her career. One inscription records that she was honored by the Athenians; the date is unknown. Another, from Hermonassa on the Kimmerian Bosporos at the north shore of the Black Sea, shows both her wide geographical reach and her connection to the imperial family at Rome. It is the dedicatory inscription on the base of a bronze statue of Augustus's wife, Livia, described as the queen's benefactor.[40] In fact, Pythodoris's relations with the imperial family were especially close: she not only named her capital city after Augustus and erected a statue of Livia in remote Hermonassa, but placed portraits of both Augustus and Tiberius on her coinage, styling herself "*Basilissa* Pythodoris."[41] This intimacy helped her escape any difficulties when her husband Archelaos was called to account by Tiberius in AD 17 and the royal couple journeyed to Rome: That Pythodoris emerged unscathed from this crisis may have been what resulted in Livia's being titled her "benefactress." Livia may also have been instrumental in ensuring that Pythodoris retained her royal rank when Archelaos died the following year.

The First Marriage of Pythodoris

It is thus possible to construct a rough chronology of Pythodoris's career. She was born in Nysa or Tralleis; the date is based on that of her marriage to Polemon I of Pontos, which lasted "for a time" and produced three children.[42] This means that it occurred a number of years before the death of Polemon, around 8 BC, and thus her birth was perhaps in the late 30s BC; any earlier chronology is less plausible. She was named after her father, but, as expected, nothing is known about her early life, education, or how she came to be married to Polemon, who had been made ruler of Pontos by Antonius. Polemon's father, the scholar Zenon of Laodikeia (probably the Pontic city of that name, about sixty miles northwest of Kabeira), had assisted the Romans when the Parthians intruded into Asia Minor in the 40s BC, which may have led Antonius to look with favor upon his son, another example of the upward mobility of the era, especially for those who were of assistance to the Romans.[43] Polemon was first made king of a portion of Cilicia, in southeastern Asia Minor, probably in the early 30s BC when the triumvir was reorganizing the region, and even before Pythodoris was born.[44] By 36 BC the Mithradatic line in Pontos had become extinct, and Polemon was given the kingship. Eventually he also ruled (for a while) Lesser Armenia to the east.[45] He quickly became one of the most powerful rulers in Asia Minor—only Archelaos of Cappadocia could claim similar status—and even though Polemon supported Antonius at Actium in 31 BC (although cautiously sending only troops, not his person), he survived the regime change and was confirmed in his position by Augustus, clearly too experienced to be removed.[46] In 15 BC he was called upon by Augustus to settle the increasing instability in Bosporos, north of the Black Sea, which involved the claims of Dynamis and various usurpers.[47] He spent the last years of his life moving between Pontos and Bosporos, entering into some kind of relationship with Dynamis, and was killed in or near Pontos by the indigenous Aspourgianians, probably in 8 BC.[48]

At some time during the last decade of his life, he married Pythodoris, probably before 15 BC, when he first went to Bosporos. In what way the daughter of Pythodoros, from southwestern Asia Minor, and the king of Pontos, from northern Asia Minor, came together remains a mystery, but presumably their union had the sanction of Augustus, who was continually involved in the marriages of the allied monarchs. Like Pythodoris, Polemon did not have a royal background but his family had long served Rome, and the elevation of such people to royal status was an inevitability of the times, due to a shortage of traditional royalty in the era that saw the collapse of the Mithradatic dynasty, the Seleukids, and the Ptolemies, as well as the problems caused by the Roman civil war. After all, even though no one dared to use the word "royal," the same thing was happening in Rome, where new families were coming into the highest levels of power.

Polemon was at least in his forties by 15 BC, and there is no evidence of any previous marriage or children. It is likely that questions about the future of the Pontic kingdom were being raised both in Rome and in Asia Minor. Marriage to a young wife of suitable status would assist in solving this problem, and in fact three heirs were produced by 7 BC.

Queen of Pontos

Yet by that time Polemon was dead, when the children of the couple would not have been more than ten years of age. The Pontic kingdom became the sole possession of Pythodoris, although in time one of her sons assisted her as an administrator.[49] Pythodoris could not have been recognized as sole ruler without the approval of Augustus, probably supported by Livia: the Romans had long been involved in the accession (and removal) of Eastern dynasts. Pythodoris would have been treated no differently, yet Roman approval of her demonstrates confidence in her ability. Probably not yet thirty years of age, she became ruler of the largest territory controlled by an independent queen since the death of Cleopatra VII a quarter century before.

The name "Pontos" was an ancient word for the open sea, older than its first documented use by Homer. By the fifth century BC, it had become a toponym, referring to what is now called the Black Sea, as a way of distinguishing it from the Mediterranean proper.[50] Eventually the name of the sea came to be applied to the territories surrounding it, especially to the south. Greeks had been on this coast ever since Jason and the Argonauts sought the Golden Fleece—a mythological starting point for local culture that was of great relevance to Pythodoris—and by the beginning of the Hellenistic period numerous Greek cities lined the Black Sea littoral. With the collapse of the Persian Empire at the time of Alexander the Great and the restructuring of the East that followed, a local leader, Mithradates I, claimed territory along the southern shore of the sea, as well as inland, and took the title King of Pontos, creating a dynasty that lasted into the 30s BC, when the lack of successors led Antonius to install Polemon.[51]

At its peak under the Mithradatic dynasty, the kingdom of Pontos extended along the southern coast of the Black Sea and through ancient Colchis up the eastern coast into the unorganized and primitive regions that today form the Black Sea coast of Russia north of modern Sochi. As Strabo noted, much of the hinterland was occupied by mountain tribesmen subject to the Pontic government. Cities, many of which were of Greek origin, lined the coast and also the great river valleys that lay inland from the southern shore. Strabo did not exaggerate in emphasizing that this was a region of great agricultural abundance. On its southern edge Pontos bordered on other kingdoms of Asia Minor, such as Cappadocia and Galatia; at times, especially under the expansionist policies of Mithradates VI, these came within the Pontic sphere. To the southeast was Armenia, which also was at times under Pontic control, especially its western region, generally called Lesser Armenia, was allied with Pontos from the early second century BC and eventually claimed by Mithradates VI.[52]

With his death in 63 BC, the Romans became directly involved in the destiny of Pontos. By the time Pythodoris became queen, nearly half a century later, the territory had been somewhat reduced. Late in the reign of Mithradates VI, as Roman forces began to exert greater pressure on the king, the western part of Pontos had become the Roman province of Bithynia. Any claim that the Pontic monarchs had to Bosporos, north of the Black Sea, was not sustained and the region reverted to Dynamis, despite any relationship between her and Polemon. Yet the territories that Pythodoris inherited were still substantial, and she ruled them in peace and prosperity for many years, well into the AD 20s if not beyond.

The Marriage to Archelaos

In one of the more peculiar developments of contemporary Eastern dynastic history, soon after the death of Polemon, Pythodoris married the most senior of the allied kings, Archelaos of Cappadocia, one of the few survivors from the era of Antonius, who had placed him on the throne by 41 BC.[53] This marriage is documented only by Strabo, in a passage written after Archelaos's death in AD 18:

> Pythodoris . . . married Archelaos and remained with him until the end, but is now a widow.[54]

Unlike the temporary arrangement between Dynamis and Polemon, this relationship lasted for a quarter of a century and was probably a formal marriage. There is no reason to doubt Strabo: he was perfectly well informed about Pythodoris and wrote this passage very shortly after Archelaos's death. Setting aside that Pythodoris had not even been born when Archelaos came to the throne, it is difficult to understand exactly what purpose the marriage served. Archelaos had been in power for more than thirty years and had seen his daughter Glaphyra marry into the Herodian family. To be sure, Pythodoris was somewhat vulnerable, since her husband had been killed while on campaign and she had three young children to raise. One can speculate that this might have been one of the factors in the marriage, with Archelaos acting more as guardian than husband. Moreover, just at the time of Polemon's death, Archelaos's arrangement with the Herodians collapsed with the execution of his son-in-law Alexander, and he may have seen possibilities in Pythodoris's young children. His later connection with Juba II of Mauretania demonstrates his broad dynastic aspirations.

It cannot be exactly determined when the marriage took place, but given that the problem with the Herodians and Polemon's death were virtually contemporary, and that Pythodoris may have needed the wisdom and advice of the astute Archelaos, it seems most probable the event occurred shortly after 7 BC. Augustus may have seen it as a better choice for maintaining the stability of the Pontic kingdom than any alternative that involved deposing Pythodoris and importing a ruler from elsewhere. It seems largely to have been a matter of convenience: no children are known, and neither ruler seems to have intervened in the territories of the other. But it did mean that in theory Pythodoris was ruler of lands from the Mediterranean coast to the eastern Black Sea littoral. Strabo's explicit but somewhat enigmatic statement, that she remained with Archelaos "until the end," has a note of surprise that the relationship survived as long as it did, well after Pythodoris's children were grown and had embarked on their own careers. It may be that Strabo was somewhat astonished that it continued through the regime change from Augustus to Tiberius in AD 14. In fact, during the last years of Augustus, it was Archelaos rather than Pythodoris who needed a guardian: he suffered a stroke and Augustus had to appoint someone to manage Cappadocia until he recovered. This may well have been Pythodoris.[55] By the time of the death of Augustus, Archelaos was in his seventies; Pythodoris was perhaps around fifty.

The "end" that Strabo referred to came in AD 18. The previous year Tiberius had summoned Archelaos to Rome, and if one is to take Strabo's statement literally, Pythodoris went with him. Tiberius complained that over the years Archelaos had not shown him sufficient respect and, more seriously, that he was fomenting rebellion.[56] Archelaos decided to make the journey to Rome because of a letter from Livia, which the emperor's critics saw as a fake yet may have been another example of her involvement in the destinies of Eastern royalty, attempting not only to restrain her son Tiberius but to encourage Archelaos to come to the city and defend himself. The seriousness of the charges of rebellion cannot be determined: there was some evidence of anti-Roman collusion with the governor of the province of Cilicia, just to the east of Cappadocia,[57] and there may have been issues in Armenia, where Archelaos's grandson (who was also a grandson of Herod the Great), Tigranes V, ruled and was having the inevitable difficulties with the Parthians.[58] At any rate, the eternally suspicious Tiberius, in office only three years, may have seen conspiracy and rebellion, and over time Archelaos had become dangerously powerful, creating alliances with practically every other major dynasty in the Mediterranean world.[59]

So Archelaos and Pythodoris arrived in Rome. The king, near if not past eighty years of age, was in poor health (something that he exploited in the hope of leniency). He was given a hearing before the Senate, whose members were more amused than threatened by the elderly invalid. Tiberius, who had proposed the death penalty, realized (perhaps encouraged by his mother) that he was in a losing situation and subject to ridicule, and dropped the charges. There was some irony in all this, because the emperor had begun his professional career, probably in 26 BC, successfully defending Archelaos before Augustus.[60]

Yet the whole matter of Archelaos's future became moot when the king died, while still in Rome. Suicide was suggested, but it is more likely that he simply succumbed to the strain of events. Pythodoris was now a widow for the second time. Remarkably she was untainted by the events surrounding her husband—one might again detect the hand of Livia—although she lost any claim, however minimal, to Cappadocia, which was promptly provincialized.[61] Yet her Pontic territories remained her own: Tiberius recognized the value of someone who had ruled Pontos successfully for twenty-five years.

Pythodoris's Last Years

Pythodoris returned to Pontos and continued her rule; it was during the immediately following years that Strabo wrote his eulogistic comments about her and her reign. She turned sixty around AD 25; there is no evidence that she ever remarried. Her children were in their thirties and had careers of their own. The daughter, Antonia Tryphaina, married Kotys VIII of Thrace.[62] One son, perhaps the elder, was Zenon, who became king of Armenia and took the name Artaxias (III) Germanicus, allegedly from Artaxata, the city in Armenia where Germanicus, the nephew of Tiberius, proclaimed him king in AD 18; the event was recorded on his coinage.[63] Yet his name was more probably chosen to commemorate his illustrious predecessor, Artaxias I, the first great ruler of Hellenistic Armenia, in power during the early second century BC.[64] Exactly why Zenon Artaxias became king of Armenia remains obscure, but Armenia and Pontos had long had connections, and his ancestry was distinguished. Moreover, he was an admirer of Armenian culture, even adopting local dress, and had wide support in the region. Before he became king, he had been honored by the citizens of Smyrna and was careful to give recognition to his mother, Pythodoris, and his grand-mother, Antonia, whose names appear on the dedicatory inscription before that of his father, Polemon, showing the prominent position of women in his family and how they contributed to his own status.[65] He brought sixteen years of peace to Armenia, which had long been a region of contention between the Romans and the Parthians, each proposing their own kings, most of whom did not last long. Yet Zenon seems to have had no descendants, and upon his death, probably in AD 34, Armenia returned to instability under rival monarchs.

Zenon's brother remains anonymous: Strabo, the source for the brief notice of his career, chose not to record the names of any of the three children of Pythodoris.[66] He may have been the only one of the three who did not attain a royal position. He served as his mother's administrator after the death of Archelaos, but other details as to his career are lacking, and depending on how closely one reads the text of the *Geography*, he may even have died before Strabo wrote. It has been suggested that he was the M. Antonius Polemo who at a later date was priest-king at the temple state of Olbe in southern Anatolia, but this is speculative and has serious chronological difficulties. There is little doubt that M. Antonius Polemo was in some way related to Pythodoris, but the exact connection remains unproved.[67]

After Strabo wrote his account of Pythodoris, there is no further in-formation that can be applied to her rule. Coins with "Year 60" are un-likely to suggest sixty years of rule in Pontos, which would be around AD 45, when her grandson Polemon II ruled. These coins have the head of either Augustus or Tiberius and may have been issued in AD 14 at the time of the regime change; the date would then refer to a chronology that began in the 40s BC, when Julius Caesar was in Asia Minor and the world was evolving, a reasonable time to start a new era.[68] There is also some joint coinage with Pythodoris's first husband, Polemon I: one in silver shows a right-facing bust of the queen, who has a rather severe-looking face and her hair drawn back into a chignon.[69] Yet these coins offer no as-sistance in determining the ultimate length of Pythodoris's rule. She may have died shortly after Strabo's eulogy, in the AD 20s, or survived for a decade or more. Her grandson Polemon II was in power by AD 38, but this

FIG. 15. Coin of Pythodoris. British Museum 1893,0406.2.
Photo © The Trustees of the British Museum

was two generations later, and the chronology of the mother of Polemon II (and daughter of Pythodoris), Antonia Tryphaina, remains a problem; she may have been on the throne of Pontos by AD 33, which would suggest a speculative date for the death of Pythodoris.[70] An epitaph from Pontic Komana of uncertain date honors Pythodoris the daughter of Antonius; "Antonius" may be an error for "Antonia," but if correctly written it is unlikely to refer to the queen but perhaps to a member of her household.[71]

Antonia Tryphaina

Pythodoris was the matriarch of a royal line that lasted into the late third century AD. All these descendants were from her daughter, Antonia Tryphaina, who assumed her mother's role as one of the prominent royal women of the era. There is no evidence that either of Pythodoris's sons had any children. Antonia Tryphaina herself had five, all of whom became royalty. Although outside the limits of this study, it is worth considering the female descendants of Pythodoris, as they continued her tradition of dynamic queens into the later Roman Empire.

Antonia Tryphaina was born around 8 BC, or a few years earlier, and named after her grandmother. Her unusual second name is enigmatic: its meaning (essentially "luxuriant") as a personal name is obscure. It occurs occasionally in the Ptolemaic dynasty, first with Cleopatra Tryphaina, the eldest daughter of Ptolemy VIII and Cleopatra III, who married the Seleukid king Antiochos VIII around 124 BC. While in Antioch in 112 BC, she killed her sister Cleopatra IV, and in turn her husband (who was also Cleopatra Tryphaina's brother-in-law), Antiochos IX, killed her. Her career is hardly a strong model for Antonia Tryphaina's parents to have followed a century later for their daughter, and there must be more to the choice of name. A better precedent might have been Cleopatra VI Tryphaina, the sister-wife of Ptolemy XII, who briefly ruled along with her daughter Berenike IV around 58 BC when her husband went into exile in Rome.[72] It is remotely possible that Pythodoris, believing herself to be a granddaughter of Antonius, sought to give her daughter a name associated with Egypt, or even the triumvir's luxuriant lifestyle, but even this seems forced.[73]

Antonia Tryphaina married Kotys VIII, the king of eastern Thrace. Thrace was the region north of the Greek peninsula, extending as far as the Istros (Danube) River. The Thracians had long been considered primitive and warlike: in the fifth century BC, Herodotos saw them as weak and disorganized. Various incursions from the south and east, beginning with the Athenians and Persians in the late sixth century BC and followed by Alexander the Great two centuries later, brought them within the sphere of the Mediterranean world. The Romans became involved in the region in the second century BC, by which time various Hellenized dynasties had been established.[74]

One of these dynasties was that of the Sapaians, who ruled a local population that had long existed: the poet Archilochos had tangled with them in the seventh century BC.[75] By AD 12, Kotys VIII had been placed on the Sapaian throne by Augustus, ruling the more civilized, or eastern, parts of Thrace, near the Greek cities along the Black Sea coast. Antonia Tryphaina had reached marriageable age a few years earlier, so it is probable that the wedding took place before Kotys's accession and while his father, Rhoimetalkes I, was still on the throne: such a marriage would make it clear that Kotys was the heir apparent. Rhoimetalkes had ruled for many years, probably since early in the Augustan period, if not before.[76]

During what would be a brief reign, Kotys proved himself a worthy husband for the daughter of Pythodoris. The epigrammatist Antipater of Thessalonike likened him to the gods and referred to his patronage of literature.[77] Ovid, living in exile at Tomis, on the borders of the kingdom, appealed to him for help, referring to the king's education and literary skills and proposing himself as a suitable addition to the Thracian court.[78] At Epidauros in the Peloponnesos, the king built a stoa and other structures; remains of the stoa are still visible. Kotys may also have become honorary archon at Athens.[79]

Yet his promising rule was not to last. Disagreements festered about the disposition of the kingdom after the death of his father, when it had been divided between Kotys and his uncle Rhescuporis. The latter felt, with perhaps some justification, that he had deliberately received the worse part of the territory, which he characterized as having poor soil and a wild population, and too close to the barbarians for comfort.[80] This may have been true, yet the division was probably based in part on the fact that Kotys, married to a princess of Pontos, would naturally receive the region closer to his wife's ancestral lands. But Rhescuporis thought otherwise. He was restrained during the last years of Augustus, but when Tiberius came to the throne he began to harass his nephew's portion militarily. Tiberius tried to calm things, but to no avail, and in AD 19 Rhescuporis killed Kotys.

At this point his widow, Antonia Tryphaina, demonstrated her fidelity to her mother's heritage by taking charge of events. She immediately went to Rome with her children and accused her husband's murderer before the Senate. One suspects that she already had contacts in the city—it had been only slightly more than a year since her mother had been there on the matter of Archelaos—and this may have given Antonia access to Livia. It is quite possible that her mother was still in town. Her case before the Senate was successful, and Rhescuporis was exiled, soon to die in Alexandria under mysterious circumstances. Tiberius divided the kingdom of Thrace between Rhoimeltakes II, who was Rhescuporis's son and was known to have been opposed to his father's ambitions, and the children of Antonia and Kotys. Antonia herself did not inherit any ruling power—unlike her mother, who had just been sustained as queen of Pontos—perhaps because there were many heirs who were direct descendants of the Thracian royal line, and Antonia had been queen for only a brief period.

After successfully prosecuting her husband's assassin, Antonia Tryphaina and her children stayed in Rome for a while, living with the imperial family, close to Livia and probably Antonia, the younger daughter of Antonius and Octavia, who was in her fifties and was becoming prominent as the younger matriarch of the Julio-Claudian family. Antonia Tryphaina's children, as was customary, were also integrated into the household.

Eventually she moved to the ancient Greek city of Kyzikos, which lay across the Propontis from the kingdom of Thrace inherited by her children, so she was near their realm but wisely not within it. The Thracian dynasty had connections with Kyzikos: when Marcus Brutus was in the region after the assassination of Caesar, local instability had led the Thracian queen Polemokratia (whose husband had just been killed) to entrust her son Kotys and the family wealth to Brutus, who deposited both in Kyzikos. The child did eventually become king, but it is difficult to place him within the Thracian king list; he may have been the grandfather of Antonia Tryphaina's husband.[81]

Antonia Tryphaina was a queen without a realm, and in Kyzikos she lived the life of a prominent wealthy woman. She retained her title of *basilissa* and was a major benefactor of the city. An inscribed pedestal in gray marble, decorated with reliefs of fish, galleys, and a trident, records that she rebuilt the harbor of this important commercial center, dedicating the works to Poseidon of the Isthmos. She and her son Rhoimetalkes III, the king of Thrace, paid for the project, and it was implemented in the name of her other sons, Polemon II (cited as king of Pontos) and Kotys IX. She also reminded the readers that she was a queen herself.[82] The incorporation of Kyzikos into the province of Asia in AD 25 may have been the stimulus for extensive public works: another inscription gives the name of the project manager (a certain Bakchios) and describes other architectural benefactions by the queen, especially in the agora.[83] The locals made a dedication to her in the Temple of Athena Polias, since she had provided financial support for the Panathenaic festival in the city, at which she was priestess of Livia (dedicating a statue of her); this was probably after Livia's death in AD 29.[84] According to the inscription, this was a major cultural event, to which people came from all over the civilized world. Antonia Tryphaina was also priestess of Drusilla, the sister of Gaius Caligula, who died in AD 38 and was deified. The inscription honors not only the "most distinguished" queen but her three sons—all of whom were kings—treating her and her family as if they were local citizens. She may also have been initiated into the mysteries of the Great Gods on the island of Samothrake.[85]

Clearly she moved at the highest levels of Kyzikene society. Even her name was imitated, as can be seen with the local Christian martyr

Tryphaina.[86] She probably spent most, if not all, of the rest of her life in the city, yet it is possible that she briefly ruled in Pontos upon the death of her mother and before the accession of her own son Polemon II, although it seems unlikely that she would have received such repeated honors from the Kyzikenes were she no longer resident in the city.[87] Nevertheless, she issued joint coinage with Polemon II that called her "*Basilissa* Tryphaina"; a portrait of her wearing the royal diadem appears on the reverse. These coins run for eighteen years, perhaps from the arrangements of AD 19 after the death of her husband to the accession of Gaius Caligula in AD 37.[88]

Despite an abundance of information about a royal woman, the exact pattern of Antonia Tryphaina's life after she left Thrace in AD 19 remains speculative. She lived in Rome in the imperial household for a while, and it is most probable that she then moved to Kyzikos and lived there for the rest of her life, becoming the doyenne of the city and an important local figure in the years of its transition from a free city to a Roman provincial one. She retained the title of queen, which was in the process of becoming as much an honorific as an actual term for reigning royalty.[89] Nevertheless, she may have ruled in Pontos after the death of her mother, in all probability dying shortly after AD 38.

The Grandchildren of Pythodoris

Royal women continued to be a feature of the next generation of the descendants of Pythodoris. The two daughters of Antonia Tryphaina, Pythodoris II and Gepaipyris, became respectively queens of Thrace and Bosporos.[90] Antonia Tryphaina's son Polemon II married into the Herodian family, to Berenike II, a great-granddaughter of Herod the Great and the only Herodian woman to have the title *basilissa*, although she never ruled, another example of the title becoming an honorific.[91] Her marriage to Polemon, in the AD 50s, was a brief moment in her rich career, which included the rebuilding of the city of Berytos, a questionable relationship with her brother King Agrippa II (which the marriage to Polemon was supposed to counteract), and her eventual desertion of Polemon to begin her famous affair with the future emperor Titus. Polemon's arrangement with Berenike may have been based, in part, on his claim of descent from Antonius the triumvir (who had also empowered the Herodian family a century previously). But Berenike had greater things in mind, and the relationship was brief.[92] By the AD 60s, instability in Pontos (fomented by the Parthians) led Polemon to resign his kingship in favor of provincialization and to withdraw to his Cilician territories, where he survived a few years longer. He is last known through coinage commemorating the brief reign of the emperor Galba, from the summer of AD 68 to the following January.[93] The long history of the independent Pontic kingdom had come to an end.

Aba of Olbe and Mousa of Parthia

There are often only glimpses of other queens who ruled alone during the Augustan era. The two best known—although the evidence remains scant and disputed—are Aba of Olbe and Mousa of Parthia. Both succeeded to the throne because of the death of a husband, and both fell victim to the usual objections to women rulers. Yet they provide hints that the political structure of the eastern Mediterranean during the second half of the first century BC and into the following century was more diverse and complex than suggested by the extant literature.

Aba of Olbe

Although she may not have survived quite into the Augustan period, Aba of Olbe (or Olba), active at least into the late 30s BC, provides a fine example of an obscure (to modern readers) ruling woman of the era. She is known only from a single passage in the *Geography* of Strabo, who was particularly well informed on the political situation in Asia Minor during the first century BC.[1] The scant surviving information provides an insight into the politics of the region in the years just before Augustus came to power.

Olbe lies in the district known in antiquity as Rough Cilicia, so named for its rugged topography, essentially the south central part of modern Turkey. The site is only fifteen miles inland but lies at more than 3,000 feet elevation and was an ancient shrine of Zeus Olbios, with a town just to its west. The locals believed that the cult had been founded by Aias, the son of the Trojan War hero Teukros, and thus the sanctuary was thought to have had its origins in the dispersal of peoples after the war. The shrine and the region around it had become a prominent temple state by the fourth century BC, with its priest-kings taking royal privileges and ruling an extensive territory, one of several such entities in central Anatolia. The priest-kings were generally named Teukros or Aias, reinforcing the mythological origins of the cult. In the early third century BC, Seleukos I paid for the repair of the temple of Zeus: Seleukid aspirations included much of southern Anatolia, but Olbe probably kept its independence.[2] By the first century BC, it may have been in decline— the collapse of the Seleukids and the rise of piracy certainly played a role—and a regional ruler named Zenophanes was guardian of the shrine, perhaps around 50 BC. His family already had some connection to Olbe, since an earlier Zenophanes had been priest-king, or the father of one, at the time of the Seleukid repairs.

The younger Zenophanes does not seem to have been priest-king himself, but his daughter, Aba, married into the priestly family. The name of her husband, presumably the priest-king, is not known. When he died, she succeeded to the rule, but her position was precarious and she eventually sought help from both Cleopatra VII and Antonius; there is a sense of desperation in her request (Strabo referred to "earnest pleas").[3] This would have been sometime between when the couple met at Tarsos in 41 BC and when they died, eleven years later. The Ptolemies had long-standing interests in Cilicia, including the region of Olbe, and under his triumviral authority Antonius had regularly restored parts of this territory to Cleopatra's control: as early as 38 BC she had a military governor of Cilicia and Cyprus in office. Aba's position was thus confirmed by both the Ptolemies and the Romans.

How long she remained in power is not recorded. Eventually she was overthrown, presumably in favor of her son, since her family continued to control the priesthood; one can only assume that she fell victim to the usual opposition to a woman ruler. There is no indication that she had any contact with Augustus, so she may have been removed due to an internal revolt before 30 BC, when Augustus (still Octavian) came to full power. After the Battle of Actium, he carried out his own reorganization of Asia Minor, upholding Antonius's appointments in some cases and not in others. Needless to say, any arrangements regarding Cleopatra tended to be voided. Strabo knew that Aba had been deposed, but the *Geography*, still being edited into the second decade of the first century AD, provides no information about the length of her tenure. In summary, she probably married into the priestly family of Olbe around 50 BC and became sole ruler a few years later, appealing to Cleopatra and Antonius after 41 BC and being removed from office in favor of her son (whose name is not recorded) by 30 BC. Whether she was killed or lived in retirement is also not known. The temple state of Olbe seems to have been dissolved sometime in the first century AD, and by AD 72, when the territory became part of the Roman province of Cilicia, it had been replaced by Diocaesarea, located west of the shrine on the townsite. The new name was more suitable for the new era, and its impressive remains are still visible.[4]

Although her life is scantily documented, Aba is unique in the history of the later first century BC. She was a dependent ruler within the expanding empire of Cleopatra VII, much like the allied monarchs of the Roman world, and her career demonstrated the wide reach of Cleopatra's power at its peak. Moreover, she ruled for several years as priestess-queen of Olbe, an office not recorded elsewhere. The official title of the priest-king was *Archiereus* (High Priest), preserved on the repair inscription of Seleukos I, and presumably she took this as her own, perhaps in the feminine form, *Archiereia*. But like so many women of power, her position and status were a threat, and she was deposed, probably when her Ptolemaic and Roman patrons were themselves eliminated. Yet she provides a momentary glimpse into a little-known world that existed just before the Augustan period.

Thea Mousa of Parthia

One of the more remarkable career paths in the Augustan period is that of Thesmousa, or Thea Mousa, an Italian slave girl who ended up as the queen of Parthia.[5] Thesmousa (Thesmusa) may have been her actual name, although, as noted later, her coinage presents her as Thea Mousa, perhaps an alteration to provide a more appropriately sounding regal name. Parthian royalty had long had a taste for Greek women—especially from Ionia—who in some cases became the mothers of Parthian kings, so there are precedents for Western women joining the royal family.[6] But Thesmousa is by far the most prominent and the best known.

In literature, she was mentioned only by Josephus, another example of his ability to provide details of Eastern dynasties not preserved in any other source. She was presented to Phraates IV, the king of Parthia, by Augustus.[7] Since she seems to have had an adult (or at most adolescent) son by 2 BC, the bestowal was perhaps around 20 BC, or just before, part of the developing arrangement between Rome and Parthia that culminated in the return of the standards lost by M. Licinius Crassus in 53 BC and Marcus Antonius some years later.[8] Crassus's ill-advised Parthian expedition, which resulted in his death, had produced thirty years of hostility between Rome and Parthia, exacerbated by Antonius's equally unwise invasions a generation later. The agreement of 20 BC, when the standards were returned, was seen by Augustus as one of his greatest achievements; he drew attention to the event in his own autobiographical *Res gestae*[9] and probably had it depicted it on the breastplate of his statue found at Prima Porta near Rome and now in the Vatican.[10] Presumably gifts were exchanged, and perhaps had been for several years, and this would have been the obvious time to present Thesmousa to the Parthian king. There were also diplomatic contacts between Rome and Parthia as early as 23 BC,[11] so any time during these several years would have been appropriate for Thesmousa to go to Parthia.

Nothing is known about her origins: even Josephus's identification of her as an Italian slave girl is not particularly informative, because it may indicate only her residence, not her ethnicity. Her name suggests that she might have been related to Augustus's physician, Antonius Musa, renowned for his cold-water cures, and his brother Euphorbos, royal botanist at the Mauretanian court.[12] Yet any association of her with this family is onomastic speculation, and in fact the name "Mousa" was common in Italy.

King Phraates IV was clearly smitten with Thesmousa, and after the couple had a child—the future king Phraates V, or Phraatakes—he declared that she would be considered his legitimate wife. Some years later, perhaps around 10 BC, Thesmousa allegedly convinced Phraates IV to send his legitimate sons to Rome. Whether this included Phraatakes is not certain: he is on the list provided by Strabo, an almost contemporary source, but there is the question of whether he could be considered legitimate.[13] Nevertheless, three other sons went to Rome, perhaps in an attempt by the queen to strengthen her position at court, although her pressure on the king need not have been the only reason for dispatching the sons: there was a long-standing tradition of sending royal children to Rome to be educated, thus removing them from a problematic life at court.

With or without Phraatakes, several potential rivals had been sent to Rome, and presumably the status of the queen was enhanced. A few years later, in AD 2, with the connivance of Phraatakes, she had her husband assassinated and her son placed on the throne as Phraates V. The two issued joint coinage, with the king on the obverse and his mother on the reverse, depicted with a three-tiered jeweled crown and her hair drawn back in a knot, and the legend "Thea Ourania Mousa, *Basilissa*," creating a play on her name to suggest divinity and association with the goddess Ourania, or Urania, either Persian Anahita or Greek Aphrodite, emphasizing the queen's fertility (fig.16). The joint series runs from AD 1 into AD 4. It is numismatically unusual, since Thea Mousa is the only Parthian queen to be named and shown on coinage.[14] "Thea Mousa"—if not solely a pun on her original name—is remindful of Cleopatra Thea, the daughter of Ptolemy VI and Cleopatra II of Egypt, who married into the Seleukid family—several times—in the late second century BC. The attribute "Thea" suggests divinity, and it was the nomenclature used on her coins.[15] Moreover, she had also been in a position of dominance over a young son, in this case the Seleukid king Antiochos VIII.

Thea Mousa's titles—queen, goddess, Ourania—all stress her legitimacy and serve to negate any memory of her former life as an Italian slave girl.[16] Yet soon the alliance between mother and son allegedly took an unusual turn, as the two were said to have entered into an incestuous relationship. This was reported by Josephus, and there may also be an allusion to it in the *Pharsalia* of Lucan, written half a century after the event (and, in fact, before the *Jewish Antiquities* of Josephus). The dramatic situation depicted in the *Pharsalia* is the civil war between Julius

FIG. 16. Coin of Thea Mousa and Phraatakes. British Museum 1918,0501.23.
Photo © The Trustees of the British Museum.

Caesar and Pompey the Great in the early 40s BC, and Lucan described Parthian royalty in the following terms:

> Their sisters lie on the couches of the kings, and also—in a sacred relationship—their mothers. The ill-fated legend condemns Oedipus of Thebes among the nations for the crime that was unknowingly committed: how frequently an Arsacid [the Parthian royal family] is born to rule the Parthians from such a mixture of blood.[17]

Although Lucan's polemic belongs in a long tradition of Roman antipathy toward the Parthians and their ways, the account seems to be grounded in specifics, and the assumed relationship of Phraatakes and Thea Mousa might have come to mind to his readers. Yet the story may be pure slander, another example of demeaning the character of a strong woman. There are examples of queens taking a younger male relative as a companion, effectively a consort, most notably Cleopatra VII and her brothers Ptolemy XIII and XIV, as well as Pythodoris and her son, who served as her administrator. In a later era, Zenobia of Palmyra had a similar relationship with her son Vaballathus. None of these cases need have involved incest, yet it was an easy charge to make, especially by enemies.

Mother–son incest was not unknown in antiquity, but was rare and considered highly objectionable. The most notorious instance is indeed that of Oedipus and his mother, Jokasta, and the fate of both—even though the relationship was entered into unknowingly—demonstrates how strict the taboo was against such a liaison. Father–daughter incest was perhaps more common, such as that between the biblical patriarch Lot and his daughters,[18] and this seems to have been allowable on occasion, probably when there was a need to produce children. Nevertheless, biblical scholars of the Roman period went to great lengths to sanction Lot's actions, given the prohibitions against incest.[19] There was alleged evidence for mother–son incest among the Persian aristocracy, although the primary documentation for it is religious sources within the Judaeo-Christian tradition that sought to denigrate pagan customs.[20] There is also a reported case of mother–son incest in Egypt involving the Nineteenth Dynasty pharaoh Amenephtes (Merenptah), who ruled in the late thirteenth century BC.[21] But the fact remains that such a relationship was rare in the ancient world and generally vigorously condemned. Thus it is not unexpected that whether or not the charge was true, it became a major factor in the prompt downfall of both Thea Mousa and her son.

Exactly what happened is not clear, but there was a violent local reaction against both the murder of Phraates IV and the supposed incest, which fed into the persistent unstable conditions in contemporary Parthia. A revolt broke out in AD 4 and Phraatakes was deposed. Josephus recorded that he also died, without indicating when the death occurred or how. Phraatakes may have fled to his mother's homeland and taken refuge with Augustus, although it is hard to believe that by this time he would have been welcomed. Whether his mother accompanied him is not known, and there is no further mention of her.[22]

Nevertheless, the couple had ruled for six years, and it is probable that Thea Mousa was the actual power in the Parthian state. Resistance to her actions took some time to coalesce; the civil war that had been brewing ever since the death of Phraates IV—if not before—lasted until after AD 10, and eventually required Roman intervention.[23] To be sure, Thea Mousa was presented negatively by Josephus, and she fell victim to some of the same prejudices against powerful women that affected Cleopatra VII and others, since she was remembered more for her personal life than for any political ability. Moreover, there are certain folktale elements to the story: the beautiful slave girl who wins the favor of the king and eventually comes to control him, in time killing him. A similar tale was reported about the legendary Assyrian queen Semiramis.[24] Yet Thea Mousa remains a remarkable example of a woman who moved astonishingly far, both geographically and in terms of social status, during her relatively short life.

8

Royal Women and Roman Women

The several royal women examined in this study had much in common. As transitional figures between the late Hellenistic world and that of Rome, they represented both the legacy of earlier queenship, going back to Penelope, and the future manifested by the women of the Roman imperial family, who were queens in all but name. They exemplified the remarkable survival of the priorities of the great opponents of Rome in the first century BC: both the granddaughter of Mithradates VI and the daughter of Marcus Antonius helped shape attitudes toward royalty in Rome as well as the eastern Mediterranean, preserving a lingering memory of their distinguished ancestors, even though those forebears had been defeated militarily and politically, and official Roman policy demeaned their memory.

A constant theme in the careers of royal women of the Augustan period is their regular contact with the women of the ruling elite at Rome, in particular Livia, the wife of Augustus. Salome, Dynamis, and Pythodoris all had personal relationships with her, and Cleopatra Selene grew up in the neighboring house of her sister-in-law Octavia, doubtless maintaining contact with the family after she went to Mauretania. This interchange between Rome and the kingdoms took the form of personal contact, correspondence, and honorific and cultic recognition. Although Livia was generally the liaison between the queens and Rome, two other prominent women of the Augustan household, Octavia and Antonia, had their own connections with royalty. Since Antonia was a daughter of Antonius the triumvir, and Octavia had been his wife, this was another example of the survival of his influence throughout and beyond the Augustan period.

MAP 5. The eastern Mediterranean during the Augustan period.

Contact between royalty and the Roman elite had existed ever since Roman power spread beyond central Italy: the Romans early realized that alliances with the ruling powers on the fringes of Roman territory could benefit their own interests and political stability.[1] Kings such as Hieron II of Syracuse (died 216 BC) and Massinissa of Numidia (died 148 BC) were the first to enter into this mutually advantageous situation where Romans educated local royalty about the value of Roman alliance and culture, and the kings had Roman assistance in preserving the stability of their kingdoms. As the Romans moved into the eastern Mediterranean and the kingdoms established by the successors of Alexander the Great, the relationship between Rome and royalty became more widespread and complex.

Because kings and queens had to balance their own interests with those of Rome, it became common for their children to be sent to the city of Rome to be educated; this was the best way to ensure that the next generation of royalty was sufficiently trained in Roman customs to be sympathetic to Roman needs. This phenomenon is particularly apparent among the Herodians. In 22 BC Herod sent his sons (and heirs apparent) Alexander (eventually to be Glaphyra's husband) and Aristoboulos to the city. They stayed in the home of the noted scholar and historian Asinius Pollio and then with Augustus himself; one can imagine no better way to become culturally Romanized. Five years later, Augustus announced that their education was complete, and Herod himself came to Rome to accompany them back to Judaea.[2] The educating and housing of royal children in Rome was a regular phenomenon of the Augustan era: both Cleopatra Selene and her future husband, Juba II, were beneficiaries of the policy.

Cleopatra Selene is a rare documented example of a royal woman raised in Rome: she was half Roman and had relatives in the Augustan household, including her half-sister Antonia, who was a few years younger and, one suspects, a childhood playmate. But the survival of evidence for Cleopatra Selene's upbringing is unusual since, typically, information on this part of a royal woman's life is even more scant than what is available on her maturity. Thus there is hardly any documentation of other royal women coming to Rome as children; in the few known cases, such as those of Berenike I of Judaea and of Antonia Tryphaina, they accompanied their mother. In both cases it was effectively the mother who initiated the trip to Rome, but in Cleopatra Selene's case, her mother was dead. Other royal women may have come to the city in their youth, but inevitably this is not recorded.

With Cleopatra Selene there was a unique situation: the joining of Eastern royalty to the Roman ruling elite. The theoretical benefits of this had been realized as early as the second century BC, when, allegedly, Ptolemy VIII asked the Roman matron Cornelia (mother of the celebrated reformers Tiberius and Gaius Gracchus) to marry him. Her husband, Tiberius Sempronius Gracchus, had just died, and as the most distinguished Roman woman of her era she would have seemed a prime candidate to marry into an Eastern royal family. But the newly widowed Cornelia rejected Ptolemy's offer as inappropriate.[3] To be sure, the story may be apocryphal—a tale of the virtue and integrity of a Roman woman who withstood the blandishments of foreign royalty— but its very existence demonstrates the plausibility and mutual political viability of a liaison between royalty and the Roman aristocracy. A century later Cleopatra VII was to fulfill this potential with her carefully chosen relationships with Julius Caesar and Antonius, connections that served all the participants well, at least at first, and in the latter case provided the link between royalty and the Roman imperial family that was to be a feature of the Augustan era.

Romans and Royalty

The joining of Eastern royalty and the imperial family was built on a paradoxical situation that had long existed in Roman society, because the Romans well remembered that hundreds of years previously, after 244 years of monarchy, they had expelled the last of their own kings and established the Republic, an event that took place around 500 BC. Laws were immediately passed providing punishment for anyone aspiring to the office, and over the years the concept of kingship became anathema in Roman society.[4] In particular, Cato the Elder, early in the second century BC, noted that a king was by nature carnivorous, an unusual metaphor that well expresses his view of the nature of royalty. Moreover, Cato wrote, kings were inferior to great Greek leaders such as Themistokles and Perikles.[5] Yet as the Romans developed necessary relationships with the kings and queens who ruled much of the territory adjacent to the ever-expanding Roman state, their attitude toward kingship became more nuanced and even contradictory, driven by the needs of foreign policy. Hieron and Massinissa were important allies against the Carthaginians and played roles in their defeat, and thus were to be supported. But even as the Romans showed a distaste for royalty within their own culture, they could stand in awe of any king who came to Rome in all his finery. The obscure Amynandros of Athamania (a remote region of northwestern Greece) visited the city in the early second century BC and was eagerly welcomed merely because of his royal position.[6]

Despite remembering the expulsion of the kings as the high point of their early history, many Romans claimed descent from royalty. The connections of the Julian family with Ascanius, king of the Latins, and the Trojan royal line were well known even before the family became the most powerful in Rome.[7] There was even a Roman family, the Marcii Reges, who saw as its eponymous ancestors Ancus Marcius and other

Roman kings. Significantly, however, the family is not known before the mid-second century BC, the very time that the Romans were developing foreign relationships, and it may represent a renewed sense of legitimization of royalty, at least among certain circles. The most famous member of the family was Q. Marcius Rex, *praetor urbanus* in 144 BC, who built the greatest of Rome's early aqueducts, the Marcia, whose remains are still visible.[8] It seems that by the second century BC, Roman society held opposing views of royalty, and Cato could condemn it while others embraced it.

Nowhere is this ambivalence more apparent than in the environment of Cleopatra VII and Julius Caesar in the mid-first century BC. The events of Caesar's last months are well known: there seems to have been some popular attempt (almost certainly staged) to acclaim him king, and he refused a conveniently produced royal diadem that his co-consul, the future triumvir Antonius, attempted to place on his head at the Lupercalia a few weeks before his death. As with so many of the events of Caesar's last days, his true intentions can never be explained, and the entire incident was perhaps a test for royalist sentiments among the Roman population.[9] Cicero even went so far as to call Caesar a *rex*, but this was more polemic than a legal title, yet again indicative of contemporary ambivalent attitudes toward royalty. Caesar knew foreign royalty well, since he was already in some difficulty because of his relationship with Cleopatra, which had produced a son, Kaisarion, whose status in the Roman world remained uncertain. It was thought that Caesar had spent far too much time in Egypt in 48-47 BC and, moreover, Cleopatra then came to Rome late the following year.[10] Shortly thereafter Caesar departed for Spain, where, among other matters, he would become friendly with the Mauretanian queen, Eunoë Maura.[11] He then returned to Rome for the last months of his life, and in early 44 BC Cleopatra came to the city again, this time with Kaisarion, seeking legal recognition of him. Thus she was probably there at the time of the diadem incident and certainly when Caesar was assassinated, remaining until April. Her presence had become disagreeable to some, and Cicero was still complaining about it as late as June, writing to his friend Atticus:

> The arrogance of the Queen herself, when she was
> living in the villa across the Tiber, cannot be
> remembered without great distress.[12]

Although much of Cicero's hostility was personal—he never called Cleopatra by name, merely "the Queen"—rather than grounded in broad political theory, it shows a contemporary attitude toward royalty even as Rome was, to some extent, captivated and moving toward it in all but name.

After Cleopatra's death and the establishment of the new regime, the official attitude toward her was one of demonization: "fatale monstrum," Horace called her.[13] But political exigency demanded an accommodation with royalty, and her daughter and sons were brought into the Augustan household to live. Juba II was already there, and within a decade the sons of Herod would also arrive. The pragmatic Romans could recognize the importance of royalty for their global plans, but only within the proper strictures of Roman policy, something that Cleopatra had overstepped. The royal children were raised and educated alongside those of the Augustan household, whose members by necessity were themselves affected by royal attitudes as they grew to maturity and became the imperial elite of the next generation.

The Roman Matron

Upper-class women in late Republican and early Imperial Rome were perhaps the most liberated in classical antiquity.[14] The Romans had a long tradition of vesting certain types of power in women, and by the late Republic influences from the Hellenistic world began to be felt. The term for the emancipated woman of Roman aristocratic society was "matron" (*matrona*), a word as old as the Latin language.[15] Originally it probably meant nothing more than a married woman, but by the late Republic it had evolved to refer to wealthy empowered women of the upper classes, who in many ways were similar to those of Hellenistic royalty.[16]

Women of Rome had had a certain status since the foundation of the city. The incident of the Sabine women, celebrated ever since in art and literature, demonstrates the early strengths of Roman women. As related by Livy, war between the Romans and their neighbors the Sabines was brought to an end when the Sabine women—who had been forcibly abducted by the Romans—rushed into the midst of the warring forces and demanded that the fighting come to an end, with the result that the two populations were peacefully assimilated.[17] Although one might argue that the Sabine women were technically not Roman, they soon became such, and the event was appropriated by the Romans as one of the defining moments of their history. From this seminal demonstration of the power of the emancipated woman the Roman matron developed. Unlike Greek women of the Classical period, Roman matrons were not confined to their homes, but from at least the early fourth century BC were encouraged to travel to festivals: as their wealth increased, they contributed to the revenue of the state.[18] When a financial crisis erupted as a result of the Gallic attack on Rome, it was the matrons who replenished the treasury. Livy reported that in return they were granted public eulogies at funerals, just as in the case of men.[19] Although his tone may seem somewhat patronizing today, this was a significant step toward equality. Yet this did not mean that women could give up their traditional roles: even Augustus was explicit about his expectation that the women of his household continue to be proficient in ancient Roman crafts such as woolworking.[20]

The exemplar of the Roman matron was Cornelia, whose reputation survived into the Imperial period as the ideal aristocratic woman and a role model for the Augustan household. Although largely remembered as the mother of Tiberius and Gaius Gracchus, the ill-fated agricultural reformers of the second century BC, her own personality transcended motherhood.[21] To be sure, her image may have been enhanced by her children, especially her daughter, Sempronia, a notable woman in her own right. Yet an alleged collection of Cornelia's correspondence was known as late as the first century AD.[22]

After the assassination of her sons in the 120s BC, the widowed Cornelia retired to an estate at Misenum, on the Bay of Naples, and became the most celebrated Roman woman of the era. Although not royalty, she lived a life that was lavish, both materially and intellectually, and without any connection to a man, an early and notable example of an independent woman with a known public profile. She was famous for her parties, and many of the intellectual luminaries of the era called upon her. Of particular interest is a statement by Plutarch, that "all the kings exchanged gifts with her."[23] This would certainly include Ptolemy VIII (whether or not an offer of marriage was made) and later his sons Ptolemy IX and X, as well as the Seleukid king Antiochos III and Mithradates VI of Pontos, and perhaps other lesser monarchs. Cornelia lived in a time of particularly prominent Eastern royalty, and it is quite reasonable that these kings would have seen her as a means of access to the Roman elite; Ptolemy VIII may not have been the only one who made a marriage proposal. At any rate, her association with the kings inaugurated the era of direct contact between royalty and Roman women that would flourish in the Augustan period. Somewhat less than a century after her death, she became the archetype of the Roman matron of the new era, and one of her successors, Octavia, the sister of Augustus, placed her statue in the portico that she had built in Rome.[24]

The well-educated and articulate Roman matrons of the late Republic had much in common with contemporary royalty. They were able to hold their own in the male-dominated world of international politics and public life. Cornelia was involved in her sons' reform plans, critiquing them when necessary.[25] Her daughter, Sempronia, testified in public when a certain Equitius claimed to be her illegitimate nephew and demanded an inheritance.[26] This increasing public role for Roman matrons—inspired both by Roman traditions as old as the Sabine women and by recent contact with Hellenistic royalty—continued to develop into the Augustan period.

Yet reaction was not always positive: Sempronia was harassed by a mob as she attempted to testify. The best example of an empowered matron who was seen negatively was Fulvia, the second wife of Marcus Antonius, who managed his affairs in Italy while he was fulfilling his triumviral responsibilities in the East. She may have been the first Roman matron actually to direct a military force, in the episode of 41-40 BC known as the Perusine War, and was compared, not in a positive sense, to the queens of the East.[27] Octavian wrote a scatological poem about her and Glaphyra, and she was also said to have prepared Antonius for his life with Cleopatra, whom she had probably met.[28] Fulvia allegedly had no interest in spinning or household management, a point of view probably intended as a direct insult, since such concerns were a necessity for any Roman matron regardless of her accomplishments in other areas.

Fulvia's reputation—which became tangled in the polemics of the last years of the Republic—showed that not all the aspirations of emancipated women were considered favorably, yet her political ambitions and military efforts demonstrated many of the characteristics of Hellenistic queens. She died in late 40 BC; a decade later Cleopatra was also gone, and the new regime that emerged, in the paradoxical manner that was typical of the Romans, built on the reputations of both women while discrediting them, as well as looking back to Sempronia, Cornelia, and even the Sabine women. A new type of Imperial Roman matron emerged, someone who did not forget old Roman virtues but who remained politically and culturally active and had strong relationships with Eastern royalty, especially its queens. Within the imperial family, this type of woman was best manifested by Octavia, the sister of Augustus, her daughter Antonia (whose father was Antonius the triumvir), and, most of all, Livia Drusilla, the wife of Augustus. All three were closely connected personally, essentially lived together, and welcomed Eastern queens (and future queens) into their households. Despite the Roman abhorrence of royalty and kingship, they were royalty in all but name: all three survived their husbands and took on the status of virtual queens. They lived in what has been called a golden age for aristocratic women, in part due to the effect of the reputation of Cleopatra, who, despite the attempts by the Augustan poets to destroy her reputation, remained the most famous woman of the preceding generation.[29]

The Women of the Augustan Household

Livia Drusilla, who was the wife of Augustus for more than half a century, was descended from some of the most ancient Roman families (fig. 17).[30] To be sure, one might be dismissive of the family's claim that Livia's ancestors included a certain Clausus, a Sabine who had assisted Aeneas,[31] but another ancestor, Appius Clausus (or Claudius), was consul in 495 BC, less than a generation after the founding of the Republic.[32] Livia was born in 58 BC, and by the end of 43 BC she was married to Tiberius Claudius Nero, a remote relative of somewhat less distinguished background. Her first son, the future emperor Tiberius, was born a year later.[33] In 39 BC she was pregnant again with her second and last child, Drusus, when she attracted the notice of Octavian, who was managing Italy and the western Mediterranean as Antonius's triumviral colleague.[34]

By January 38 BC she had divorced her husband, given birth to Drusus, and married Octavian. This childless marriage lasted until the death of Augustus fifty-two years later. She served as her husband's adviser and participated in the Augustan building program, including the construction of the highly popular Porticus Liviae, on the Oppian Hill.[35] Most important in the present context, she regularly cultivated relationships with the queens of the allied kingdoms. Her power was such that Ovid even called her "femina princeps," almost suggesting an independent political role and certainly an indication of why the Eastern queens sought contact with her.[36] In fact, the prominent role

FIG. 17. Portrait of Livia.

Courtesy Musée du Louvre. Photo © RMN-Grand Palais/Art Resource, NY.

of royal and wealthy women in the eastern Mediterranean was to some extent modeled on Livia's role in Rome and another example of the cross-fertilization between East and West typical of the era. She survived Augustus by fifteen years, dying at the age of eighty-six in AD 29. Tacitus preserved part of the eulogy at her funeral, delivered by her great-grandson, the future emperor Gaius Caligula:

> In the integrity of her household, her customs were those
> of former times. Her affability was beyond that approved by
> women of antiquity.[37]

When she met Octavian, in 39 BC, she would have soon encountered his sister, Octavia, who was a decade older than Livia (fig.18). She had been married to C. Claudius Marcellus, the consul of 50 BC, who had

FIG. 18. Cast of portrait of Octavia. Museo dell'Ara Pacis, Rome.

recently died, and she had just married Antonius the triumvir, whose own wife, Fulvia, had also just died. The couple took up residence in Antonius's ancestral home on the Palatine, but he was increasingly absent and never returned to Rome after 37 BC. Several children were part of the household, including those of both parents from their previous marriages, and one dispossessed royal child, Juba II. Octavia was more conservative than her sister-in-law Livia, demonstrated in part by her devotion to raising children, especially those whose parents had died. Soon she and Antonius had children of their own, including two daughters, both named Antonia. The elder is largely remembered as the grandmother of the emperor Nero, but the younger became a dominant figure in the imperial family and was the mother of the emperor Claudius.

After Antonius took up permanent residence with Cleopatra in 37 BC, Octavia remained true to his memory, running the household as if he were still in Rome and becoming the only serious rival that Cleopatra ever had. Antonius's treatment of his wife was quickly and vigorously exploited by her brother, and her reputation increased as Antonius's declined: she was pictured as a person of great beauty, dignity, and intelligence who had to endure much.[38]

In 32 BC Octavia and Antonius divorced.[39] Antonius ordered that she leave his family home, and she and the children promptly did so (an act of nobility that only added to her reputation), moving into the developing imperial compound on the southwest corner of the Palatine, a neighbor to her brother and sister-in-law and Livia's children.[40] Two years later, with the deaths of Cleopatra and Antonius, their children—Cleopatra Selene as well as her brothers—moved into Octavia's home to be raised by her.[41] The boys promptly vanished from the historical record and probably soon died, but for a while Octavia had four royal refugees in her household: the two survivors, Juba II and Cleopatra Selene, were married in five years and sent on their way to Mauretania.

Octavia never remarried and lived out her life in her home next to her brother, raising the children and promoting their eventual marriages. Like her sister-in-law, Livia, she contributed to the Augustan building program, with her Porticus Octaviae, whose remains are still visible at the southern edge of the Campus Martius.[42] The structure contained the statue of her illustrious symbolic forebear, Cornelia; public statues of women were rare in Rome but not unknown, and in fact the one of Cornelia probably dated from shortly after her lifetime, but the reestablishment of it in the new porticus demonstrates a rejuvenation of her reputation in the Augustan period.[43] When Octavia died in 11 BC at the age of fifty-eight, her body lay in state in the Temple of the Divine Julius. Virtuous Octavia was widely mourned.[44] Present at her funeral, certainly, were many of the children she had raised, including the younger Antonia, now married to Livia's son Drusus. Antonia is the third member of the group of Augustan women who were particularly connected to Eastern royalty (fig.19).

She was of a different generation than Octavia or Livia, but carried on the traditions of the Roman imperial matron, including its associations with Eastern royalty. As Octavia's daughter, born in 36 BC, she was raised in the same household as Cleopatra Selene and Juba II. She never knew

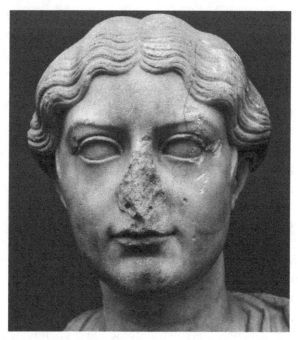

FIG. 19. Portrait of Antonia the Younger, from Leptis Magna.

her father, Antonius, although ironically she inherited his extensive estates in Egypt, mostly in the Fayum, where a district was named after her.[45] As a major Egyptian landowner, she thus acquired some of the characteristics of Eastern royalty, especially those of her mother's nemesis, Cleopatra VII, who, in a strange turn of events, had originally given the estates to Antonia's father.

Antonia married Drusus, the younger son of Livia, around 18 BC: the court poet Krinagoras may have commemorated this wedding, as he had done previously for that of Cleopatra Selene and Juba.[46] Yet the marriage lasted only nine years, until Drusus's death in Germany in 9 BC.[47] Among their children were Germanicus and the future emperor Claudius. When Drusus died, Antonia settled into the life of a respectable widow, never remarrying (despite her youth, only twenty-seven years of age) and remaining in the imperial compound, living in the suite that she had occupied with her husband and sleeping in the same bed. She was an *univira* (one-man woman) and devoted herself to educating her children, even hiring the historian Livy to teach Claudius.[48] Yet as an aristocratic woman of the empire, she became more involved in politics and business than her mother or mother-in-law.

She lived as a virtuous widowed matron for nearly half a century after her husband's death, with Cornelia as her primary role model. Her Egyptian estates, with which she was regularly involved, gave her a substantial income. When her son Germanicus embarked on his lengthy and fatal mission to the East in late AD 17, Antonia may have accompanied him at least part of the time. Details are sparse, but several dedications to her along Germanicus's route imply her presence, most notably one from Ilion, ancient Troy. Visits to royal courts were part of the program; Nabataea and Armenia were specifically mentioned.[49] There was a symbolic tone to this Eastern journey of Germanicus and his family, as, in a way, they were reliving the career of Antonius the triumvir, grandfather of Germanicus and father of Antonia. Yet it all ended in tragedy: in October AD 19 Germanicus suddenly died at Antioch in Syria, under mysterious circumstances that have never been satisfactorily explained.[50]

After her son's death, Antonia lived in Rome and became the primary local hostess of Eastern royalty, especially the Herodians. She and Salome's daughter Berenike became close friends, and Antonia was a major beneficiary in Berenike's will.[51] With the death of Livia in AD 29, Antonia became the most influential woman in the imperial family, instrumental in uncovering the plot of Sejanus in AD 31.[52] She became an important adviser to her brother-in-law Tiberius, and when her grandson Gaius Caligula became emperor in early AD 37, she received many honors. But he soon turned against her, and she died, the last surviving child of Antonius, on the first of May of that year, at age seventy-two, allegedly by suicide.[53]

Matrons and Royal Women

Each of the prominent women in the Augustan family had her own relationship with those of Eastern royalty. At first, this may have been merely a recognition by the royal women that Roman wives were able to influence their husbands. In the last days of her life, in early August 30 BC, Cleopatra VII met with Octavian in Alexandria, the final stage of long negotiations about her future. Antonius had killed himself a few days previously, and Cleopatra realized that her options were decreasing.[54] She gave Octavian an account of her wealth, and when it was demonstrated that the list was incomplete, she told him that she had held some back as "small gifts to Octavia and Livia." This was all part of a complex game that the queen was playing, and the promise of gifts may not have been totally sincere, but the incident reveals that the astute Cleopatra well knew the power of Roman women, especially insofar as their husbands and brothers were concerned. The offer of gifts came to nothing, and the queen was soon dead, but this is the earliest documented example of an Eastern queen appealing to Roman matrons. Plutarch's account—more thorough and reliable than others, since he had access to reports from within the palace at Alexandria—is the only one to mention Octavia as well as Livia, probably an accurate assessment of the contemporary situation.[55] Livia was not as well known as Octavia and maintained a lower profile.[56] She and Cleopatra had probably never met. Octavia, on the other hand, had been an important player in the events of the preceding decade—much of the time she had been Antonius's wife—and she and Cleopatra may have come into contact during one of the queen's trips to Rome. Octavia also had come close to destroying the relationship between queen and triumvir. Having seen her in action, Cleopatra knew the status and importance of a well-situated Roman matron, and her appeal—centered on the sister, rather than the wife, of Octavian—was her primary and last hope.

Moreover, it was Octavia who housed the queen's children after their mother's death; Cleopatra may have had some hint that this could happen, or even suggested it to Octavian, knowing that Octavia had taken in another royal refugee, Juba, for a number of years. Cleopatra Selene lived in Rome for only five years, but she did so from the age of ten to fifteen, certainly a seminal period in any young person's development. In 25 BC Octavia implemented the marriage of the two royal refugees, and they were sent to Mauretania.[57] With Greek, Roman, and probably Egyptian blood, the young princess found that her years in Rome well prepared her for her new role as queen.

But it was Livia who had the longest and most thorough relationship with the women of Eastern royalty and who was honored most directly, especially with statues. Statues of her, as well as of Octavia, existed in Rome from 35 BC, perhaps located in the Forum Julium near the cult statue of Venus, the ancestor of the Julian family. This would have meant that the two women were commemorated next to Cleopatra VII, whose gilded statue had been placed in the temple some years previously. If this were the case, there would have been no more visible symbol of the connection of the Roman matron of the Augustan period with the queens of the East, as well as the continuity between the old and new eras.[58]

From the time of Cleopatra's appeal to her, and for the rest of her life, Livia was in regular contact with the queens and royal woman of the allied kingdoms. She attained cultic status in the East from at least 29 BC, when she may have been honored in a Temple of Roma and Augustus at Pergamon, and there were other examples elsewhere in the Greek world.[59] One place of particular interest where she was honored was Tralleis, the home of Pythodoris's family, whose members were probably involved in this recognition of her status.[60] When Germanicus visited Egypt in AD 19, the locals gave his grandmother Livia divine honors. It is not surprising that the queens of the East understood the importance of commemorating her as much as possible.

Livia's complex relationship with Judaea has already been discussed. She was of importance to Pythodoris, who honored her at Hermonassa in the Bosporos, as well as Dynamis, who erected a statue of her in Phanagoreia.[61] In both cases the services that Livia provided are unknown, but if the data regarding Salome provide any parallel, they included assistance in sorting out the complex dynastic relationships of the queens. Livia seems to have been the last resort when things were not going well; this was certainly the case with Cleopatra VII and Salome, and the poet Ovid appealed to her regarding his exile.[62] Interestingly, all these requests were unsuccessful, and in the case of Salome, Livia specifically told her to do something other than what she wanted, a decision that was respected.

Most of these exchanges were carried out by correspondence—the letters in the matter of Salome, although forged, demonstrate that this was the usual medium[63]—and Livia may have had few actual meetings with the queens themselves unless they came to Rome. But there may have been an important case of personal contact during Augustus's extended Eastern trip of 22–19 BC, which included visits to much of Greece, Asia Minor, and Syria.[64] Although the evidence is elusive, this was most likely Livia's trip to the East mentioned some years later by her grandson Drusus the Younger. It was probably while she was in Antioch or Judaea in 20 BC that she met Salome, establishing the long and fruitful relationship that would last for several decades. But there is no evidence that Livia ever went to Pontos or Bosporos—neither did her husband—although in early 20 BC the couple was near Pontos, in northwestern Asia Minor at Ilion and Kyzikos.

Even if Roman women rarely visited royal women in their kingdoms—which, after all, were not Roman territory—the queens came to Rome on a regular basis. Cleopatra VII was perhaps the first, followed by her daughter. Salome was there during the succession struggle upon the death of her brother Herod in 4 BC and may have stayed in the city for a while; her daughter Berenike I, part of the same group of travelers, certainly did. If Dynamis actually appears on the Ara Pacis, that implies a visit to the city before the completion of the altar in 9 BC, but nothing more is known. Pythodoris came with her husband Archelaos in AD 17—summoned by a letter from Livia, demonstrating that she had the interests of the royal couple in mind—and after Archelaos's death the following year she stayed for a while. She may have still been in the city when her daughter Antonia Tryphaina arrived in AD 19, seeking justice for the death of her husband; she and her children seem to have lived in the city for several years. Only Glaphyra is not recorded as having come to Rome, but the sparseness of the evidence for her means that such a trip should not be ruled out; she did visit Athens.

These trips to Rome by royal women were of the utmost importance for the maintenance of their positions. Because they lived at the borders of the empire, outside Roman territory, they often had little chance to relate directly with the Roman governing powers, and coming to the city allowed them to visit the political and cultural center of the Mediterranean world, as well as to develop a personal relationship with the ruling elite. They could be housed in the imperial family complex on the west side of the Palatine, which grew steadily over the years, in part because of the constant flow of visitors. They could marvel at the physical splendor of the city, which was being rebuilt in marble during the Augustan era, and carry knowledge of its innovative architecture back to their own capitals, invariably named Kaisareia or Sebaste. They could visit the tourist sites of the city. One that was certainly on every queen's list was the Forum Julium, renowned for its golden statue of Cleopatra VII; the survival of this statue seemingly into the third century AD would have been visible evidence of the ambivalent attitudes of early Imperial Rome.[65] The queens could leave their children in the city to be educated and incidentally remove them from the temptations of revolt at home.

The values of the Augustan period did not end with Augustus's death in AD 14. His successors ruled, with various degrees of ability, for another half century. The queens were in charge of their kingdoms as long as they survived; Pythodoris was probably the last to die, in the early AD 30s. Despite their closeness to Augustus and Livia, in many ways Cleopatra and Antonius remained their model. She was the archetype of many of the values that the queens held, and all of them had some sort of association with the triumvir, even if not a direct one, celebrating his memory either as a real or putative ancestor or as the one who created or sustained their kingdoms. Antonius's reputation also survived in Rome; when he died in Alexandria in August 30 BC, few would have anticipated that his descendants would rule Rome in an unbroken line from AD 37 (the accession of Gaius Caligula, his great-grandson) through the rule of Claudius (his grandson) and to the death of Nero (another great-grandson) in AD 68. The spirit of Antonius provided the continuity upon which the queens held their power.

Information about the royal women of the Augustan period is frustratingly sparse, with lengthy gaps in the historical record. Often the raw data reveal very little about their personalities. But the conceptual goal for all of them, beginning with Cleopatra Selene (and even her mother), was to be, as best expressed by Strabo, writing about Pythodoris, "a wise woman capable of managing the government."[66]

APPENDIX 1

A Note on Flavius Josephus and Nikolaos of Damascus

Readers of this volume cannot fail to notice the extensive reliance on the two works by Josephus—the *Jewish War* and the *Jewish Antiquities*—for so much of the material, especially where the Herodian family is concerned. Ancient historiography must often contend with too little evidence or vast gaps in the record, but in the case of Herod and his dynasty there is the opposite problem: remarkably detailed information that all comes from one source, with numerous events and personalities known nowhere else, and biases that may not always be apparent. So much of the Augustan period suffers from inadequate documentation, yet that for the Herodian era in the southern Levant is unique, since there is great detail from Josephus but practically nothing from other writers.

Flavius Josephus was a religious and political leader in Judaea during the second half of the first century AD, who became close to the Roman imperial elite and lived his later years in Italy. Several of his works survive, including the two historical ones mentioned. The *Jewish War*, in seven books and completed in the AD 70s, describes the conflict between the Jews and the Romans, with the narrative extending from the Maccabean period in the early second century BC to Josephus's own time; he was a major player in the later years of the account. The Herodian period is discussed in Books 1 and 2. Some years later he wrote the *Jewish Antiquities*, in twenty books, which was completed by

AD 95. This was a broader survey of Jewish history, from the Creation to his own era, but again with a detailed focus on the Herodian period, which is covered in Books 14–17. Thus the Herodian era was examined in both works, although in a more thorough and nuanced manner in the *Jewish Antiquities*. Nevertheless, there is material in the *Jewish War* that was not considered in the other work, hence the frequent dual citations necessary for historians discussing the Herodian period.[1] Moreover, Josephus's knowledge was not limited to the Herodians: when the family had an impact on events in Rome, he supplied details not otherwise preserved. The closeness of the younger Antonia to it led to unique biographical information about her, most notably details of her role in uncovering the plot of Sejanus in AD 31.[2]

Needless to say, in regard to the world of Herod the Great, Josephus relied on earlier sources. Herod's own memoirs played a role; although cited only once, for events of 30 BC, they would have been used more than this implies. Yet they certainly did not include Herod's turbulent last years and perhaps went no farther than the early 20s BC. They may never have been published and were merely notes used by his confidante, Nikolaos of Damascus.[3]

Nikolaos was Josephus's primary source for the Herodian era. He tutored the children of Cleopatra VII and arrived at the Herodian court after the collapse of the Ptolemaic world, spending the rest of his political career as an adviser and ambassador for Herod, and then for his son Archelaos. He is not documented after the succession struggle at Herod's death and probably retired to Italy and wrote. His writings were varied and included an autobiography and a universal history in 144 books, the longest known.[4] The history ended with the death of Herod, in 4 BC, and thus the succession struggle—in which Nikolaos was deeply involved—may have been reported only in the autobiography.[5] All the strengths and weaknesses of this genre—both the intense detail and a self-serving attitude—were inevitably a factor in Nikolaos's account, but it and the history, as preserved in Josephus's recension, provide the most detailed report on any of the late Hellenistic dynasties.

APPENDIX 2

The Girl Who Danced for the Head of John the Baptist

One of the best-known incidents involving the Herodian family was the death of John the Baptist, the peculiar circumstances of which are familiar through countless works of art as well as the drama by Oscar Wilde and the opera by Richard Strauss (fig. 20). Both of these are prime examples—along with the reputation of Cleopatra VII—of significant modern divergence from the historical record for the sake of artistic impact.

The major ancient sources for the death of John are the gospels of Matthew and Mark and the *Jewish Antiquities* of Josephus.[1] All were written in the last quarter of the first century AD; the exact date of the two gospels remains uncertain, but the *Jewish Antiquities* was completed by AD 95.[2] The date of the death of John cannot be determined with precision, but it may have been around the spring of AD 29.[3]

The earliest report is probably that of Mark, who recounted how John had condemned the tetrarch Herod (Antipas) because he had married his brother's wife, Herodias. She wanted John killed, although Antipas did not. But on Antipas's birthday, Herodias's daughter danced during the festivities, and when the tetrarch told her that she could have anything she wanted, her mother persuaded her to request the head of John on a platter. This was granted, and the head was given to Herodias. Neither mother nor daughter was mentioned again in the narrative. The version of Matthew differs only in details of wording. Josephus did not

FIG. 20. Lovis Corinth, *Salome II*. Museum der Bildenden Künste, Leipzig.

record any role by Herodias or her daughter in the death of John, but placed it within the political context of the era and the common fear of the seditious potential of contemporary holy men. Josephus added that the imprisonment and death of John occurred at Machairous (modern Mukawir), the Hasmonean fortress high above the northeastern side of the Dead Sea, which had been rebuilt by Herod the Great to protect his Nabataean frontier, becoming in time one of Antipas's primary residences.[4] What is common to all three accounts is that the daughter of Herodias was neither named nor killed.

Antipas, upon the death of his father, Herod the Great, had been awarded parts of his kingdom by Augustus with the title of tetrarch. His territory consisted of Galilee, west of the sea of the same name, and Peraia, the region east of the southern Jordan River and the northern Dead Sea.[5] He ruled these districts until he was removed by Gaius Caligula, probably in AD 39, and went into exile in Spain, or more probably Gaul, accompanied by Herodias and dying there at an unknown date.[6]

Herodias was a granddaughter of both Herod the Great and his sister Salome; her parents were Herod's son Aristoboulos and his cousin Berenike.[7] She had been married to Antipas's brother Philip, tetrarch of Batanaea (east of the Sea of Galilee), who was another of the sons of Herod, who came to power in 4 BC. How this marriage ended is not certain, and the exact chronology of events is almost impossible to determine, but Herodias eventually married Antipas. Since she and Philip had had at least one child, she was thus in the same position as Glaphyra had been with her final marriage and according to Jewish law should not have married her husband's brother.[8]

As tetrarch, Antipas came into contact with the holy men of his day, including John the Baptist and Jesus of Nazareth, both of whom were closely watched by the authorities. When Antipas married Herodias, John's reaction was swift and explicit: the accounts are consistent that he condemned the marriage. This was probably the last in a series of perceived offenses on the part of John, and it led Antipas to imprison him at Machairous. In time he was executed.

What has made the account particularly interesting, however, is the identity of the girl who danced and brought about the death of John, who is not named in the sources. The manuscripts of Mark vary, and some suggest that she was a daughter of Antipas named Herodias, but there is no evidence that Antipas and his wife Herodias had any children, and the presumed recent date of their marriage means that any issue would have been exceedingly young, hardly in a position to make unusual and dangerous requests of her father. But the genealogical account of Josephus explicitly states that Herodias had a daughter named Salome (probably named after her great-grandmother, the sister of Herod), which is the reason that her name became attached to the story.[9] Salome's father was identified only as "Herod" and was probably Philip the tetrarch, often called Herod Philip. As expected, the date of her birth is uncertain: Matthew and Mark called her a *korasion*, a rare Greek word of Hellenistic and Roman times and a diminutive of *kore*, or girl; the use of an unusual term gives credence to the story. It is probable that she was born in the second decade of the first century AD and was in her adolescence when she danced.[10] Yet all this is speculative, because of chronological and homonymic problems with both the career of John the Baptist and members of the wide-ranging Herodian family.

A peculiar point, however, is the dance itself, perhaps the most famous element of the Salome story in later tradition. The account is limited to the two biblical reports and may be nothing more than an early Christian tale about the decadence of the Herodian court. It is certainly a unique element in ancient history. To be sure, dancing girls at festivals were not unusual—the Phoenician town of Gadeira (modern Cádiz) in the Iberian Peninsula was well known for them[11]—but to have a female relative dance for the ruler, even if at a major party for him (probably Antipas's fiftieth or sixtieth birthday),[12] is strange, to say the least.

Moreover, portions of the tale are certainly formulaic: similar elements can be found as early as the story of the entanglement of the Persian king Xerxes with his brother's wife and her daughter Artaynte, which involves both a question that should not be answered and a banquet on the king's birthday, although with a totally different outcome.[13] A closer parallel is the tale of the Roman magistrate Lucius Quinctius Flamininus, who in the early second century BC was persuaded by a paramour at a dinner party to behead a prisoner.[14]

According to the contemporary popular tradition about Salome and her dance, she was killed immediately after being presented with John's head, as in the final line of Wilde's play: "Tuez cette femme!" Yet this is a modern evolution of the story: it does not seem to have been known in the Renaissance or immediately thereafter, nor does it appear in the visual arts, and as late as Gustave Flaubert's short story *Hérodias* (1877) Salome's fate is not mentioned. Jules Massenet's opera *Hérodiade* (1881) has Salome commit suicide, but a full account of her death came only with Wilde (1891) and was perpetuated in Strauss's opera (1905).

In fact, Salome's death—by whatever means—at the time of John's execution has no authority in ancient sources, since her career continued after the event. She survived to marry her cousin the younger Aristoboulos, a great-grandson of both Herod the Great and his sister Salome, who was placed on the throne of Lesser Armenia by Nero in AD 54, remaining there until the region was provincialized in AD 71/2.[15] How long Salome survived is not known, but she was represented on joint coinage with her husband (he was on the obverse and she was on the reverse) and holding the title *basilissa*.[16] She and Aristoboulos had three children: Herod, Agrippa, and another Aristoboulos, who seem to have been of little importance yet who were the last known members of this branch of the Herodian family.[17]

Abbreviations

AClass	*Acta Classica*
AJA	*American Journal of Archaeology*
AJN	*American Journal of Numismatics*
AJPh	*American Journal of Philology*
AncWE	*Ancient West and East*
ANRW	*Aufstieg und Niedergang der Römischen Welt*
AR	*Archaeological Reports*
BAR	*British Archaeological Reports*
BMC	*British Museum Catalogue of Greek Coins*
BNP	*Brill's New Pauly*
BSR	*Papers of the British School at Rome*
CAH	*Cambridge Ancient History*
CÉFR	*Collection de l'École française de Rome*
CIL	*Corpus inscriptionum latinarum*
CIRB	*Corpus Inscriptionem Regni Bosporani* (Moscow, 1965)
ClAnt	*Classical Antiquity*
CP	*Classical Philology*
CQ	*Classical Quarterly*
CRAI	*Comptes Rendus de Séances de l'Académie des Inscriptions et Belles-Lettres*
EA	*Epigraphica Anatolica*
FGrHist	*Die Fragmente der Griechischen Historiker*
G&R	*Greece and Rome*
HSCP	*Harvard Studies in Classical Philology*
IA	*Iranica Antiqua*
IEJ	*Israel Exploration Journal*
IG	*Inscriptiones Graecae*
IGRR	*Inscriptiones Graecae ad res Romanas pertinentes*
JBL	*Journal of Biblical Literature*
JHS	*Journal of Hellenic Studies*

JRA	*Journal of Roman Archaeology*
JRS	*Journal of Roman Studies*
JThS	*Journal of Theological Studies*
NC	*Numismatic Chronicle*
NEAEHL	*The New Encyclopedia of Archaeological Excavations in the Holy Land*
OGIS	*Orientis Graeci inscriptiones selectae*
OP	*Ordia Prima*
OxyPap	*The Oxyrhynchus Papyri*
PAAJR	*Proceedings of the American Academy for Jewish Research*
PECS	*Princeton Encyclopedia of Classical Sites*
PEQ	*Palestine Exploration Quarterly*
RE	Pauly-Wissowa, *Real Encyclopädie der classischen Altertumswissenschaft*
RÉA	*Revue des études anciennes*
SchwMbll	*Schweizer Münzblätter*
SCI	*Scripta classica israelica*
SCO	*Studi classici e orientali*
SEG	*Supplementum Epigraphicum Graecum*
SIG	*Sylloge Inscriptionum Graecarum*
TAPA	*Transactions of the American Philological Society*
VDI	*Vestnik drevnej istorii*
ZAG	*Zeitschrift für Alte Geschichte*
ZfN	*Zeitschrift für Numismatik*
ZPE	*Zeitschrift für Papyrologie und Epigraphik*

Notes

Introduction

1. The third member of the triumvirate, Lepidus, had been marginalized. For a good summary of these years, see Christopher Pelling, "The Triumviral Period," *CAH* 10, 2d ed. (Cambridge, 1996), 1–69.

2. David C. Braund, *Rome and the Friendly King: The Character of the Client Kingship* (London, 1984).

Chapter 1

1. Elizabeth D. Carney, *Women and Monarchy in Macedonia* (Norman, OK, 2000), xii–xiii, avoided the use of "queen" entirely.

2. A good example is Clytaemnestra: Aeschylus, *Agamemnon* 84 and *Persians* 623 (used adjectively).

3. Michael Ventris and John Chadwick, *Documents in Mycenaean Greek* (Cambridge, 1953), 121–2; Barbara A. Olsen, *Women in Mycenaean Greece* (London, 2014), 63–4.

4. For Penelope, see Homer, *Odyssey* 4.697, 770; 16.332, 337; 17.370, 468, 513, 583; 18.314, 351; 21.275; 23.149; for Tyro, 11.258; for Arete and Nausikaa, 6.115, 7.241, 11.345, 13.59.

5. R. Hope Simpson and J. F. Lazenby, *The Catalogue of the Ships in Homer's "Iliad"* (Oxford, 1970), 103–6.

6. Homer, *Odyssey* 1.328–35.

7. Homer, *Odyssey* 15.16–19.

8. Homer, *Odyssey* 19.509–34.

9. Homer, *Odyssey* 2.91–109, 19.137–9. The logistics of the stratagem, which have long been questioned (see John Scheid and Jesper Svenbro, *The Craft of Zeus*, trans. Carol Volk [Cambridge, MA, 1996], 68–70), are not of particular concern here, since it was more the idea itself than its execution that showed Penelope's astuteness.

10. Homer, *Odyssey* 19.571–4, 21.68–79.

11. Homer, *Odyssey* 24.192–202.

12. Herodotos 1.11, 185–7, 205. The term was probably also applied to Semiramis of Babylon—although not explicitly so in Herodotos's narrative (1.184)—who had the same characteristics as the others.

13. Aristotle, *Politics* 2.6.6, 5.9.6; see also Diodoros 2.45 (as a verb); Plutarch, *Antonius* 10.3.

14. Homer, *Iliad* 3.189, 6.186; Strabo 11.5.4; Adrienne Mayor, *The Amazons* (Princeton, NJ, 2014), 170–2.

15. Diodoros 17.77.1–3; Strabo 11.5.4; Plutarch, *Alexander* 46.1–2.

16. Xenophon, *Hellenika* 3.1.10–28; Polyainos 8.54; Charles Brian Rose, *The Archaeology of Greek and Roman Troy* (Cambridge, 2014), 150–1.

17. Xenophon, *Anabasis* 7.8.8–20.

18. Herodotos 7.99; 8.68, 87, 101; Rosaria Vignolo Munson, "Artemisia in Herodotus," *ClAnt* 7 (1988): 91–106; Amadeo Visconti, "Artemisia di Alicarnasso ovvero il potere visibile," in *Il potere invisibile: Figure del femminile tra mito e storia*, ed. Simona Marino et al. (Naples, 2002), 63–75.

19. Pausanias 3.11.3; Justin, *Epitome* 2.12.23–4.

20. Diodoros 14.98.3, 16.36.2; Strabo 14.2.17; Arrian, *Anabasis* 1.23.7–8; Kyra L. Nourse, "Women and the Early Development of Royal Power in the Hellenistic East" (PhD dissertation, University of Pennsylvania, 2002), 75–123.

21. A. B. Bosworth, *A Historical Commentary on Arrian's History of Alexander* (Oxford, 1980–95), 1: 152–4.

22. Her younger brother Pixodaros is documented with the title, both in an inscription (Bosworth, *Historical Commentary*, 1: 153) and by Plutarch (*Alexander* 10); see also Elizabeth D. Carney, "Women and Dunasteia in Caria," *AJPh* 126 (2005): 68–9.

23. The creation of a catalogue of the Seven Wonders of the World was an example of the Hellenistic taste for producing such lists, often in order to demonstrate the superior cultural history of the eastern Mediterranean and ancient Near East in a world of expanding Roman power. The earliest documentation of the Wonders is by the poet Antipatros of Sidon in the mid-second century BC (*Greek Anthology* 9.58; see also Strabo 14.2.16). The components vary but the Mausoleion was always included.

24. Andrew Stewart, *Greek Sculpture: An Exploration* (New Haven, CT, 1990), 180–2.

25. Demosthenes, *For the Liberty of the Rhodians* 11–12, 23; Vitruvius 2.8.14–15; Violaine Sebillotte Cuchet, "The Warrior Queens of Caria (Fifth to Fourth Centuries BCE)," in *Women and War in Antiquity*, ed. J. Fabre-Serris and A. Keith (Baltimore, 2015), 228–46. The veracity of Artemisia's capture of Rhodes has been called into question (Carney, "Women and Dunasteia," 67–8).

26. Matthew A. Sears, "Alexander and Ada Reconsidered," *CP* 109 (2014): 211–21. A rich tomb in the Halikarnassos nekropolis of a royal woman, from this era, may belong to one of the Hekatomnids, perhaps Ada: A. J. N. W. Prag and R. A. H. Neave, "Who Is the 'Carian Princess'?," in *Hekatomnid Caria and the Ionian Renaissance*, ed. Jacob Isager (Odense, 1994), 97–109.

27. Elizabeth D. Carney, *Olympias: Mother of Alexander the Great* (New York, 2006).

28. Elizabeth D. Carney, " 'What's in a Name?': The Emergence of a Title for Royal Women in the Hellenistic Period," in *Women's History and Ancient History*, ed. Sarah B. Pomeroy (Chapel Hill, NC, 1991), 154–72.

29. Xenophon, *Oikonomikos* 7.32–4; 9.15; Elizabeth Wayland Barber, *Women's Work: The First 20,000 Years* (New York, 1994), 275–7.

30. Diodoros 20.53; Plutarch, *Demetrios* 18.

31. Diodoros 19.59; Plutarch, *Demetrios* 14, 27–32, 45; Claude Wehrli, "Phila, fille d'Antipater et épouse de Démétrius, roi des macédoniens," *Historia* 13 (1964): 140–6; Waldemar Heckel, *Who's Who in the Age of Alexander the Great* (London, 2006), 207–8.

32. Carney, " 'What's in a Name?,' " 161, 170.

33. Diodoros 20.109.7; Strabo 12.3.10; Arrian, *Anabasis* 7.4.5; Stanley M. Burstein, *Outpost of Hellenism: The Emergence of Heraclea on the Black Sea* (Berkeley, CA, 1976), 79–86; Heckel, *Who's Who*, 21, 113–14.

34. Barclay V. Head, *Historia Numorum* (Oxford, 1911), 505–6.

35. The seminal work on the topic is Grace Macurdy, *Hellenistic Queens* (Baltimore, 1932), out of date but still valuable, supplemented by Sarah B. Pomeroy, *Women in Hellenistic Egypt from Alexander to Cleopatra* (Detroit, 1984), and John Whitehorne, *Cleopatras* (London, 1994).

36. Sarah P. Pomeroy, *Goddesses, Whores, Wives, and Slaves* (New York, 1975), 38–9.

37. Aristotle, *Politics* 2.6.5–11.

38. Pomeroy, *Women*, 13–24.

39. Jan Quaegebeur, "Cleopatra VII and the Cults of the Ptolemaic Queens," in *Cleopatra's Egypt: Age of the Ptolemies* (Brooklyn, 1988), 41–2.

40. Ptolemy XII and his sister Cleopatra VI were probably the last to practice it, in the first half of the first century BC. Cleopatra VII may have been technically married to her brother Ptolemy XIII in 51 BC, but since he was only eleven years of age this was probably a legal fiction, and neither he nor the relationship lasted long.

41. Pausanias 1.6.8, 1.7.1; Heckel, *Who's Who*, 71.

42. Plutarch, *Pyrrhos* 4.4; Pausanias 1.11.5; for Arete, see Homer, *Odyssey* 7.66–74; Pomeroy, *Women*, 18–19.

43. Pausanias 3.8.1; the account of Berenike's victories was preserved by the contemporary epigrammatist Poseidippos of Pella (*Hippika* 87–8), who, as a Macedonian, may have had connections with the Ptolemaic court: Elizabeth D. Carney, *Arsinoë of Egypt and Macedon* (New York, 2013), 27–9.

44. Theokritos 17.34–52, 121–5; Athenaios 5.202d; Judith McKenzie, *The Architecture of Alexandria and Egypt, c. 300 BC–AD 700* (New Haven, CT, 2007), 51.

45. Strabo 16.4.7; Ptolemy, *Geographical Guide* 4.7.6; P. M. Fraser, *Ptolemaic Alexandria* (Oxford, 1972), 1: 228, 232.

46. Plutarch, *Antonius* 54.6.

47. Strabo 16.4.5; Pliny, *Natural History* 6.168; Steven E. Sidebotham, *Berenike and the Ancient Maritime Spice Route* (Berkeley, CA, 2011).

48. Strabo 16.4.10; Getzel M. Cohen, *The Hellenistic Settlements in Syria, the Red Sea Basin, and North Africa* (Berkeley, CA, 2006), 315–16.

49. Head, *Historia Numorum*, 851; Carney, *Arsinoë*, 121.

50. Carney, *Arsinoë*, 73. For the possible exception of Thea Mousa of Parthia, see infra, pp. 123–7.

51. Justin, *Epitome* 26.3; Dee L. Clayman, *Berenice II and the Golden Age of Ptolemaic Egypt* (New York, 2014), 36–9; Günther Hölbl, *A History of the Ptolemaic Empire,* trans. Tina Saavedra (London, 2001), 127–8.

52. Kallimachos, *Aitia* F110; Catullus 66; Clayman, *Berenice II*, 97–104; Mark R. Chartrand, *National Audubon Society Field Guide to the Night Sky* (New York, 1991), 498–90.

53. Whitehorne, *Cleopatras*, 80–8; Hölbl, *History*, 140.

54. Homer, *Iliad* 9.556; Pindar, *Pythian* 11.17; Aeschylus, *Libation Bearers* 733; Heckel, *Who's Who*, 90.

55. Plutarch, *Antonius* 27.4.

56. Pomeroy, *Women*, 23–4.

57. Livy 35.13.4; Appian, *Syriaka* 5.

58. Polybios 24.6; Hölbl, *History*, 141–2.

59. Pomeroy, *Women*, 23.

60. *BMC Ptolemies*, 78–9.

61. Hölbl, *History*, 143–5.

62. Whitehorne, *Cleopatras*, 89–131; Fraser, *Ptolemaic Alexandria*, 1: 121–2.

63. Strabo 2.3.4.

64. Whitehorne, *Cleopatras*, 174–7; Hölbl, *History*, 213–14.

65. Cicero, *Pro Rabiro Postumo* 6; Plutarch, *Pompeius* 49; Dio 39.12.

66. John Whitehorne, "The Supposed Co-Regency of Cleopatra Tryphaena and Berenice IV (58–55 BC)," in *Akten des 21. Internationalen Papyrologenkongresses, Berlin 1995*, ed. Barbel Kramer et al. (Stuttgart, 1997), 1009–13.

67. Strabo 12.3.34, 17.1.11; Dio 39.57–8; infra, p. 50.

68. Plutarch, *Antonius* 3.

69. Duane W. Roller, *Cleopatra: A Biography* (New York, 2010), 26–7.

Chapter 2

1. Plutarch, *Antonius* 25–6.

2. Plutarch, *Antonius* 28–30; Appian, *Civil War* 5.10–11.

3. Plutarch, *Antonius* 36.

4. W. W. Tarn, "Alexander Helios and the Golden Age," *JRS* 22 (1932): 135–60. It must be remembered that the Fourth Eclogue has no bearing on Cleopatra's children but is representative of the ideals of the era: Philip Hardie, "Virgil's Ptolemaic Relations," *JRS* 96 (2006): 29–41.

5. Dio 50.6; C. B. R. Pelling, *Plutarch: Life of Antony* (Cambridge, 1988), 219.

6. Duane W. Roller, *The World of Juba II and Kleopatra Selene* (London, 2003), 76–90.

7. Livy, *Summary* 132; Dio 49.32.5; Roller, *Cleopatra*, 69–70.

8. Plutarch, *Antonius* 36, 54; Dio 49.32, 41; Pelling, *Plutarch*, 217–18, 248–52.

9. Cicero, *De lege agraria* 2.51; Livy, *Summary* 70; Tacitus, *Annals* 14.18.

10. Livy, *Summary* 100; Plutarch, *Pompeius* 29; Hölbl, *History*, 42, 195.

11. *BMC Cyrenaica*, #24–6; Plutarch, Antonius 42.4, 56.1. The coins may also have been minted on Crete: Jane Draycott, "The Symbol of Cleopatra Selene: Reading Crocodiles on Coins in the Late Republic and Early Principate," *AClass* 55 (2012): 50–2.

12. Augustus, *Res gestae* 27.

13. *FGrHist*, #90; infra, pp. 147–8.

14. Dio 49.44.

15. Roller, *Cleopatra*, 137–50.

16. Dio 51.19.6.

17. Plutarch, *Antonius* 87.1.

18. Braund, *Rome and the Friendly King*, 136–7.

19. Livy F54; Dio 51.21.8.

20. The earliest known Antonius was one Titus Antonius Merenda, a magistrate of 451 BC: Livy 3.35.11; Dionysios of Halikarnassos, *Roman Archaeology* 10.58.

21. Roller, *Cleopatra*, 165–8.

22. Suetonius, *Augustus* 48; Ann-Cathrin Harders, "An Imperial Family Man: Augustus as Surrogate Father to Marcus Antonius' Children," in *Growing Up Fatherless in Antiquity*, ed. Sabine R. Hübner and David M. Ratzan (Cambridge, 2009), 217–40.

23. Diane E. E. Kleiner and Bridget Buxton, "Pledges of Empire: The Ara Pacis and the Donations of Rome," *AJA* 112 (2008): 65–9.

24. She may appear as an adult; infra pp. 44–5.

25. Suetonius, *Augustus* 18.2; Dio 51.1.3.

26. Konstantinos I. Zachos, "The *Tropaeum* of the Sea Battle of Actium at Nikopolis: Interim Report," *JRA* 16 (2003): 65–92; John Pollini, *From Republic to Empire* (Norman, OK, 2012), 191–6. A problem is that Dio's account (51.21.8) seems to imply that Octavian appeared separately from the children, but Dio's reports are often imprecise as to detail and the physical evidence is unequivocal.

27. Susan Treggiari, *Roman Marriage*: Iusti Coniuges *from the Time of Cicero to the Time of Ulpian* (Oxford, 1991), 39–43.

28. *De bello Africo* 91–7.

29. Roller, *World of Juba*, 61–3.

30. A few fragments survive, including the eyewitness account of Massinissa and his court (*FGrHist*, #234).

31. Polybios 36.16; Cicero, *Republic* 6.9; Livy 37.53.20–2; Plutarch, *Tiberius Graccus* 1.4; infra, pp. 131-2.

32. This is probably the modern el-Kebir in eastern Algeria: Pomponius Mela 1.30; Pliny, *Natural History* 5.22.

33. Roller, *World of Juba*, 39–58.

34. Strabo 8.4.3; Dio 49.43.7, 50.11.3.

35. Pliny, *Natural History* 5.2–5, 5.20–1.

36. Dio 53.22–5; Helmut Halfmann, *Itinera principum* (Stuttgart, 1986), 157.

37. Plutarch, *Antonius* 87; Suetonius, Augustus 26.3; Dio 51.15.6; *Suda*, "Iobas."

38. Jean Mazard, *Corpus Nummorum Numidiae Mauretaniaeque* (Paris, 1955), #357.

39. For a discussion of the arguments for various dates, see Roller, *World of Juba*, 86–7.

40. *Greek Anthology* 7.645; for Philostratos and Cleopatra VII, see Philostratos (not the same individual), *Lives of the Sophists* 5.

41. *Greek Anthology* 9.235.

42. Infra, pp. 43–4.

43. 1 Kings 16:31; 2 Kings 9:30–7; Josephus, *Jewish Antiquities* 9.122–4.

44. Vergil, *Aeneid* 1.697–756; Pelling, *Plutarch*, 190.

45. Ammianus Marcellinus 22.15.8.

46. Timaios (*FGrHist*, #566) F82.

47. Justin, *Epitome* 18.4–6; Duane W. Roller, *Scholarly Kings: The Writings of Juba II of Mauretania, Archelaos of Kappadokia, Herod the Great and the Emperor Claudius* (Chicago, 2004), 35–42.

48. Philippe Leveau, *Caesarea de Maurétanie: Une ville romaine et ses campagnes*, *CÉFR* 70 (Paris, 1984), 11.

49. Strabo 17.3.12; Roller, *World of Juba*, 121–8.

50. Vergil, *Aeneid* 8.688; Horace, *Odes* 1.37.

51. Good examples are Cherchel Museum S65 (28) and S66 (31), although it is difficult to distinguish between portraits of mother and daughter, and none has a certain attribution.

52. Mazard, *Corpus*, #345, 357–74, 392–5.

53. Jean Mazard, "Un denier inédit de Juba II et Cléopâtre-Séléné," *SchwMbll* 31 (1981): 1–2.

54. Cherchel Museum S74 (95); for a catalogue of the sculpture at Caesarea, see Nacéra Benseddik et al., *Cherchel* (Algiers, 1983).

55. Cherchel Museum 66; Mazard, *Corpus*, #355–6.

56. Cherchel Museum S75 (94).

57. Paris, Musée du Louvre Bj 1969; Susan Walker and Peter Higgs, eds., *Cleopatra of Egypt: From History to Myth* (London, 2001), 312; see also 242; Jane Draycott, "Dynastic Politics, Defeat, Decadence and Dining: Cleopatra Selene on the So-Called 'Africa' Dish from the Villa della Pisanella at Boscoreale," *BSR* 80 (2012): 45–64.

58. *CIL* 8.9344; Michèle Coltelloni-Trannoy, *Le royaume de Maurétanie sous Juba II et Ptolémée* (Paris, 1997), 215.

59. John Boardman, *Greek Gems and Finger Rings: Early Bronze Age to Late Classical* (London, 1970), pl. 1013; Marie-Louise Vollenweider, *Die Steinschneidekunst und Ihre Künstler in spätrepublikanischer und Augusteischer Zeit* (Baden-Baden, 1966), 45–6.

60. *Greek Anthology* 9.752; Roller, *World of Juba*, 88–9.

61. Pliny, *Natural History* 5.16, 25.77–8.

62. Dioskourides 3.82; Galen, *On the Combining of Drugs According to Place* 1; Roller, *World of Juba*, 178–9.

63. Roller, *World of Juba*, 160.

64. Ammianus Marcellinus 22.15.8.

65. *OxyPap* 71 (2007), no. 4809.

66. Roller, *World of Juba*, 163–243.

67. Duane W. Roller, *Ancient Geography: The Discovery of the World in Classical Greece and Rome* (London, 2015), 158.

68. The writings of Ptolemy II, IV, and VIII were cited by Juba; see his *Roman Archaeology* F10; *Libyka* F2, 25, 27, 31. Fragment numbers are as in Roller, *Scholarly Kings*.

69. Juba, *Libyka* F7–11, 13, 15, 17, 19, 35; *On Arabia* F2; Roller, *Ancient Geography*, 110–13.

70. Juba, *Libyka* F7, 10.

71. Strabo 17.3.7; Suetonius, *Gaius Caligula* 26.1; other sources record that Juba was his father: Strabo 17.3.12, 25; Pliny, *Natural History* 5.16; Tacitus, *Annals* 4.23; Dio 59.25.1.

72. Mazard, *Corpus*, #375.

73. The child is figure N-37, and his possible mother N-35: Kleiner and Buxton, "Pledges of Empire," 82–5. Most figures on the Ara Pacis are enigmatic, and identification of them is speculative and varied, but these suggestions have a compelling logic about them.

74. Juba's last dated coinage is in his forty-eighth year, and notices of his death by Strabo (17.3.9) and Tacitus (*Annals* 4.1.5, 23) conform to this date.

75. Infra, pp. 48–8.

76. Mazard, *Corpus*, #398, 399, 429; Dio 59.25.1.

77. Tacitus, *Annals* 4.26.

78. S. J. V. Malloch, "The Death of Ptolemy of Mauretania," *Historia* 53 (2004): 38–45.

79. Chris Bennett, "Drusilla Regina," *CQ* 53 (2003): 315.

80. *IG* 3.1.1309; Roller, *Cleopatra*, 22.

81. Tacitus, *Histories* 5.9.

82. Bennett, "Drusilla Regina," 315–19; Roller, *World of Juba*, 251–2.

83. *Greek Anthology* 7.633.

84. Theodor Oppolzer, *Canon of Eclipses*, trans. Owen Gingerich (New York, 1962); one year has been added to his BC dates to account for his use of a Year Zero. See also Maud Worcester Makemson, "Note on Eclipses," in Grace Harriet Macurdy, *Vassal Queens* (Baltimore, 1937), 60–2.

85. Velleius 2.101–2; Pliny, *Natural History* 6.141, 12.56, 32.10; Tacitus, *Annals* 2.4, 42; Suetonius, *Tiberius* 12, *Nero* 5; Dio 55.10–12, 57.17.4; Roller, *World of Juba*, 212–26.

86. Treggiari, *Roman Marriage*, 235–6.

87. Kurt Regling, "Zum Fund von Iubadenaren in Alkasar," *ZfN* 28 (1910): 9–27.

88. For these suggestions, see Roller, *World of Juba*, 250–1.

89. Mazard, *Corpus*, #384; one coin in the Alkasar hoard (#64) has the legend "rex Ptolemaeus." For Numidian posthumous coins see Stéphane Gsell, *Histoire ancienne de l'Afrique du Nord* (Paris, 1914–28), 8: 220–3.

90. Pomponius Mela 1.31; Marcel Christofle, *Le Tombeau de la Chrétienne* (Paris, 1951); Mounir Bouchenaki, *Le Mausolée Royal de Maurétanie* (Algiers, 1979).

91. Coltelloni-Trannoy, *Royaume*, 200, 206.

92. The best evidence for this is that several members of the royal household died in the city: *CIL* 6.9046, 10110, 35602; Coltelloni-Trannoy, *Royaume*, 217.

93. Unlike her mother, Cleopatra Selene had only a slight impact on post-antique culture, but it was similar to her mother's, since her modern legacy had little to do with her actual career. She is a character in the wide-ranging epistolary romance of Gauthier de Costes, *Cléopâtre* (1648) and in Johann Matheson's 1704 opera, *Die unglückselige Cleopatra*.

Chapter 3

1. Strabo 12.3.1–2.

2. Herodotos 1.72.

3. Tacitus, *Annals* 2.42; Appian, *Civil* War 5.7; Dio 49.32.3; Richard D. Sullivan, "The Dynasty of Cappadocia," *ANRW* 2.7 (1980): 1147–8; *BNP Chronologies*, 105–6.

4. Strabo 12.2.8.

5. Plutarch, *Sulla* 22–4; Appian, *Mithridateios* 30–64; Pausanias 1.20.5.

6. Strabo 12.3.34; Appian, *Mithradateios* 114; Richard D. Sullivan, "Priesthoods of the Eastern Dynastic Aristocracy," in *Studien zur Religion und Kultur Kleinasiens*, ed. S. Şahin et al. (Leiden, 1978), 919–23.

7. Plutarch, *Antonius* 3; supra, p. 24.

8. *De bello Alexandrino* 66.

9. Appian, *Civil War* 5.7.

10. Strabo 12.2.6; Ronald Syme, *Anatolica: Studies in Strabo*, ed. Anthony Birley (Oxford, 1995), 148–50.

11. Sullivan, "Dynasty of Cappadocia," 1147–61. At roughly the same time, it took three years for Herod the Great to obtain his throne.

12. Martial 11.20; I. A. Ruffell, "Beyond Satire: Horace, Popular Invective and the Segregation of Literature," *JRS* 93 (2003): 45.

13. Nevertheless, some have been dismissive of its historical significance; see Meyer Reinhold, *From Republic to Principate* (Atlanta, 1988), 63.

14. Pelling, *Plutarch*, 199; Kathryn E. Welch, "Antony, Fulvia, and the Ghost of Claudius in 47 B.C.," *G&R* 42 (1995): 192–5.

15. Plutarch, *Antonius* 30.3.

16. Appian, *Civil War* 5.7; Dio 49.32.3.

17. *OGIS* 361; Sullivan, "Dynasty of Cappadocia," 1153–4.

18. Josephus, *Jewish War* 1.507.

19. Eleanor Goltz Huzar, *Mark Antony: A Biography* (London, 1978), 254.

20. Infra, pp. 111–15.

21. Strabo 14.5.6; Josephus, *Jewish Antiquities* 16.131. Elaioussa-Sebaste is a rich archaeological site today, with the possible location of Archelaos's palace identified on a promontory overlooking the harbor: Eugenia Equini Schneider, *Elaiussa Sebaste: A Port City between East and West* (Istanbul, 2008).

22. Strabo 14.5.6; Tacitus, *Annals* 6.41; Sullivan, "Dynasty of Cappadocia," 1167–8.

23. Homer, *Iliad* 2.712; Hope Simpson and Lazenby, *Catalogue*, 136.

24. Josephus, *Jewish Antiquities* 15.342–3; Nikos Kokkinos, *The Herodian Dynasty: Origins, Role in Society and Eclipse* (Sheffield, 1998), 369–70.

25. Josephus, *Jewish Antiquities* 16.6, 11; Duane W. Roller, *The Building Program of Herod the Great* (Berkeley, CA, 1998), 66–8.

26. Sullivan, "Dynasty of Cappadocia," 1161–3.

27. Josephus, *Jewish War* 1.476; Josephus, *Jewish Antiquities* 16.193; for more on Salome, infra, pp. 59–78.

28. Josephus, *Jewish War* 1.499–501; Josephus, *Jewish Antiquities* 16.261–70, 325–34.

29. Josephus, *Jewish War* 1.552–3; Josephus, *Jewish Antiquities* 17.11–12.

30. Josephus, *Jewish Antiquities* 18.139–40; Tacitus, *Annals* 6.40; Sullivan, "Dynasty of Cappadocia," 1163–5.

31. Tacitus, *Annals* 14.26, 15.1–6; Kokkinos, *Herodian Dynasty*, 246–63.

32. Josephus, *Jewish Antiquities* 18.139–41.

33. F. E. Romer, "A Numismatic Date for the Departure of C. Caesar?" *TAPA* 108 (1978): 187–202; Roller, *World of Juba*, 212–26.

34. Roller, *Scholarly Kings*, 170–6.

35. *OGIS*, 359, 363; Josephus, *Jewish War* 1.427; Nikos Kokkinos, "Re-Assembling the Inscription of Glaphyra from Athens," *ZPE* 68 (1987): 288–90.

36. Supra, pp. 46–8.

37. The date is based on the chronology of Archelaos's ethnarchy (infra, p. 75).

38. Sullivan, "Dynasty of Cappadocia," 1165–6. The only literary notices of the marriage—those by Josephus—are confused, since he said that it ended when Juba died. This is simply an error—Juba survived until AD 23 or 24—and the best explanation is that Josephus had little knowledge about the Mauretanian kingdom and simply got his facts wrong (Roller, *World of Juba*, 248–9).

39. Josephus, *Jewish War* 2.93; Josephus, *Jewish Antiquities* 17.317; Richard D. Sullivan, "The Dynasty of Judaea in the First Century," *ANRW* 2.8 (1977): 308–10; Kokkinos, *Herodian Dynasty*, 226–9.

40. Strabo 16.2.46; Josephus, *Jewish Antiquities* 17.342–4.

41. Leviticus 18:16, 20:21; Deuteronomy 25:5.

42. Josephus, *Jewish War* 2.114–16; Josephus, *Jewish Antiquities* 17.349–53.

43. Louis H. Feldman, "Prophets and Prophecy in Josephus," *JThS* 41 (1990): 408–9.

44. Infra, pp. 112–13.

Chapter 4

1. Josephus, *Jewish War* 1.36; Josephus, *Jewish Antiquities* 12.265; M. Avi-Yonah, "The Hasmonean Revolt and Judah Maccabee's War against the Syrians," in *The World*

History of the Jewish People, 1st ser., vol. 6: *The Hellenistic Age*, ed. Abraham Schalit (New Brunswick, NJ, 1972), 147–82.

2. Daniel R. Schwartz, "One Temple and Many Synagogues: On Religion and State in Herodian Judaea and Augustan Rome," in *Herod and Augustus*, ed. David M. Jacobson and Nikos Kokkinos (Leiden, 2009), 387.

3. *BNP Historical Atlas of the Ancient World*, 131.

4. Josephus, *Jewish War* 1.437; Josephus, *Jewish Antiquities* 15.53–6; Kokkinos, *Herodian Dynasty*, 211–13.

5. Amos Kloner, "Mareshah (Marisa)," *NEAEHL*, 948–57.

6. Josephus, *Jewish Antiquities* 13.257–8.

7. Lawrence E. Stager, "Ashkelon," *NEAEHL*, 103–12; Roller, *Building Program*, 215–19.

8. Josephus, *Jewish War* 1.181; Josephus, *Jewish Antiquities* 14.121; Kokkinos, *Herodian Dynasty*, 95–7.

9. Josephus, *Jewish War* 1.187–94, 226; Josephus, *Jewish Antiquities* 14.127–39, 277–84.

10. Josephus, *Jewish Antiquities* 15.184.

11. Roller, *Building Program*, 182–3, 131–2.

12. Josephus, *Jewish War* 1.264; Josephus, *Jewish Antiquities* 14.353–4; Kokkinos, *Herodian Dynasty*, 177–8.

13. Kokkinos, *Herodian Dynasty*, 152.

14. Josephus, *Jewish War* 1.566; Josephus, *Jewish Antiquities* 17.9.

15. Josephus, *Jewish Antiquities* 15.62–87.

16. Roller, *Cleopatra*, 120–1.

17. Josephus, *Jewish War* 1.439.

18. Josephus, *Jewish War* 1.486; Josephus, *Jewish Antiquities* 15.253–66; Kokkinos, *Herodian Dynasty*, 179–82. The name is a Hellenized version of Qos-gabar.

19. Dio 49.32.

20. Josephus, *Jewish Antiquities* 15.260–6. The personal name "Baba" is known from Marisa, the original home of Herod's family (Kokkinos, *Herodian Dynasty*, 180).

21. Josephus, *Jewish Antiquities* 15.223–39.

22. Martin Goodman, "Judaea," *CAH* 10, 2d ed. (1996), 742.

23. Josephus, *Jewish Antiquities* 15.247–52.

24. Josephus, *Jewish Antiquities* 15.259–66.

25. Josephus, *Jewish Antiquities* 17.92.

26. Boaz Cohen, "Concerning Divorce in Jewish and Roman Law," *PAAJR* 21 (1952): 28–9, 34.

27. Kokkinos, *Herodian Dynasty*, 182.

28. Supra, p. 53–4.

29. Josephus, *Jewish War* 1.552–3; Josephus, *Jewish Antiquities* 16.11, 18.165.

30. Josephus, *Jewish War* 1.566; Josephus, *Jewish Antiquities* 16.227; Kokkinos, *Herodian Dynasty*, 192–3.

31. Glen W. Bowersock, *Roman Arabia* (Cambridge, MA, 1983), 47–52.

32. Strabo 15.4.21–4; Shelagh Jameson, "Chronology of the Campaigns of Aelius Gallus and C. Petronius," *JRS* 58 (1968): 71–84; Duane W. Roller, *A Historical and Topographical Guide to the "Geography" of Strabo* (Cambridge, 2018), 935–9.

33. Josephus, *Jewish Antiquities* 15.343, 360.

34. Josephus, *Jewish Antiquities* 16.220–4.

35. Josephus, *Jewish War* 1.399–400.

36. Josephus, *Jewish Antiquities* 16.271–5; Roller, *Building Program*, 74; Kokkinos, *Herodian Dynasty*, 182; Halfmann, *Itinera*, 158.

37. Josephus, *Jewish War* 1.487, 566; Josephus, *Jewish Antiquities* 16.225, 17.10–11.

38. Infra, pp. 137–8.

39. Anthony A. Barrett, *Livia: First Lady of Imperial Rome* (New Haven, CT, 2002), 37.

40. Josephus, *Jewish Antiquities* 17.190, 18.31; infra, pp. 73, 76.

41. Strabo 16.4.24; Josephus, *Jewish War* 1.577; Josephus, *Jewish Antiquities* 16.351–3; 17.54–7; Bowersock, *Roman Arabia*, 53.

42. Josephus, *Jewish War* 1.566; Josephus, *Jewish Antiquities* 17.7–10; Kokkinos, *Herodian Dynasty*, 185–6.

43. Supra, pp. 53–5, 147–8.

44. Josephus, *Jewish* War 1.486–7; Josephus, *Jewish Antiquities* 16.201–19.

45. Josephus, *Jewish War* 1.498, 534–5; Josephus, *Jewish Antiquities* 16.256.

46. Josephus, *Jewish War* 1.641–3; Josephus, *Jewish Antiquities* 17.93.

47. Kokkinos, *Herodian Dynasty*, 208–11; the exact sequence of these events remains speculative.

48. Josephus, *Jewish War* 1.536–51; Josephus, *Jewish Antiquities* 16.356–94.

49. Strabo 16.2.46; Josephus, *Jewish Antiquities* 18.143–5, 156, 165; Kokkinos, *Herodian Dynasty*, 275–6.

50. Josephus, *Jewish War* 1.578–83; Josephus, *Jewish Antiquities* 17.58–67; Kokkinos, *Herodian Dynasty*, 171–3.

51. Josephus, *Jewish War* 1.661–4; Josephus, *Jewish Antiquities* 17.36–53, 133–47, 182–7; on problems with the account of Herod's final days, see Mark Toher, "Herod's Last Days," *HSCP* 106 (2011): 209–28.

52. Josephus, *Jewish War* 1.660 (quotation); Josephus, *Jewish Antiquities* 17.175 (paraphrase).

53. Infra, pp. 147–8.

54. Josephus, *Jewish War* 1.666; Josephus, *Jewish Antiquities* 17.193–4.

55. Josephus, *Jewish War* 1.646; Josephus, *Jewish Antiquities* 17.147, 189.

56. It is perhaps first documented for the southern Levant at 1 Maccabees 11:28, from the early second century BC.

57. For example, Medea: Euripides, *Medea* 17.

58. Shimon Dar, "The Agrarian Economy in the Herodian Period," in *The World of the Herods*, ed. Nikos Kokkinos (Stuttgart, 2007), 305–11.

59. Herodotos 2.157; Moshe Dothan, "Ashdod," *NEAEHL*, 102.

60. Pliny, *Natural History* 5.68; Ben-Zion Rosenfeld, "The 'Boundary of Gezer' Inscriptions and the History of Gezer at the End of the Second Temple Period," *IEJ* 38 (1988): 235–45.

61. Kokkinos, *Herodian Dynasty*, 158–9.

62. Menahem Stern, "The Reign of Herod," in *The World History of the Jewish People*, 1st ser., vol. 7: *The Herodian Period*, ed. Michael Avi-Yonah (New Brunswick, NJ, 1975), 117–23.

63. Josephus, *Jewish War* 2.14–38, 80–100; Josephus, *Jewish Antiquities* 17.220–49, 299–323.

64. Tal Ilan, "Josephus on Women," in *A Companion to Josephus*, ed. Honora Howell Chapman and Zuleika Rodges (Malden, MA, 2016), 216.

65. Josephus, *Jewish War* 2.111–13; Josephus, *Jewish Antiquities* 17.339–44; Michael Grant, *The Jews in the Roman World* (London, 1973), 83–7.

66. Archelaos's erratic nature and the opposition to his rule were recalled some years later by Jesus of Nazareth in the parable of the nobleman (Luke 19:12–27).

67. Strabo 16.2.46.

68. G. H. R. Horsley, "Epigraphy as an Ancilla to the Study of the Greek Bible," *Biblica* 79 (1998): 263.

69. *BMC Palestine*, 110–11.

70. Roller, *Building Program*, 240.

71. Horace, *Epistles* 2.2.184.

72. Pliny, *Natural History* 13.45; Plutarch, *Symposium* 8.1; Athenaios 14.652ab; Asaph Goor, "The History of the Date through the Ages in the Holy Land," *Economic Botany* 21 (1967): 326–7.

73. Josephus, *Jewish War* 2.167–8; Josephus, *Jewish Antiquities* 18.29–31.

74. Goodman, "Judaea," 750–1.

75. Pliny, *Natural History* 5.68.

76. Josephus, *Jewish Antiquities* 18.158, 163.

77. Josephus, *Jewish Antiquities* 13.405–17; Grant, *Jews*, 49.

78. Simonetta Segenni, "Antonia Minore e la 'Domus Augusta,'" *SCO* 44 (1995): 319–20.

79. Strabo 16.2.46.

80. *Chrestomathia* 14.3.11; Herbert Musurillo, *Acts of the Pagan Martyrs* (Oxford, 1954), 1: 128–30.

81. Galen, *On the Composition of Medicines* 2.7; Kokkinos, *Herodian Dynasty*, 191.

Chapter 5

1. Roller, *Ancient Geography*, 8–12; John Boardman, *The Greeks Overseas: Their Early Colonies and Trade*, 4th ed. (London, 1999), 242; Alexander M. Butyagin, "The History of the Northern Black Sea Region," in *Greeks on the Black Sea: Ancient Art From the Hermitage*, ed. Anna A. Trofimova (Los Angeles, 2007), 8–16.

2. Aeschylus, *Prometheus Bound* 732–4.

3. Stephanos of Byzantion, "Pantikapaion"; David C. Braund, *Georgia in Antiquity* (Oxford, 1994), 68–9.

4. Diodoros 12.31.

5. Strabo 7.4.4; Gocha R. Tsetskhladze, "A Survey of the Major Urban Settlements in the Kimmerian Bosporos (with a Discussion of Their Status as *Poleis*)," in *Yet More Studies in the Ancient Greek Polis*, ed. Thomas Heine Nielsen (Stuttgart 1997), 44–9.

6. Thomas S. Noonan, "The Grain Trade of the Northern Black Sea in Antiquity," *AJPh* 94 (1973): 231–42.

7. Strabo 11.2.12; Philip de Souza, *Piracy in the Graeco-Roman World* (Cambridge, 1999), 9.

8. Strabo 7.4.4; V. F. Gajdukevič, *Das Bosporanische Reich* (Berlin, 1971).

9. Strabo 11.2.11, 11.5.8; Appian, *Mithridateios* 113.

10. Strabo 7.3.18.

11. Agatharchides F67 = Diodoros 3.34.7–8.

12. *IGRR* 1.905; Strabo 11.2.11; Appian, *Mithridateios* 110–13; M. Rostovtzeff, "Queen Dynamis of Bosporus," *JHS* 39 (1919): 88–109; Richard D. Sullivan, *Near Eastern Royalty and Rome, 100–30 BC* (Toronto, 1990), 159–60.

13. Dio 42.46–7.

14. "Veni, vidi, vici": Suetonius, *Divine Julius* 37.

15. Strabo 13.4.3; Appian, *Mithridateios* 120.

16. Homer, *Iliad* 8.294, 13.787, etc. There are a few citations of the name from Asia Minor in the first century BC, essentially contemporary with Pharnakes's daughter, but no known earlier examples: P. M. Fraser and E. Matthews, eds., *A Lexicon of Greek Personal Names* (Oxford, 1987–),4: 113; 4a: 126.

17. The title appears on his coinage ("Asandros, Archon of Bosporos"): David MacDonald, *An Introduction to the History and Coinage of the Kingdom of Bosporus* (Lancaster, PA, 2005), 49–50.

18. Sullivan, *Near Eastern Royalty*, 158–9.

19. MacDonald, *Introduction*, 51.

20. Dio 54.24.4–6; Fergus Millar, *A Study of Cassius Dio* (Oxford, 1964), 34–8.

21. Appian, *Civil War* 2.91.

22. Lucian, *Makrobioi* 17.

23. Krzysztof Nawotka, "The Attitude towards Rome in the Political Propaganda of the Bosporan Monarchs," *Latomus* 48 (1989): 328–9.

24. It is possible that he, or perhaps his son, was the Pantaleon who was in the service of Aspourgos, Dynamis's presumed son and successor: Heinz Heinen, "Zwei Briefe des bosporanischen Königs Aspurgos (*AE* 1994, 1538)," *ZPE* 124 (1999): 140–1.

25. Strabo 7.4.6, 11.2.11.

26. Demosthenes, *Against Leptines* 30–1.

27. M. Rostovtzeff, *The Social and Economic History of the Roman Empire*, 2d ed. (Oxford, 1957), 154.

28. M. Rostovtzeff, *The Social and Economic History of the Hellenistic World* (Oxford, 1941), 1243.

29. *IGRR* 1.879; Sullivan, *Near Eastern Royalty*, 160; Rostovtzeff, "Queen Dynamis," 103–4; Glen W. Bowersock, *Augustus and the Greek World* (Oxford, 1965), 53.

30. Lucian, *Makrobioi* 17; Dio 54.24.4–6.

31. Bowersock, *Augustus*, 50–1.

32. Josephus, *Jewish Antiquities* 16.16–21; Dio 54.24.6; Halfmann, *Itinera*, 163; Meyer Reinhold, *Marcus Agrippa: A Biography* (Geneva, NY, 1933), 113–15.

33. Infra, pp. 108–9.

34. Aeschylus, *Libation Bearers* 909; Richard D. Sullivan, "Dynasts in Pontus," *ANRW* 2.7 (1980): 920.

35. For a credible account of the opposing view, see Erich S. Gruen, "The Expansion of the Empire under Augustus," *CAH* 10, 2d ed. (1996), 151–2.

36. Strabo 12.3.29.

37. Glen W. Bowersock, "Strabo and the Memory of Mithradates Eupator," in *Monumentum Gregorianum*, ed. A. I. Ivanchik (Moscow, 2013), 382–3.

38. Andrea Primo, "The Client Kingdom of Pontus Between Mithradatism and Philoromanism," in *Kingdoms and Principalities in the Roman Near East*, ed. Ted Kaizer and Margherita Facella (Stuttgart, 2010), 165–6.

39. Strabo 11.2.3, 11.

40. Rostovtzeff, "Queen Dynamis," 101–2.

41. Primo, "Client Kingdom," 168.

42. Anthony A. Barrett, "Polemo II of Pontus and M. Antonius Polemo," *Historia* 27 (1978): 438–9.

43. Dio 59.12.2 (mistakenly reported to be the son, not the grandson); Sullivan, "Dynasts in Pontus," 925–30.

44. Heinen, "Zwei Briefe," 140–1; Fergus Millar, "Emperors, Kings and Subjects: The Politics of Two-Level Sovereignty," *SCI* 15 (1996): 168–70. The inscription reporting his visit is from the summer of AD 15, but there is no date for the journey, and it is uncertain whether Augustus (who had died in August of the previous year) or Tiberius was on the throne.

45. *IGRR* 1.879.

46. Kokkinos, *Herodian Dynasty*, 260–3.

47. *CIRB* 38, 1046.

48. Étienne Bernand, *Les inscriptions grecques et latines de Philae*, 2: *Haut et bas Empire* (Paris, 1969), no. 142. The inscription is dated to 7 BC. Catilius, known also through an-other epigram from Philai (no. 143), was probably a member of the entourage of the prefect of Egypt, C. Turranius. See also Vergil, *Aeneid* 1.286–8; Ovid, *Metamorphoses* 15.830–1.

49. *CIRB* 978; see also *SEG* 44.658; Heinz Heinen, "Rome et le Bosphore: Notes épigraphiques," *Cahiers du Centre Gustav Glotz* 7 (1996): 86.

50. Boardman, *Greeks Overseas*, 253–4; Barrett, *Livia*, 195–6.

51. *Greeks on the Black Sea: Ancient Art from the Hermitage*, ed. Anna A. Trofimova (Los Angeles, 2007), 187–8.

52. Roller, *World of Juba*, 267–75.

53. Supra, pp. 44–5.

54. *CIRB* 979; Nawotka, "Attitude," 328–9.

55. *CIRB* 31.

56. Nikolai Povalahev, "Eine Bauinschrift aus Phanagoreia von 220/1 n. Chr. und ihr historischer Hintergrund: Text und Kommentar," *ZPE* 177 (2011): 152.

57. *SEG* 57.697, 45.1022; see also 59.860.

58. Head, *Historia Numorum*, 495. For other coins of Dynamis, see A. N. Zograf, *Ancient Coinage*, trans. H. Bartlett Wells, *BAR* Supplementary Series 33 (Oxford, 1977), 2: 415–17; Konstantin V. Golenko, "The Numismatic Department of the Pushkin State Museum of Fine Arts, Moscow," *NC* 13 (1973): 212.

59. Roller, *Building Program*, 128–9.

60. Rostovtzeff, "Queen Dynamis," 100–1.

61. J. M. C. Toynbee, *Roman Historical Portraits* (London, 1978), 116–17; see also J. G. F. Hind, "Archaeology of the Greeks and Barbarian Peoples around the Black Sea (1982–1993)," *AR* 39 (1992–3): 99.

62. Krzysztof Nawotka, "Asander of the Bosporos: His Coinage and Chronology," *AJN* 3/4 (1992): 31.

63. Anna A. Trofimova, "The Sculpted Portrait in the Bosporus," in *Greeks on the Black Sea: Ancient Art from the Hermitage*, ed. Anna A. Trofimova (Los Angeles, 2007), 51–2. It has also been suggested to be Gepaipyris of Bosporos (infra, p. 119).

64. Rostovtzeff, "Queen Dynamis," 104.

65. C. R. Whittaker, "Roman Africa: Augustus to Vespasian," *CAH* 10, 2d ed. (1996), 597.

66. Kostantin V. Golenko and P. J. Karyszkowski, "The Gold Coinage of King Pharnaces of the Bosporus," *NC* 12 (1972): 25–38; Zograf, *Ancient Coinage*, 2: 308; Karsten Dahmen, "With Rome in Mind? Case Studies in the Coinage of the Client Kings," in *Kings and Principalities in the Roman Near East*, ed. Ted Kaizer and Margherita Facella (Stuttgart, 2010), 110.

67. Charles Brian Rose, "'Princes' and Barbarians on the Ara Pacis," *AJA* 94 (1990): 455–9; Rose, "The Parthians in Augustan Rome," *AJA* 109 (2005): 40–2; V. N.

Parfenov, "Dynamis, Agrippa und der Friedensaltar: Zur Militärischen und Politischen Geschichte des Bosporanischen Reiches Nach Asandros," *Historia* 45 (1996): 95–103.

68. Strabo 7.3.18.

69. Fraser and Matthews, *Lexicon*, 1: 144; 2: 136; 3a: 135; 3b: 127; 4: 113; 5a: 12.

70. See the genealogical chart in Richard D. Sullivan, "King Marcus Antonius Polemo," *NC* 19 (1979): 12; *BNP Chronologies of the Ancient World*, 112–13.

Chapter 6

1. Hatto H. Schmitt, "Pythodoris" (#1), *RE* 24 (1963): 581–6.

2. Getzel M. Cohen, *The Hellenistic Settlements in Europe, the Islands, and Asia Minor* (Berkeley, CA, 1995), 256–9.

3. Strabo 14.1.43, 48; George E. Bean, "Nysa," *PECS*, 636–7.

4. Supra, pp. 13–15

5. This and the rest of what is known about Chairemon's career are recorded on an inscription from Nysa, *SIG* 741; for an English translation, see Robert K. Sherk, *Rome and the Greek East to the Death of Augustus* (Cambridge, 1984), no. 60.

6. Jonathan Roth, *The Logistics of the Roman Army at War* (Leiden, 1999), 18–24.

7. Strabo 14.1.42.

8. There are chronological problems with the genealogy from Chairemon to Pythodoris, and it is possible that he was actually her great-grandfather: Christopher P. Jones, "An Inscription Seen by Agathias," *ZPE* 179 (2011): 107–15.

9. Strabo 14.1.42.

10. It is not clear whether Pythodoros's thousands of talents were his total wealth or annual income, but as a point of reference the annual income of Ptolemy XII, the king of Egypt at this time, was 12,500 talents: Strabo 17.1.13; see also Ronald Syme, *The Roman Revolution* (Oxford, 1939), 262.

11. Cicero, *Pro Flacco* 52.

12. Seneca the Elder, *Controversiae* 2.4.8.

13. Andrea Raggi, "The First Roman Citizens among Eastern Dynasts and Kings," in *Kingdoms and Principalities in the Roman Near East*, ed. Ted Kaizer and Margherita Facella (Stuttgart, 2010), 89–90.

14. Peter Thonemann, "Polemo, Son of Polemo (Dio, 59.12.2)," *EA* 37 (2004): 144–50.

15. Bowersock, *Augustus*, 8; Peter Thonemann, *The Maeander Valley* (Cambridge, 2011), 205–9.

16. *OGIS* 377; the feminist orientation of the inscription is discussed infra, p. 114.

17. *OGIS* 103–23.

18. Herodotos 8.85.

19. David C. Braund, "Polemo, Pythodoris and Strabo," in *Roms auswärtige Freunde in der späten Republik und im frühen Prinzipat*, ed. Altay Coksun (Göttingen 2005), 259–60.

20. Tacitus, *Annals* 2.43.

21. Sullivan, "Dynasts in Pontus," 920–1.

22. Plutarch, *Antonius* 87.

23. Cicero, *Letters to Atticus* #420; *Philippics* 2.3, 3.17, 13.23.

24. Plutarch, *Antonius* 9.2; Charles L. Babcock, "The Early Career of Fulvia," *AJPh* 86 (1966): 13.

25. Dio 49.44.2.

26. Alexander Helios was also soon dead, but Iotape survived to marry Mithradates III of Kommagene, around 20 BC, and her descendants, including Eastern monarchs and even a Roman consul, are known into the following century: Richard D. Sullivan, "The Dynasty of Commagene," *ANRW* 2.8 (1977): 780–1.

27. Cicero, *Letters to Friends* 2.18; Domitilla Campanile, "Pitodoride e la sua famiglia," *SCO* 56 (2010): 71–3, who argued for Lucius Antonius as the ancestor. For his career, see T. R. S. Broughton, *The Magistrates of the Roman Republic* (New York, 1951–60), 2: 249.

28. Plutarch, *Antonius* 87; Richard D. Sullivan, "Papyri Reflecting the Eastern Dynastic Network," *ANRW* 2.8 (1977): 920.

29. David Konstan, "Women, Ethnicity and Power in the Roman Empire," *OP* 1 (2002): 19–21.

30. Katherine Clarke, "In Search of the Author of Strabo's *Geography*," *JRS* 87 (1997): 100–1.

31. Strabo 14.1.42.

32. Duane W. Roller, *The "Geography" of Strabo* (Cambridge, 2014), 15.

33. Strabo 12.3.29; Braund, "Polemo," 255–6.

34. Strabo 11.2.18.

35. Strabo 12.3.29.

36. Supra, pp. 88–9.

37. Strabo 12.2.1–11.

38. Strabo 11.2.16; Roller, *Historical and Topographical Guide*, 640–1; Braund, *Georgia*, 193–4; Everett L. Wheeler, "Roman Fleets in the Black Sea: Mysteries of the 'Classis Pontica,'" *AClass* 55 (2012): 139.

39. Strabo 14.1.42.

40. *OGIS* 376; *SEG* 39.695; Braund, "Polemo," 258; Yu. G. Vinogradov, "Greek Epigraphy of the North Black Sea Coast, the Caucasus and Central Asia (1985–1990)," *Ancient Civilizations from Scythia to Siberia* 1 (1994): 69. The statue in honor of Livia may have been erected shortly after Polemon's death, around 7 BC, when Pythodoris might have felt especially vulnerable and was seeking new alliances: A. I. Boltunova, "The Inscription of Pythodoris from Hermonassa," *VDI* 188 (1989): 86–91.

41. Head, *Historia Numorum*, 503.

42. Strabo 12.3.29.

43. Strabo 14.2.24.

44. Strabo 12.8.16; Appian, *Civil War* 5.75.

45. Dio 49.33.1–2.

46. Strabo 12.8.16; Plutarch, *Antonius* 61.2.

47. Supra, pp. 87–8.

48. Strabo 11.2.11; Sullivan, "Dynasts in Pontus," 915–20.

49. Strabo 12.3.29; his identity is discussed infra, pp. 113–14.

50. Homer, *Iliad* 1.350, etc.; Aeschylus, *Persians* 878; Herodotos 7.147. The modern name "Black Sea" is derived from the Persian *aesaena*, meaning "dark" or "somber": Duane W. Roller, *Through the Pillars of Herakles: Greco-Roman Exploration of the Atlantic* (London, 2006), 1.

51. *BNP Chronologies*, 110–11.

52. Polybios 25.2.

53. Supra, pp. 50–2.

54. Strabo 12.3.29.

55. Dio 57.17.4.

56. Tacitus, *Annals* 2.42; Dio 57.17.3–7; Sullivan, "Dynasty of Cappadocia," 1159–61.

57. Philostratos, *Life of Apollonios* 1.12.

58. Tacitus, *Annals* 2.43.

59. F. E. Romer, "A Case of Client-Kingship," *AJPh* 106 (1985): 75–100.

60. The charges in this action are unknown; see Suetonius, *Tiberius* 8; Barbara Levick, *Tiberius the Politician* (London, 1976), 20, 140.

61. Strabo 12.1.4; Tacitus, *Annals* 2.56.

62. Infra, pp. 115–19.

63. Tacitus, *Annals* 2.56; Sullivan, "Dynasts in Pontus," 923–5.

64. Head, *Historia Numorum*, 755; L. A. Saryan, "An Unpublished Silver Drachm Attributed to Artaxias III (A.D. 18–34) of Armenia," *AJN* 9 (1977): 14–15.

65. *OGIS* 377.

66. Strabo 12.3.29.

67. Barrett, "Polemo II," 437–48. Olbe was where Aba had ruled a century previously: infra, pp. 121–3.

68. Théodore Reinach, "Some Pontic Eras," *NC* 2 (1902): 1–2.

69. Toynbee, *Roman Historical Portraits*, 117.

70. *BNP Chronologies*, 111; Hans Roland, Baldus, "Die Daten von Münzprägung und Tod der Königen Pythodoris von Pontus," *Chiron* 13 (1983): 537–43.

71. *SEG* 40.1170.

72. Supra, pp. 23–4.

73. Justin, *Epitome* 39.3.4–12; Hölbl, *History*, 203–7; J. Tondriau, "La tryphè: Philosophie royale ptolémaïque," *RÉA* 50 (1948): 49–54.

74. Herodotos 5.3–10; Sullivan, *Near Eastern Royalty*, 25–30.

75. Archilochos F5 (= Strabo 10.2.17, 12.3.20); Tacitus, *Annals* 2.64.

76. Richard D. Sullivan, "Thrace in the Eastern Dynastic Network," *ANRW* 2.7 (1979): 200–4.

77. *Greek Anthology* 16.75.

78. Ovid, *Epistulae ex Ponto* 2.9.

79. Pausanias 2.27.6; R. A. Tomlinson, *Epidauros* (Austin, TX, 1983), 47–54; Sullivan, "Thrace," 202–3.

80. Velleius 2.129; Tacitus, *Annals* 2.65–7.

81. Appian, *Civil War* 4.75.

82. F. W. Hasluck, "An Inscribed Basis from Cyzicus," *JHS* 22 (1902) 126–34; see also Adolf Wilhelm, "Zu Inschriften Aus Kleinasien," in *Anatolian Studies Presented to Sir William Mitchell Ramsay*, ed. W. H. Buckler and W. M. Calder (Manchester, 1923). 418–31.

83. *SIG* 779.

84. Barrett, *Livia.* 196.

85. *SIG* 798. The inscription is highly fragmentary, and attribution is not certain: Slavtcho Kirov, "Gaius Iulius Rhascos," *ZPE* 178 (2011): 215–20.

86. The queen Tryphaina who appears in the apocryphal *Acts of Paul and Thekla*, written in the second century AD but set at the time of the emperor Claudius, is a fictional character, but probably based on popular knowledge of the historical queen, whose memory was kept alive by her inscriptions and perhaps also a public monument. The account may also have been influenced by the conversion of her son Polemon II to Judaism: Jan N. Bremmer, "Magic, Martyrdom and Women's Liberation, in *The Apocryphal Acts of Paul and Thecla*, ed. Jan N. Bremmer (Kampen, 1996), 44–59.

87. Schmitt, "Pythodoris," 585–6; *BNP Chronologies*, 111.

88. Toynbee, *Roman Historical Portraits*, 119; *BMC Pontus, Paphlagonia, Bithynia, and the Kingdom of Bosporus*, 47; Sullivan, "Dynasts in Pontus," 922–3.

89. This was a process that reached its culmination some years later with King Alexander, a descendant of Herod the Great and Glaphyra, who became king of Cilicia around AD 75 and then, when he lost his position, moved to Rome, becoming a senator and eventually consul, but was always officially addressed by his royal title: Sullivan, "Dynasty of Commagene," 794–5.

90. Sullivan, "Thrace," 204–7; *BNJ Chronologies*, 113–14; Macurdy, *Vassal Queens*, 48–50.

91. Josephus, *Jewish Antiquities* 20.145–7; Dio 59.12.2; Tacitus, *Histories* 2.81; Josephus, *Life* 119; Juvenal 6.153–60; Roller, *Building Program*, 250; Sullivan, *Papyri*, 923; Sviatoslav Dmitriev, "Claudius' Grant of Cilicia to Polemo," *CQ* 53 (2003): 286–91.

92. Sullivan, "Dynasty of Judaea," 310–13.

93. Suetonius, *Nero* 18; Tacitus, *Histories* 3.47; Sullivan, "Dynasts in Pontus," 925–30.

Chapter 7

1. Strabo 14.5.10.

2. A. H. M. Jones, *Cities of the Eastern Roman Provinces*, 2d ed. (Oxford, 1971), 199, 207.

3. In a classic case of male-dominated scholarship, David Magie, in his generally valuable *Roman Rule in Asia Minor to the End of the Third Century after Christ* (Princeton, NJ, 1950), 494, did not even mention Cleopatra's role in Aba's fortunes, but credited everything to Antonius alone, despite Strabo's explicit statement that the queen was involved.

4. Theodora S. Mackay, "The Major Sanctuaries of Pampyhlia and Cilicia," *ANRW* 2.18 (1990): 2082–2103.

5. Emma Strugnell, "Thea Musa, Roman Queen of Parthia," *IA* 43 (2008): 275–98; J. M. Bigwood, "Queen Mousa, Mother and Wife (?) of King Phraatakes of Parthia: A Re-evaluation of the Evidence," *Mouseion* 4 (2004): 35–70.

6. Plutarch, *Crassus* 32.5.

7. Josephus, *Jewish Antiquities* 18.40–3. Josephus's text reads "Julius Caesar," but Phraates did not come to the throne until 38 BC, several years after Caesar's death, although it is possible Thesmousa was given to him before he became king.

8. Velleius 2.91.1; Dio 54.8.1–2.

9. Augustus, *Res gestae* 29.

10. This long-standing view has recently been disputed in a credible argument that suggests the scene represents a western European context: Bridget Buxton, "A New Reading of the Prima Porta Augustus: The Return of the Eagle of Legio V Alaudae," *Latomus* 338 (2012): 277–306.

11. Dio 53.33.1–2.

12. Suetonius, *Augustus* 59; Pliny, *Natural History* 25.77, 29.6; Dio 53.30.

13. Strabo 16.2.24.

14. Bigwood, "Queen Mousa," 47–50.

15. Hölbl, *History*, 192–3; *BMC Seleukid Kings*, 85–6.

16. A portrait bust from Susa of a Parthian queen has also been tentatively identified as her: Franz Cumont, "Portrait d'une reine parthe trouvé à Suse," *CRAI* 83 (1939): 330–41.

17. Lucan, *Pharsalia* 8.404–9.

18. Genesis 19:31–8.

19. Leviticus 20:17, etc.; Philo, *Questions and Answers: Genesis* 4.56–8.

20. Philo, *Special Laws* 3.13–14; Minucius Felix, *Octavius* 31.3; see also Tertullian, *Apology* 9.16, who cited Ktesias, a historian of Persia from about 400 BC, whose reliability is questionable.

21. P. B. Adamson, "Consanguineous Marriages in the Ancient World," *Folklore* 93 (1982): 86.

22. Augustus, *Res gestae* 32; *BNJ Chronologies*, 121.

23. Josephus, *Jewish Antiquities* 18.43–52.

24. Aelian, *Historical Miscellany* 7.1.

Chapter 8

1. The main source on the phenomenon of allied royalty remains Braund, *Rome and the Friendly King*.

2. Josephus, *Jewish Antiquities* 15.342–3; 16.6; Roller, *Building Program*, 66–8.

3. Plutarch, *Tiberius Gracchus* 1.4; Linda-Marie Günther, "Cornelia und Ptolemaios VIII: Zur Historizität des Heiratantrages (Plut. TG 1,3)," *Historia* 39 (1990): 124–8.

4. Dionysios of Halikarnassos, *Roman Archaeology* 4.84–5; Livy 1.59–60, 2.8.2.

5. Plutarch, *Marcus Cato* 8.7–8.

6. Polybios 18.10.7.

7. Elizabeth Rawson, "Caesar's Heritage: Hellenistic Kings and Their Roman Equals," *JRS* 65 (1975): 152–4.

8. Pliny, *Natural History* 31.41–2; Frontinus, *De aquis* 1.7; L. Richardson, Jr., *A New Topographical Dictionary of Ancient Rome* (Baltimore, 1992), 17–18.

9. Cicero, *Philippics* 2.85; Rawson, "Caesar's Heritage," 148–50.

10. Cicero, *Letters to Atticus* #226, 229–31; Dio 43.27.1; Roller, *Cleopatra*, 71–4.

11. Suetonius, *Divine Julius* 52.

12. Cicero, *Letters to Atticus* #393.

13. Horace, *Ode* 1.37.21.

14. J. P. V. D. Balsdon, *Roman Women: Their History and Habits* (London, 1962), 45–9.

15. Ennius, *Annals* 371; Plautus, *Casina* 585; Plautus, *Mostellaria* 190; Terence, *Eunuch* 37.

16. Pomeroy, *Goddesses*, 150–89; on the Roman matron of the Imperial period, see Susan Fischler, "Social Stereotypes and Historical Analysis: The Case of the Imperial Women at Rome," in *Women in Ancient Societies*, ed. Léonie J. Archer et al. (New York, 1994), 115–33.

17. Livy 1.9–13; Dionysios of Halikarnassos, *Roman Archaeology* 2.45–6.

18. Livy 5.25.9.

19. "Sicut virorum," Livy 5.50.7.

20. Suetonius, *Augustus* 64.2.

21. The phrase "mother of the Gracchi" (*mater Gracchorum*) became almost an addendum to her name: Cicero, *Brutus* 211; Tacitus, *Dialogue on Oratory* 28.5.

22. Cicero, *Brutus* 211; Quintilian, *Institutes* 1.1.6; Suzanne Dixon, *Cornelia: Mother of the Gracchi* (London, 2007), 12–14.

23. Plutarch, *Gaius Gracchus* 19.2.

24. *CIL* 6.31610; Pliny, *Natural History* 34.31; Dixon, *Cornelia*, 56–7.

25. Diodoros 34(35).25; Plutarch, *Gaius Gracchus* 4, 13.2; Pomeroy, *Goddesses*, 170–6.

26. Valerius Maximus 3.8.6.

27. Appian, *Civil War* 5.32–49; Babcock, "Early Career," 1–24; Judith Hallett, "Fulvia," in *Women and War in Antiquity*, ed. J. Fabre-Serris and A. Keith (Baltimore, 2015), 247–65.

28. Plutarch, *Antonius* 10.3.

29. Diana E. E. Kleiner, "Imperial Women as Patrons of the Arts in the Early Empire," in *I Claudia: Women in Ancient Rome*, ed. Diana E. E. Kleiner and Susan B. Matheson (New Haven, CT, 1996), 28–41; Phyllis Culham, "Did Roman Women Have an Empire?," in *Inventing Ancient Culture*, ed. Mark Golden and Peter Toohey (London, 1997), 192–204; Maria Wyke, "Augustan Cleopatras: Female Power and Poetic Authority," in *Roman Poetry and Propaganda in the Age of Augustus*, ed. A. Powell (Bristol, 1997), 98–140.

30. Tacitus, *Annals* 5.1; Barrett, *Livia* 9–16. On women of the Augustan family generally, see Richard A. Bauman, *Women and Politics in Ancient Rome* (London, 1994), 91–129.

31. Vergil, *Aeneid* 7.706–9.

32. Livy 2.21.5; Suetonius, *Tiberius* 1.1.

33. Suetonius, *Tiberius* 5.

34. Dio 48.34.3, 44.

35. Marleen B. Flory, "*Sic Exempla Parantur*: Livia's Shrine to Concordia and the Porticus Liviae," *Historia* 33 (1984): 309–30; Richardson, *New Topographical Dictionary*, 314.

36. Ovid, *Tristia* 1.6.25; see also his *Consolatio ad Liviam* 356. Livia's son, the emperor Tiberius, was said to be eternally annoyed at her power and the honors she accumulated: Suetonius, *Tiberius* 50.3; Stéphane Benoist, "Women and *Imperium* in Rome," in *Women and War in Antiquity*, ed. J. Fabre-Serris and A. Keith (Baltimore, 2015), 266–88.

37. Tacitus, *Annals* 5.1; R. A. Kearsley, "Women and Public Life in Imperial Asia Minor: Hellenistic Tradition and Augustan Ideology," *AncWE* 4 (2005): 98–121.

38. Plutarch, *Antonius* 31, 53–5.

39. Plutarch, *Antonius* 57; Dio 50.3.2.

40. Richardson, *New Topographical Dictionary*, 281.

41. Plutarch, *Antonius* 87; Roller, *World of Juba*, 83–4.

42. Richardson, *New Topographical Dictionary*, 317–18.

43. Marleen B. Flory, "Livia and the History of Public Honorific Statues for Women in Rome," *TAPA* 123 (1993): 290–2.

44. Dio 54.35.4–5.

45. Nikos Kokkinos, *Antonia Augusta: Portrait of a Great Roman Lady* (London, 1992), 70–86.

46. *Greek Anthology* 6.435. Krinagoras also commemorated her first pregnancy (*Greek Anthology* 6.244).

47. Livy, *Summary* 142; Strabo 7.1.3; Valerius Maximus 5.5.3.

48. Valerius Maximus 4.3.3; Josephus, *Jewish Antiquities* 18.180; Suetonius, *Claudius* 41.1.

49. *IGRR* 4.206; Tacitus, *Annals* 2.56–7; Kokkinos, *Antonia*, 43–5.

50. Tacitus, *Annals* 2.69–75, 3.2–5; Suetonius, *Gaius Caligula* 5.

51. Josephus, *Jewish Antiquities* 18.143, 156, 164–7.

52. Josephus, *Jewish Antiquities* 18.181–2; Dio 65.14.

53. Suetonius, *Gaius Caligula* 15.2, 23; Dio 59.3.1–6.

54. Plutarch, *Antonius* 83.4; Dio 51.13.

55. Roller, *Cleopatra*, 7–8.

56. Barrett, *Livia*, 28.

57. Plutarch, *Antonius* 87.

58. Appian, *Civil* War 2.102; Dio 49.38.1, 55.2.5; Flory, "Livia," 292–6.

59. Tactius, *Annals* 4.37; see also Dio 51.20.

60. Gertrude Grether, "Livia and the Roman Imperial Cult," *AJPh* 67 (1946): 231, 243.

61. Supra, pp. 90–1.

62. Ovid, *Tristia* 2.161–2; *Epistulae ex Ponto* 4.9.105–8; Barrett, *Livia*, 195.

63. Supra, p. 71.

64. Barrett, *Livia*, 36–8; Halfmann, *Itinera*, 158.

65. Appian, *Civil War* 2.102; Dio 51.22.3; Richardson, *New Topographical Dictionary*, 165–7.

66. Strabo 12.3.29.

Appendix 1

1. Jonathan Edmondson, "Introduction: Flavius Josephus and Flavian Rome," in *Flavius Josephus and Flavian Rome*, ed. Jonathan Edmondson et al. (Oxford, 2005), 3–7.

2. Josephus, *Jewish Antiquities* 18.181–2.

3. *FGrHist*, #236; Josephus, *Jewish Antiquities* 15.174; Roller, *Scholarly Kings*, 177–85.

4. *FGrHist*, #90; Ben Zion Wacholder, *Nicolaus of Damascus* (Berkeley, CA, 1962); Bowersock, *Augustus*, 134–6.

5. Mark Toher, "Herod, Augustus, and Nikolaos of Damascus," in *Herod and Augustus*, ed. David M. Jacobson and Nikos Kokkinos (Leiden, 2009), 65–81.

Appendix 2

1. Matthew 14:3–12; Mark 6.17–29; Josephus, *Jewish Antiquities* 18.118–19. The biblical accounts refer only to "Herod" or "Herod the tetrarch," but there is no question that Antipas is meant.

2. It was the thirteenth year of the emperor Domitian: *Jewish Antiquities* 20.267.

3. Harold W. Hoehner, *Herod Antipas* (Cambridge, 1972), 169–70.

4. Roller, *Building Program*, 184–6.

5. Josephus, *Jewish War* 1.664; Josephus, *Jewish Antiquities* 17.188, 317–20.

6. Josephus, *Jewish War* 2.183 (Spain); Josephus, *Jewish Antiquities* 18.252 (Gaul).

7. Josephus, *Jewish War* 1.552; Kokkinos, *Herodian Dynasty*, 267–70.

8. Supra, pp. 55–6.

9. Josephus, *Jewish Antiquities* 18.136–7. Onomastics of the Herodian family are always particularly difficult to untangle, compounded by the fact that Salome is one of the two most popular woman's names among contemporary Jewish populations and is even the name of one of the few known female followers of Jesus of Nazareth (Mark 15:40, 16:1; Kokkinos, *Herodian Dynasty*, 177).

10. Hoehner, *Herod Antipas*, 154–6.

11. Strabo 2.3.4.

12. He was probably born around 25–20 BC, as best as can be determined: Kokkinos, *Herodian Dynasty*, 225.

13. Herodotos 9.109–12.

14. Livy 39.43.3–4.

15. Josephus, *Jewish Antiquities* 18.136–7, 20.158; Tacitus, *Annals* 13.7.

16. Nikos Kokkinos, "Which Salome Did Aristobulus Marry?" *PEQ* 113 (1996): 33.

17. For a thorough study of the story of the death of John the Baptist, see Ross S. Kraemer, "Implicating Herodias and Her Daughter in the Death of John the Baptist: A (Christian) Theological Strategy," *JBL* 125 (2006): 321–49.

Bibliography

Adamson, P. B. "Consanguinous Marriages in the Ancient World." *Folklore* 93 (1982): 85–92.

Avi-Yonah, M. "The Hasmonean Revolt and Judah Maccabee's War against the Syrians." In *The World History of the Jewish People*, 1st ser., vol. 6: *The Hellenistic Age*, edited by Abraham Schalit, 147–82. New Brunswick, NJ, 1972.

Babcock, Charles L. "The Early Career of Fulvia." *AJPh* 86 (1965): 1–32.

Baldus, Hans Roland. "Die Daten von Münzprägung und Tod der Königen Pythodoris von Pontus." *Chiron* 13 (1983): 537–43.

Balsdon, J. P. V. D. *Roman Women: Their History and Habits*. London, 1962.

Barber, Elizabeth Wayland. *Women's Work: The First 20,000 Years*. New York, 1994.

Barrett, Anthony A. *Livia: First Lady of Imperial Rome*. New Haven, CT, 2002.

———. "Polemo II of Pontus and M. Antonius Polemo." *Historia* 27 (1978): 437–48.

Bauman, Richard A. *Women and Politics in Ancient Rome*. London, 1994.

Bean, George E. "Nysa." *PECS*, 636–7.

Bennett, Chris. "Drusilla Regina." *CQ* 53 (2003): 315–19.

Benoist, Stéphane. "Women and *Imperium* in Rome." In *Women and War in Antiquity*, edited by J. Fabre-Serris and A. Keith, 266–88. Baltimore, 2015.

Benseddik, Nacéra et al. *Cherchel*. Algiers, 1983.

Bernand, Étienne. *Les inscriptions grecques et latines de Philae 2: Haut et bas Empire*. Paris, 1969.

Bigwood, J. M. "Queen Mousa, Mother and Wife (?) of King Phraatakes of Parthia: A Re-evaluation of the Evidence." *Mouseion* 4 (2004): 35–70.

Boardman, John. *Greek Gems and Finger Rings: Early Bronze Age to Late Classical*. London, 1970.

———. *The Greeks Overseas: Their Early Colonies and Trade*, 4th ed. London, 1999.

Boltunova, A. I. "The Inscription of Pythodoris from Hermonassa." *VDI* 188 (1989): 86–91.

Bosworth, A. B. *A Historical Commentary on Arrian's History of Alexander*. Oxford, 1980–95.

Bouchenaki, Mounir. *Le Mausolée Royal de Maurétanie*. Algiers, 1979.

Bowersock, Glen W. *Augustus and the Greek World*. Oxford, 1965.

———. *Roman Arabia*. Cambridge, MA, 1983.

———. "Strabo and the Memory of Mithradates Eupator." In *Monumentum Gregorianum*, edited by A. I. Ivanchik, 318–87. Moscow, 2013.

Braund, David C. *Georgia in Antiquity*. Oxford, 1994.

———. "Polemo, Pythodoris and Strabo." In *Roms auswärtige Freunde in der späten Republik und im frühen Prinzipat*, edited by Altay Coksun, 253–70. Göttingen, 2005.

———. *Rome and the Friendly King: The Character of the Client Kingship*. London, 1984.

Bremmer, Jan N. "Magic, Martyrdom and Women's Liberation. In *The Apocryphal Acts of Paul and Thecla*, edited by Jan N. Bremmer, 36–59. Kampen, 1996.

Broughton, T. R. S. *The Magistrates of the Roman Republic*. New York, 1951–60.

Burstein, Stanley M. *Outpost of Hellenism: The Emergence of Heraclea on the Black Sea*. Berkeley, CA, 1976.

Butyagin, Alexander M. "The History of the Northern Black Sea Region." In *Greeks on the Black Sea: Ancient Art from the Hermitage*, edited by Anna A. Trofimova, 8–17. Los Angeles, 2007.

Buxton, Bridget. "A New Reading of the Prima Porta Augustus: The Return of the Eagle of Legio V Alaudae." *Latomus* 338 (2012): 277–306.

Campanile, Domitilla. "Pitodoride e la sua famiglia." *SCO* 56 (2010): 57–85.

Carney, Elizabeth D. *Arsinoë of Egypt and Macedon*. New York, 2013.

———. *Olympias: Mother of Alexander the Great*. New York, 2006.

———. " 'What's in a Name?' The Emergence of a Title for Royal Women in the Hellenistic Period." In *Women's History and Ancient History*, edited by Sarah B. Pomeroy, 154–72. Chapel Hill, NC, 1991.

———. "Women and Dunasteia in Caria." *AJPh* 126 (2005): 65–91.

———. *Women and Monarchy in Macedonia*. Norman, OK, 2000.

Chartrand, Mark R. *National Audubon Society Field Guide to the Night Sky*. New York, 1991.

Christofle, Marcel. *Le Tombeau de la Chrétienne*. Paris, 1951.

Clarke, Katherine. "In Search of the Author of Strabo's *Geography*." *JRS* 87 (1997): 92–110.

Clayman, Dee L. *Berenice II and the Golden Age of Ptolemaic Egypt*. New York, 2014.

Cleopatra of Egypt: From History to Myth (ed. Susan Walker and Peter Higgs, London 2001).

Cohen, Boaz. "Concerning Divorce in Jewish and Roman Law." *PAAJR* 21 (1952): 3–34.

Cohen, Getzel M. *The Hellenistic Settlements in Europe, the Islands, and Asia Minor*. Berkeley, CA, 1995.

———. *The Hellenistic Settlements in Syria, the Red Sea Basin, and North Africa*. Berkeley, 2006.

Coltelloni-Trannoy, Michèle. *Le royaume de Maurétanie sous Juba II et Ptolémée*. Paris, 1997.

Corpus Inscriptionum Regni Bosporani. Edited by Vasilii Struve. Moscow, 1965.

Cuchet, Violaine Sebillotte. "The Warrior Queens of Caria (Fifth to Fourth Centuries BCE)." In *Women and War in Antiquity*, edited by J. Fabre-Serris and A. Keith, 228–46. Baltimore, 2015.

Culham, Phyllis. "Did Roman Women Have an Empire?" In *Inventing Ancient Culture*, edited by Mark Golden and Peter Toohey, 192–204. London, 1997.

Cumont, Franz. "Portrait d'une reine parthe trouvé à Susa." *CRAI* 83 (1939): 330–41.

Dahmen, Karsten. "With Rome in Mind? Case Studies in the Coinage of the Client Kings." In *Kings and Principalities in the Roman Near East*, edited by Ted Kaizer and Margherita Facella, 99–112. Stuttgart, 2010.

Dar, Shimon. "The Agrarian Economy in the Herodian Period." In *The World of the Herods*, edited by Nikos Kokkinos, 305–11. Stuttgart, 2007.

de Souza, Philip. *Piracy in the Graeco-Roman World*. Cambridge, 1999.

Dixon, Suzanne. *Cornelia: Mother of the Gracchi*. London, 2007.

Dmitriev, Sviatoslav. "Claudius' Grant of Cilicia to Polemo." *CQ* 53 (2003): 286–91.

Dothan, Moshe. "Ashdod." *NEAEHL*, 93–102.

Draycott, Jane. "Dynastic Politics, Defeat, Decadence and Dining: Cleopatra Selene on the So-Called 'Africa' Dish from the Villa della Pisanella at Boscoreale." *BSR* 80 (2012): 45–64.

———. "The Symbol of Cleopatra Selene: Reading Crocodiles on Coins in the Late Republic and Early Principate." *AClass* 55 (2012): 43–56.

Edmondson, Jonathan. "Introduction: Flavius Josephus and Flavian Rome." In *Flavius Josephus and Flavian Rome*, edited by Jonathan Edmondson et al., 1–33. Oxford, 2005.

Feldman, Louis H. "Prophets and Prophecy in Josephus." *JThS* 41 (1990): 386–422.

Fischler, Susan. "Social Stereotypes and Historical Analysis: The Case of the Imperial Women at Rome." In *Women in Ancient Societies*, edited by Léonie J. Archer et al., 115–33. New York, 1994.

Flory, Marleen B. "Livia and the History of Public Honorific Statues for Women in Rome." *TAPA* 123 (1993): 287–308.

———. "*Sic Exempla Parantur*: Livia's Shrine to Concordia and the Porticus Liviae." *Historia* 33 (1984): 309–30.

Forrer, Leonard. *Portraits of Royal Ladies on Greek Coins*. Chicago, 1969.

Fraser, P. M. *Ptolemaic Alexandria*. Oxford, 1972.

Fraser, P. M., and E. Matthews, eds. *A Lexicon of Greek Personal Names*. Oxford, 1987–.

Gajdukevič, V. F. *Das Bosporanische Reich*. Berlin, 1971.

Golenko, Konstantin V. "The Numismatic Department of the Pushkin State Museum of Fine Arts, Moscow." *NC* 13 (1973): 208–14.

Golenko, Konstantin V., and P. J. Karyszkowski. "The Gold Coinage of King Pharnaces of the Bosporus." *NC* 12 (1972): 25–38.

Goodman, Martin. "Judaea." *CAH* 10, 2d ed., 1996: 737–81.

Goor, Asaph. "The History of the Date through the Ages in the Holy Land." *Economic Botany* 21 (1967): 320–40.

Grant, Michael. *The Jews in the Roman World*. London, 1973.

Grether, Gertrude. "Livia and the Roman Imperial Cult." *AJPh* 67 (1946): 222–52.

Gruen, Erich S. "The Expansion of the Empire under Augustus." *CAH* 10, 2d ed., 1996: 147–97.

Gsell, Stéphane. *Histoire ancienne de l'Afrique du Nord*. Paris, 1914–28.

Günther, Linda-Marie. "Cornelia und Ptolemaios VIII: Zur Historizität des Heiratsantrages (Plut. TG 1.3)." *Historia* 39 (1990): 124–8.

Halfmann, Helmut. *Itinera principum*. Stuttgart, 1986.

Hallett, Judith. "Fulvia." In *Women and War in Antiquity*, edited by J. Fabre-Serris and A. Keith, 247–65. Baltimore, 2015.

Harders, Ann-Cathrin. "An Imperial Family Man: Augustus as Surrogate Father to Marcus Antonius' Children." In *Growing Up Fatherless in Antiquity*, edited by Sabine R. Hübner and David M. Ratzan, 217–40. Cambridge, 2009.

Hardie, Philip. "Virgil's Ptolemaic Relations." *JRS* 96 (2006): 25–41.

Hasluck, F. W. "An Inscribed Basis from Cyzicus." *JHS* 22 (1902): 126–34.

Head, Barclay V. *Historia Numorum*. Oxford, 1911.

Heckel, Waldemar. *Who's Who in the Age of Alexander the Great*. London, 2006.

Heinen, Heinz. "Rome et le Bosphore: Notes épigraphiques." *Cahiers du Centre Gustav Glotz* 7 (1996): 81–101.

———. "Zwei Briefe des bosporanischen Königs Aspurgos (AE 1994, 1538)." *ZPE* 124 (1999): 133–42.

Hind, J. G. F. "Archaeology of the Greeks and Barbarian Peoples around the Black Sea (1982–1993)." *AR* 39 (1992–3): 82–112.

Hoehner, Harold W. *Herod Antipas*. Cambridge, 1972.

Hölbl, Günther. *A History of the Ptolemaic Empire*. Translated by Tina Saavedra. London, 2001.

Hope Simpson, R., and J. F. Lazenby. *The Catalogue of the Ships in Homer's "Iliad."* Oxford, 1970.

Horsley, G. H. R. "Epigraphy as an Ancilla to the Study of the Greek Bible." *Biblica* 79 (1998): 258–67.

Huzar, Eleanor Goltz. *Mark Antony: A Biography*. London, 1978.

Ilan, Tal. "Josephus on Women." In *A Companion to Josephus*, edited by Honora Howell Chapman and Zuleika Rodgers, 210–21. Malden, MA, 2016.

Jameson, Shelagh. "Chronology of the Campaigns of Aelius Gallus and C. Petronius." *JRS* 58 (1968): 71–84.

Jones, A. H. M. *Cities of the Eastern Roman Provinces*, 2d ed. Oxford, 1971.

Jones, Christopher P. "An Inscription Seen by Agathias." *ZPE* 179 (2011): 107–15.

Kearsley, R. A. "Women and Public Life in Imperial Asia Minor: Hellenistic Tradition and Augustan Ideology." *AncWE* 4 (2005): 98–121.

Kirov, Slavtcho. "Gaius Iulius Rhascos." *ZPE* 178 (2011): 215–20.

Kleiner, Diana E. E. "Imperial Women as Patrons of the Arts in the Early Empire." In *I Claudia: Women in Ancient Rome*, edited by Diana E. E. Kleiner and Susan B. Matheson, 28–41. New Haven, CT, 1996.

Kleiner, Diana E. E., and Bridget Buxton. "Pledges of Empire: The Ara Pacis and the Donations of Rome." *AJA* 112 (2008): 57–89.

Kloner, Amos. "Mareshah (Marisa)." *NEAEHL*, 948–57.

Kokkinos, Nikos. *Antonia Augusta: Portrait of a Great Roman Lady*. London. 1992.

———. *The Herodian Dynasty: Origins, Role in Society and Eclipse*. Sheffield, 1998.

———. "Re-Assembling the Inscription of Glaphyra from Athens." *ZPE* 68 (1987): 288–90.

———. "Which Salome Did Aristobulus Marry?" *PEQ* 118 (1996): 33–50.

Konstan, David. "Women, Ethnicity and Power in the Roman Empire." *OP* 1 (2002): 11–23.

Kraemer, Ross S. "Implicating Herodias and Her Daughter in the Death of John the Baptist: A (Christian) Theological Strategy." *JBL* 125 (2006): 321–49.

Leveau, Philippe. *Caesarea de Maurétanie: Une ville romaine et ses campagnes. CÉFR 70*. Paris, 1984).

Levick, Barbara. *Tiberius the Politician*. London, 1976.

MacDonald, David. *An Introduction to the History and Coinage of the Kingdom of the Bosporus*. Lancaster, PA, 2005.

Mackay, Theodora W. "The Major Sanctuaries of Pamphylia and Cilicia." *ANRW* 2.18 (1990): 2045–2129.

Macurdy, Grace. *Hellenistic Queens*. Baltimore, 1932.

———. *Vassal Queens*. Baltimore, 1937.

Magie, David. *Roman Rule in Asia Minor to the End of the Third Century after Christ*. Princeton, NJ, 1950.

Makemson, Maud Worcester. "Note on Eclipses." In *Vassal Queens*, by Grace Macurdy, 60–2. Baltimore, 1937.

Malloch, S. J. V. "The Death of Ptolemy of Mauretania." *Historia* 53 (2004): 38–45.

Mayor, Adrienne. *The Amazons*. Princeton, NJ, 2014.

Mazard, Jean. *Corpus Nummorum Numidiae Mauretaniaeque*. Paris, 1955.

———. "Un denier inedit de Juba II et Cléopâtre-Séléné." *SchwMbll* 31 (1981): 1–2.

McKenzie, Judith. *The Architecture of Alexandria and Egypt*, c. 300 BC–A D 700. New Haven, CT, 2007.

Millar, Fergus. "Emperors, Kings and Subjects: The Politics of Two-Level Sovereignty." *SCI* 15 (1996): 159–73.

———. *A Study of Cassius Dio*. Oxford, 1964.

Munson, Rosaria Vignolo. "Artemisia in Herodotus." *ClAnt* 7 (1988): 91–106.

Musurillo, Herbert. *Acts of the Pagan Martyrs*. Oxford, 1954.

Nawotka, Krzysztof. "Asander of the Bosporos: His Coinage and Chronology." *AJN* 3/4 (1992): 21–48.

———. "The Attitude towards Rome in the Political Propaganda of the Bosporan Monarchs." *Latomus* 48 (1989): 326–38.

Noonan, Thomas S. "The Grain Trade of the Northern Black Sea in Antiquity." *AJPh* 94 (1973): 231–42.

Nourse, Kyra L. "Women and the Early Development of Royal Power in the Hellenistic East." PhD dissertation, University of Pennsylvania, 2002.

Olsen, Barbara A. *Women in Mycenaean Greece.* London, 2014.

Oppolzer, Theodor. *Canon of Eclipses.* Translated by Owen Gingerich. New York, 1962.

Parfenov, V. N. "Dynamis, Agrippa und der Friedensaltar: Zur Militärischen und Politischen Geschichte des Bosporanischen Reiches Nach Asandros." *Historia* 45 (1996): 95–103.

Pelling, Christopher. *Plutarch: Life of Antony.* Cambridge, 1988.

———. "The Triumviral Period." *CAH* 10, 2d ed., 1996: 1–69.

Pollini, John. *From Republic to Empire.* Norman, OK, 2012.

Pomeroy, Sarah B. *Goddesses, Whores, Wives, and Slaves.* New York, 1975.

———. *Women in Hellenistic Egypt from Alexander to Cleopatra.* Detroit, 1984.

Povalahev, Nikolai. "Eine Bauinschrift aus Phanagoreia von 220/1 n. Chr. und ihr historischer Hintergrund: Text und Kommentar." *ZPE* 177 (2011): 141–56.

Prag, A. J. N. W., and R. A. H. Neave. "Who Is the 'Carian Princess'?" In *Hekatomnid Caria and the Ionian Renaissance*, edited by Jacob Isager, 97–109. Odense, 1994.

Primo, Andrea. "The Client Kingdom of Pontus Between Mithradatism and Philoromanism." In *Kingdoms and Principalities in the Roman Near East*, edited by Ted Kaizer and Margherita Facella, 159–79. Stuttgart, 2010.

Quaegebeur, Jan. "Cleopatra VII and the Cults of the Ptolemaic Queens." In *Cleopatra's Egypt: Age of the Ptolemies*, 41–54. Brooklyn, 1988.

Raggi, Andrea. "The First Roman Citizens among Eastern Dynasts and Kings." In *Kingdoms and Principalities in the Roman Near East*, edited by Ted Kaizer and Margherita Facella, 81–97. Stuttgart, 2010.

Rawson, Elizabeth. "Caesar's Heritage: Hellenistic Kings and Their Roman Equals." *JRS* 65 (1975): 148–59.

Regling, Kurt. "Zum Fund von Iubadenaren in Alkasar." *ZfN* 28 (1910): 9–27.

Reinach, Théodore. "Some Pontic Eras." *NC* 2 (1902): 1–10.

Reinhold, Meyer. *From Republic to Principate.* Atlanta, 1988.

———. *Marcus Agrippa: A Biography.* Geneva, NY, 1933.

Richardson, Jr., L. *A New Topographical Dictionary of Ancient Rome.* Baltimore, 1992.

Roller, Duane W. *Ancient Geography: The Discovery of the World in Classical Greece and Rome.* London, 2015.

———. *The Building Program of Herod the Great.* Berkeley, CA, 1998.

———. *Cleopatra: A Biography.* New York, 2010.

———. *The "Geography" of Strabo.* Cambridge, 2014.

———. *A Historical and Topographical Guide to the "Geography" of Strabo.* Cambridge, 2018.

———. *Scholarly Kings: The Writings of Juba II of Mauretania, Archelaos of Kappadokia, Herod the Great and the Emperor Claudius.* Chicago, 2004.

———. *Through the Pillars of Herakles: Greco-Roman Exploration of the Atlantic.* London, 2006.

———. *The World of Juba II and Kleopatra Selene.* London, 2003.

Romer, F. E. "A Case of Client-Kingship." *AJPh* 106 (1985): 75–100.

――――. "A Numismatic Date for the Departure of C. Caesar?" *TAPA* 108 (1978): 187–202.

Rose, Charles Brian. *The Archaeology of Greek and Roman Troy*. Cambridge, 2014.

――――. "The Parthians in Augustan Rome." *AJA* 109 (2005): 425–67.

――――. " 'Princes' and Barbarians on the Ara Pacis." *AJA* 94 (1990): 453–67.

Rosenfeld, Ben-Zion. "The 'Boundary of Gezer' Inscriptions and the History of Gezer at the End of the Second Temple Period." *IEJ* 38 (1988): 235–45.

Rostovtzeff, M. "Queen Dynamis of Bosporus." *JHS* 39 (1919): 88–109.

――――. *The Social and Economic History of the Hellenistic World*. Oxford, 1941.

――――. *The Social and Economic History of the Roman Empire*, 2d ed. Oxford, 1957.

Roth, Jonathan. *The Logistics of the Roman Army at War*. Leiden 1999.

Ruffell, I. A. "Beyond Satire: Horace, Popular Invective and the Segregation of Literature." *JRS* 93 (2003): 35–65.

Saryan, L. A. "An Unpublished Silver Drachm Attributed to Artaxias III (A.D. 18–34) of Armenia." *AJN* 9 (1977): 7–16.

Scheid, John, and Jesper Svenbro, *The Craft of Zeus*. Translated by Carol Volk. Cambridge, MA, 1996.

Schmitt, Hatto H. "Pythodoris" (#1). *RE* 24 (1963): 581–6.

Schneider, Eugenia Equini. *Elaiussa Sebaste: A Port City between East and West*. Istanbul, 2008.

Schwartz, Daniel R. "One Temple and Many Synagogues: On Religion and State in Herodian Judaea and Augustan Rome." In *Herod and Augustus*, edited by David M. Jacobson and Nikos Kokkinos, 385–98. Leiden, 2009.

Sears, Matthew A. "Alexander and Ada Reconsidered." *CP* 109 (2014): 211–21.

Segenni, Simonetta. "Antonia Minore e la 'Domus Augusta.' " *SCO* 44 (1995): 297–331.

Sherk, Robert K. *Rome and the Greek East to the Death of Augustus*. Cambridge, 1984.

Shillam, Matthew William. "Imperial Matchmaker: The Involvement of the Roman Emperor in the Arrangement of Marriages between Client Kings." PhD dissertation, University of New England, 2016.

Sidebotham, Steven E. *Berenike and the Ancient Maritime Spice Route*. Berkeley, CA, 2011.

Stager, Lawrence E. "Askhelon." *NEAEHL*, 103–12.

Stern, Gaius. "Women, Children, and Senators on the Ara Pacis Augustae: A Study of Augustus' Vision of a New World." PhD dissertation, University of California–Berkeley, 2006.

Stern, Menahem. "The Reign of Herod." In *The World History of the Jewish People*, 1st ser., vol. 7: *The Herodian Period*, edited by Michael Avi-Yonah, 71–123. New Brunswick, NJ, 1975.

Stewart, Andrew. *Greek Sculpture: An Exploration*. New Haven, CT, 1990.

Strugnell, Emma. "Thea Musa, Roman Queen of Parthia." *IA* 43 (2008): 275–98.

Sullivan, Richard D. "Dynasts in Pontus." *ANRW* 2.7 (1980): 913–30.

――――. "The Dynasty of Cappadocia." *ANRW* 2.7 (1980): 1125–68.

――――. "The Dynasty of Commagene." *ANRW* 2.8 (1977): 732–98.

――――. "The Dynasty of Judaea in the First Century." *ANRW* 2.7 (1977): 296–354.

------. "King Marcus Antonius Polemo." *NC* 19 (1979): 6–20.

------. *Near Eastern Royalty and Rome, 100–30 BC.* Toronto, 1990.

------. "Papyri Reflecting the Eastern Dynastic Network." *ANRW* 2.8 (1977): 908–39.

------. "Priesthoods of the Eastern Dynastic Aristocracy." In *Studien zur Religion und Kultur Kleinasiens*, edited by S. Şahin et al., 914–39. Leiden, 1978.

------. "Thrace in the Eastern Dynastic Network." *ANRW* 2.7 (1979): 186–211.

Syme, Ronald. *Anatolica: Studies in Strabo.* Edited by Anthony Birley, Oxford, 1995.

------. *The Roman Revolution.* Oxford, 1939.

Tarn, W. W. "Alexander Helios and the Golden Age." *JRS* 22 (1932): 135–60.

Thonemann, Peter J. *The Maeander Valley.* Cambridge, 2011.

------. "Polemo, Son of Polemo (Dio, 59.12.2)." *EA* 37 (2004): 144–50.

Toher, Mark. "Herod, Augustus, and Nikolaos of Damascus." In *Herod and Augustus*, edited by David M. Jacobson and Nikos Kokkinos, 65–81. Leiden, 2009.

------. "Herod's Last Days." *HSCP* 106 (2011): 209–28.

Tomlinson, R. A. *Epidauros.* Austin, TX, 1983.

Tondriau, J. "La tryphè: Philosophie royale Ptolémaïque." *RÉA* 50 (1948): 49–54.

Toynbee, J. M. C. *Roman Historical Portraits.* London, 1978.

Treggiari, Susan. *Roman Marriage: Iusti Coniuges from the Time of Cicero to the Time of Ulpian.* Oxford, 1991.

Trofimova, Anna A., ed. *Greeks on the Black Sea: Ancient Art from the Hermitage.* Los Angeles, 2007.

------. "The Sculpted Portrait in the Bosporus." In *Greeks on the Black Sea: Ancient Art from the Hermitage*, edited by Anna A. Trofimova, 46–55. Los Angeles, 2007.

Tsetskhladze, Gocha R. "A Survey of the Major Urban Settlements in the Kimmerian Bosporos (with a Discussion of Their Status as *Poleis*)." In *Yet More Studies in the Ancient Greek Polis*, edited by Thomas Heine Nielsen, 39–81. Stuttgart, 1997.

Ventris, Michael, and John Chadwick. *Documents in Mycenaean Greek.* Cambridge, 1953.

Vinogradov, Yu. G. "Greek Epigraphy of the North Black Sea Coast, the Caucasus and Central Asia (1985–1990)." *Ancient Civilizations from Scythia to Siberia* 1 (1994): 63–74.

Visconti, Amedeo. "Artemisia di Alicarnasso ovvero il potere visibile." In *Il potere invisibile: Figure del femminile tra mito e storia*, edited by Simona Marino et al., 63–75. Naples, 2002.

Vollenweider, Marie-Louise. *Die Steinschneidekunst und Ihre Künstler in spätrepublikanischer und Augusteischer Zeit.* Baden-Baden, 1966.

Wacholder, Ben Zion. *Nicolaus of Damascus.* Berkeley, CA, 1962.

Walker, Susan, and Peter Higgs, eds. *Cleopatra of Egypt: From History to Myth.* London, 2001.

Wehrli, Claude. "Phila, fille d'Antipater et épouse de Démétrius, roi des macédoniens." *Historia* 13 (1964): 140–6.

Welch, Kathryn E. "Antony, Fulvia, and the Ghost of Claudius in 47 B. C." *G&R* 42 (1995): 182–201.

Wheeler, Everett. "Roman Fleets in the Black Sea: Mysteries of the 'Classis Pontica.'" *AClass* 55 (2012): 119–54.

Whitehorne, John. *Cleopatras*. London, 1994.

———. "The Supposed Co-Regency of Cleopatra Tryphaena and Berenice IV (58–55 BC)." In *Akten des 21. Internationalen Papyrorologenkongresses, Berlin 1995*, edited by Bärbel Kramer et al., 1009–13. Stuttgart, 1997.

Whittaker, C. R. "Roman Africa: Augustus to Vespasian." *CAH* 10, 2d ed., 1996: 586–618.

Wilhelm, Adolf. "Zu Inschriften Aus Kleinasien." In *Anatolian Studies Presented to Sir William Mitchell Ramsay*, edited by W. H. Buckler and W. M. Calder, 415–39. Manchester, 1923.

Wood, Susan E. Imperial Women: A Study in Public Images, 40 BC–AD 68. Leiden 2000.

Wyke, Maria. "Augustan Cleopatras: Female Power and Poetic Authority." In *Roman Poetry and Propaganda in the Age of the Augustus*, edited by A. Powell, 98–140. Bristol, 1997.

Zachos, Konstantinos I. "The *Tropaeum* of the Sea Battle of Actium at Nikopolis: Interim Report." *JRA* 16 (2003): 65–92.

Zograf, A. N. *Ancient Coinage*. Translated by H. Bartlett Wells. BAR Supplementary Series 33. Oxford, 1977.

List of Passages Cited

Italicized numbers are citations in ancient sources; romanized numbers are pages in this volume.

Greek and Latin Literary Sources

Acts of the Pagan Martyrs, Chrestomathia 14.3.11, 165n80
Acts of Paul and Thekla, 170n86
Aelian, *Historical Miscellany 7.1*, 172n24
Aeschylus:
  Agamemnon 84, 155n2
  Libation Bearers 733, 157n54; *909*, 166n34
  Persians 623, 155n2; *878*, 169n50
  Promethus Bound 732–4, 165n2
Agatharchides *F67*, 165n11
Ammianus Marcellinus *22.15.8*, 159n45, 160n64
Appian:
  Civil War 2.91, 160n21; *2.102*, 174n58, 174n65; *4.75*, 170n81; *5.7*, 161n9, 161n13, 161n16; *5.10–11*, 158n2; *5.32–49*, 173n27; *5.75*, 169n44
  Mithridateios 30–6, 161n5; *110–13*, 165n12; *113*, 165n9; *114*, 161n6; *120*, 166n15
  Syriaka 5, 157n57
Archilochos *F5*, 170n75
Aristotle, *Politics 2.6.5–11*, 157n37; *2.6.6*, 156n13; *5.9.6*, 156n13
Arrian, *Anabasis 1.23.7–8*, 156n20; *7.4.5*, 157n33
Athenaios *5.202d*, 157n44; *14.652ab*, 165n72
Augustus, *Res gestae 27*, 158n12; *29*, 171n9; *32*, 172n22

de bello Africo 91–7, 159n28
de bello Alexandrino 66, 161n8

Catullus *66*, 157n52
Cicero:
    Brutus 211, 172n21, 172n22
    pro Flacco 52, 168n11
    de lege agraria 2.51, 158n9
    Letters to Atticus #226, 172n10; *#229–31*, 172n10; *#393*, 172n12; *#420*, 168n23
    Letters to Friends 2.18, 169n27
    Philippics 2.3, 168n23; *2.85*, 172n9; *3.17*, 168n23; *13.23*, 168n23
    pro Rabiro Postumo 6, 158n65
    Republic 6.9, 159n31

Demosthenes:
    Against Leptines 30–1, 166n26
    For the Liberty of the Rhodians 11–12, 156n25; *23*, 156n25
Dio:
    Book 39: 12, 158n65; *57–8*, 158n67
    Book 42: 46–7, 165n13
    Book 43: 27.1, 172n10
    Book 48: 34.3, 173n34; *44*, 173n34
    Book 49: 32, 158n8, 163n19; *32.3*, 161n3, 161n16; *32.5*, 158n7; *33.1–2*, 169n45; *38.1*, 174n58;
        41, 158n8; *43.7*, 159n34; *44*, 158n14; *44.2*, 169n25
    Book 50: 6, 158n5; *11.3*, 159n34; *30.2*, 173n39
    Book 51: 1.3, 159n25; *13*, 174n54; *15.6*, 159n37; *19.6*, 158n16; *20*, 174n59; *21.8*, 158n19;
        22.3, 174n65
    Book 53: 22.5, 159n36; *30*, 171n12; *33.1–2*, 171n11
    Book 54: 8.1–2, 171n8; *24.4–6*, 166n20, 166n30; *24.6*, 166n32, 35.4–5, 173n44
    Book 55: 2.5, 174n58; *10–12*, 161n85
    Book 57: 17.3–7, 170n56; *17.4*, 161n85, 169n55
    Book 59: 3.1–6, 174n53; *12.2*, 166n43, 168n14, 171n91; *25.1*, 160n71, 160n76
    Book 65: 14, 173n52
Diodoros:
    Book 2: 45, 156n13
    Book 3: 34.7–8, 165n11
    Book 12: 31, 165n4
    Book 14: 98.3, 156n20
    Book 16: 36.2, 156n20
    Book 17: 77.1–3, 156n15
    Book 19: 59, 156n31

Book 20: 53, 156n30; 109.7, 157n33

Book 34(35): 25, 173n25

Dionysios of Halikarnassos, *Roman Archaeology* 2.45–6, 172n17; 4.84–5, 172n4; 10.58, 158n20

Dioskourides 3.82, 160n62

Ennius, *Annals* 371, 172n15

Euripides, *Medea* 17, 164n57

Frontinus, *de aquis* 1.7, 172n8

Galen:

On the Combining of Drugs According to Place 1, 160n62

On the Composition of Medicines 2.7, 165n81

Greek Anthology:

Book 6: 244, 173n46; 435, 173n46

Book 7: 633, 160n83; 645, 159n40

Book 9: 58, 156n23; 235, 159n41; 752, 160n60

Book 16: 75, 170n77

Herodotos:

Book 1: 11, 155n12; 72, 161n2; 184, 155n12; 185–7, 155n12; 205, 155n12

Book 2: 157, 164n59

Book 5: 3–10, 170n74

Book 7: 99, 156n18; 147, 169n50

Book 8: 68, 156n18; 85, 168n18; 87, 156n18; 101, 156n18

Book 9: 109–12, 175n13

Homer:

Iliad:

Book 1: 350, 169n50

Book 2: 712, 162n23

Book 3: 189, 156n14

Book 6: 186, 156n14

Book 8: 294, 166n16

Book 9: 556, 157n54

Book 13: 787, 166n16

Odyssey:

Book 1: 328–35, 155n6

Book 2: 91–109, 155n8

Book 4: 697, 155n4; 770, 155n4

Book 6: 115, 155n4

Book 7: 66–74, 157n42; 241, 155n4

Book 11: 258, 155n4; 345, 155n4

Book 13: 59, 155n4

Book 15: 16–19, 155n6

Book 16: 332, 155n4; 337, 155n4

Book 17: 37, 155n4; 468, 155n4; 513, 155n4; 583, 155n4

Book 18: 314, 155n9; 351, 155n9

Book 19: 137–9, 155n9; 509–34, 155n8; 571–4, 155n10

Book 21: 68–79, 155n10; 275, 155n4

Book 23: 149, 155n4

Book 24: 192–202, 155n81

Horace:

Epistles 2.2.184, 165n71

Odes 1.37, 159n50; 1.37.21, 172n13

Josephus:

Jewish Antiquities:

Book 9: 122–4, 159n43

Book 12: 265, 162n1

Book 13: 257–8, 163n6; 405–17, 165n77

Book 14: 121, 163n8; 127–39, 163n9; 277–84, 163n9; 353–4, 163n12

Book 15: 53–6, 163n4; 62–87, 163n15; 174, 174n3; 184, 163n10; 223–39, 163n21; 247–52, 163n23; 253–66, 163n18; 259–66, 163n24; 260–6, 163n20; 342–3, 162n24, 172n2; 343, 163n33; 360, 163n33

Book 16: 6, 162n25, 172n2; 11, 162n25, 163n29; 16–21, 166n32; 131, 162n21; 193, 162n27; 193–4, 164n54; 201–19, 164n44; 220–4, 163n34; 225, 164n37; 227, 163n30; 256, 164n45; 261–70, 162n28; 271–5, 163n36; 325–34, 162n28; 351–3, 164n41; 356–94, 164n48

Book 17: 7–10, 164n42; 9, 163n14; 10–11, 162n29; 11–12, 162n29; 36–53, 164n51; 54–7, 164n41; 58–67, 164n50; 92, 163n25; 93, 164n46; 133–47, 164n51; 147, 164n55; 175, 164n52; 182–7, 164n51; 188, 174n5; 189, 164n55; 190, 164n40; 193–4, 164n54; 220–49, 164n63; 299–323, 164n63; 317, 162n39; 317–20, 174n5; 339–44, 164n65; 342–4, 162n40; 349–53, 162n42

Book 18: 29–31, 165n73; 31, 164n40; 40–3, 171n7; 43–52, 173n23; 118–19, 174n1; 136–7, 174n9, 175n15; 139–40, 162n30; 139–41, 162n32; 143, 173n51; 143–5, 164n49; 156, 164n49, 173n51; 158, 165n76; 163, 165n76; 164–7, 173n51; 165, 163n29, 164n49; 180, 173n48; 181–2, 173n52, 174n2; 252, 174n6

Book 20: 145–7, 171n91; 158, 175n15; 267, 174n2

Jewish War:

Book 1: 36, 162n1; 181, 163n8; 187–94, 163n9; 226, 163n9; 264, 163n12; 399–400, 163n25; 427, 162n35; 437, 163n4; 439, 163n17; 476, 162n27; 486, 163n18; 486–7,

164n44; *487*, 164n37; *498*, 164n45; *499–501*, 162n28; *507*, 161n18; *534–5*, 164n45; *536–51*, 164n48; *552*, 174n7; *552–3*, 162n29, 163n29, 163n30; *566*, 163n14, 163n30, 164n37, 164n42; *577*, 164n41; *578–83*, 164n50; *641–3*, 164n46; *646*, 164n55; *660*, 164n52; *661–4*, 164n51; *664*, 174n5; *666*, 164n54

    Book 2: *14–38*, 164n63; *80–100*, 164n63; *93*, 162n39; *111–13*, 164n65; *114–16*, 162n42; *167–8*, 165n73; *183*, 174n6

  Life *119*, 171n91

Juba II of Mauretania (Roller, *Scholarly Kings*):

  On Arabia F2, 160n69

  Libyka F2, 160n68; F7, 160n70; F7–11, 160n69; F10, 160n70; F13, 160n69; F15, 160n69; F17, 160n69; F19, 160n69; F25, 160n68; F27, 160n68; F31, 160n68; F35, 160n69

  Roman Archaeology F10, 160n68

Justin, *Epitome* 2.12.23–4, 156n19; 18.4–6, 159n47; 26.3, 157n51; 39.3.4–12, 170n73

Juvenal 6.153–60, 171n91

Kallimachos, *Aitia* F110, 157n52

Livy:

  Book 1: *9–13*, 172n17; *59–60*, 172n4

  Book 2: 8.2, 172n4; 21.5, 173n32

  Book 3: 35.11, 158n20

  Book 5: 25.9, 172n18; 50.7, 172n19

  Book 35: 13.4, 157n54

  Book 37: 53.20–2, 159n31

  Book 39: 43.3–4, 175n14

  F54, 158n19

  Summary 70, 158n9; 100, 158n10; 132, 158n7; 142, 173n47

Lucan, *Pharsalia* 8.404–9, 172n17

Lucian, *Makrobioi* 17, 166n22, 166n30

Martial *11.20*, 161n12

Minucius Felix, *Octavius* 31.3, 172n30

Ovid:

  Consolatio ad Liviam 356, 173n36

  Epistulae ex Ponto 2.9, 170n78; 4.9.105–8, 174n62

  Metamorphoses 15.830–1, 167n48

  Tristia 1.6.25, 173n36; 2.161–2, 174n62

Pausanias, *1.6.8*, 157n41; *1.7.1*, 157n41; *1.11.5*, 157n42; *1.20.5*, 161n5; *2.27.6*, 170n79; *3.8.1*, 157n43; *3.11.3*, 156n19

Philo:

    Questions and Answers: Genesis 4.56–8, 172n19

    Special Laws 3.13–14, 172n20

Philostratos:

    Life of Apollonios 1.12, 170n57

    Lives of the Sophists 5, 159n40

Pindar, *Pythian* 11.17, 157n54

Plautus:

    Casina 585, 172n5

    Mostellaria 190, 172n5

Pliny, *Natural History*:

    Book 5: *2–5*, 157n35; *16*, 160n61, 160n71; *20–1*, 157n35; *22*, 159n32; *68*, 164n60, 165n75

    Book 6: *141*, 161n85; *168*, 157n47

    Book 12: *56*, 161n85

    Book 13: *45*, 165n72

    Book 25: *77*, 171n12; *77–8*, 160n61

    Book 29: *6*, 171n12

    Book 31: *41–2*, 172n8

    Book 32: *10*, 161n85

    Book 34: *31*, 173n24

Plutarch:

    Alexander 10, 156n22; 46.1–2, 156n15

    Antonius 3, 158n68, 161n7; *9.2*, 168n24; *10.3*, 156n13, 173n28; *25–6*, 158n1; *27.4*, 157n55; *28–30*, 158n2; *30.3*, 161n15; *31*, 173n38; *36*, 158n3, 158n8; *42.4*, 158n11; *53–5*, 173n38; *54*, 158n8; *54.6*, 157n46; *56.1*, 158n11; *57*, 173n39; *61.2*, 169n46; *83.4*, 174n54; *87*, 159n37, 168n22, 169n28, 173n41, 174n57; *87.1*, 158n57

    Crassus 32.5, 171n6

    Demetrios 14, 156n30; *18*, 156n30; *27–32*, 156n30; *45*, 156n30

    Gaius Gracchus 4, 173n25; *13.2*, 173n25; *19.2*, 172n23

    Marcus Cato 8.7–8, 172n5

    Pompeius 29, 158n10; *49*, 158n65

    Pyrrhos 4.4, 157n42

    Sulla 22–4, 161n5

    Symposium 8.1, 165n72

    Tiberius Gracchus 1.4, 159n31, 172n3

Polyainos 8.54, 156n16

Polybios *18.10.7*, 172n6; *24.6*, 157n58; *25.2*, 169n52; *36.16*, 159n31

Pomponius Mela *1.30*, 159n32; *1.31*, 161n90

Poseidippos of Pella, *Hippika* 87–8, 157n43

Ptolemy, *Geographical Guide* 4.7.6, 157n45

Quintilian, *Institutes 1.1.6*, 172n22

Seneca the Elder, *Controversiae 2.4.8*, 168n12
Stephanos of Byzantion, "Pantikapaion," 165n3
Strabo, *Geography*:
  Book 2: 3.4, 158n63, 175n11
  Book 7: 1.3, 173n47; *3.18*, 165n10, 168n68; *4.4*, 165n5, 165n8; *4.6*, 166n25
  Book 8: 4.3, 159n34
  Book 10: 2.17, 170n75
  Book 11: 2.3, 166n39; *2.11*, 165n9, 165n12, 166n25, 166n39, 169n48; *2.12*, 165n7; *2.16*, 169n38; *2.18*, 169n34; *5.4*, 156n14, 156n15; *5.8*, 165n9
  Book 12: 1.4, 170n61; *2.1–11*, 169n37; *2.6*, 161n10; *2.8*, 160n4; *3.1–2*, 161n1; *3.10*, 157n33; *3.20*, 170n75; *3.29*, 166n36, 169n33, 169n35, 169n42, 169n49, 169n54, 169n66, 174n66; *3.34*, 158n67, 161n6; *8.16*, 169n44, 169n46
  Book 13: 4.3, 166n15
  Book 14: 1.42, 168n7, 168n9, 169n31, 169n39; *1.43*, 168n3; *1.48*, 168n3; *2.16*, 156n23; *2.17*, 156n20; *2.24*, 169n43; *5.6*, 162n21, 162n22; *5.10*, 171n1
  Book 15: 4.21–4, 163n32
  Book 16: 2.24, 171n13; *2.46*, 162n40, 164n49, 165n67, 165n79; *4.5*, 157n47; *4.7*, 157n45; *4.10*, 157n48; *4.24*, 164n41
  Book 17: 1.11, 158n67; *1.13*, 168n10; *3.7*, 160n71; *3.9*, 160n74; *3.12*, 159n49, 160n71; *3.25*, 160n71
Suda, "Iobas," 159n37
Suetonius:
  Augustus 18.2, 159n25; *26.3*, 159n37; *48*, 158n22; *59*, 171n12; *64.2*, 172n20
  Claudius 41.1, 173n48
  Divine Julius 37, 166n14; *52*, 172n11
  Gaius Caligula 5, 173n50; *15.2*, 174n53; *23*, 174n53; *26.1*, 160n71
  Nero 5, 161n85; *18*, 171n93
  Tiberius 1.1, 173n32; *5*, 173n32; *8*, 170n60; *12*, 161n85; *50.3*, 173n36

Tacitus
  Annals
    Book 2: 4, 161n85; *42*, 161n3, 161n85, 170n56; *43*, 168n20, 170n58; *56*, 170n61, 170n63; *56–7*, 173n49; *64*, 170n75; *65–7*, 170n80; *69–75*, 173n50
    Book 3: 2–5, 173n50
    Book 4: 1.5, 160n74; *23*, 160n71, 160n74; *26*, 160n77; *37*, 174n59
    Book 5: 1, 173n30, 173n37
    Book 6: 40, 162n30; *41*, 162n22
    Book 13: 7, 175n15
    Book 14: 18, 158n9; *26*, 162n31

Book 15: 1–6, 162n31

Dialogue on Oratory 28.5, 172n21

Histories 2.81, 171n91; 3.47, 171n93; 5.9, 160n81

Terence, *Eunuch* 37, 172n15

Tertullian, *Apology* 9.16, 172n20

Theokritos 17.34–52, 157n44; 17.121–5, 157n44

Timaios (*FGrHist* #565) F82, 159n46

Valerius Maximus 3.8.6, 173n26; 4.3.3, 173n48; 5.5.3, 173n47

Velleius 2.91.1, 171n8; 2.101–2, 161n85; 2.129, 170n80

Vergil, *Aeneid* 1.286–8, 167n48; 1.697–756, 159n44; 7.706–9, 173n31; 8.688, 159n50

Vitruvius 2.8.14–15, 156n25

Xenophon:

Anabasis 7.8.8–20, 156n17

Hellenika 3.1.10–28, 156n16

Oikonomikos 7.32–4, 156n29; 9.15, 156n29

Biblical Sources

Genesis 4.56–8, 172n19; *19:31–8*, 172n18

Deuteronomy 25:5, 162n41

1 Kings *16:31*, 159n43

2 Kings *9:30–7*, 159n43

Leviticus *18:16*, 162n41; *20:17*, 172n19; *20:21*, 162n41

Luke *19:12–27*, 164n66

1 Maccabees *11:28*, 164n56

Matthew *14:3–12*, 174n1

Mark 6:17–29, 174n1; *15.40*, 174n9; *16.1*, 174n9

Epigraphical Texts

Bernand, *Les Inscriptions 142*, 167n48

CIL 6.9046, 161n92; 6.10110, 161n92; 6.31610, 173n24; 6.35602, 161n92; 8.9344, 160n58

CIRB 31, 167n55; 38, 167n47; 978, 167n49; 979, 167n54; 1046, 167n47

IG 3.1.1309, 160n80

IGRR 1.879, 166n29, 167n45; 1.905, 165n12; 4.206, 173n49

OGIS *103–23*, 168n17; *359*, 162n35; *361*, 161n17; *363*, 162n35; *376*, 169n40; *377*, 168n16, 170n65

SEG *39.695*, 169n40; *40.1170*, 170n71; *44.658*, 167n49; *45.1022*, 167n57; *57.697*, 167n57; *59.860*, 167n57

SIG *741*, 168n5; *779*, 170n83; *798*, 170n85

Papyri

OxyPap *4809*, 160n65

Index

Aba of Olbe, 121–3, 170n67

Achaian Federation, 22

Actium, locality in Greece, 30, 32, 62, 66, 109, 122

Ada, Hekatomnid ruler, 14–15, 18, 156n26

Adramyttion, district in Greece, 12

Aegean Sea, 79, 100

Aelius Gallus, Roman prefect, 67–8

Africa, 34–6, 38, 43, 45; Cleopatra Selene's claim to, 37, 48; symbols of, 36, 40

Agamemnon, Greek hero, 9

Agrippa I, Judaean king, 67

Agrippa II, Judaean king, 67, 119

Agrippa, son of Salome, 152

Agrippa, M. Vipsanius, Roman magistrate, 84, 86–8, 92–3, 96

Agrippa, as toponym, 93

Agrippia, Bosporan city, 92–3

Agrippias, Levantine city, 93

Aias, Greek hero, 121

Aias, priest-king of Olbe, 122

Aietes, Colchian ruler, 79

Aigialeia, wife of Diomedes, 8

Aigisthos, Greek hero, 8

el-'Ain, Ras, Israeli locality, 62

Aischinos Antonianus, Mauretanian freedman, 41

Alexander the Great, 11, 14–18, 21, 28, 49, 110, 116; successors of, 15–16, 19, 31–2, 130

Alexander IV, son of Alexander the Great, 18

Alexander Helios, 26, 30–3, 104, 169n26

Alexander Jannaios, 59, 77

Alexander of Cilicia, 55, 171n89

Alexander, son of Glaphyra, 54

Alexander, son of Herod the Great, 53–4, 56, 70–1, 111, 131

Alexandra, Hasmonean princess, 63–7, 77

Alexandra Salome, Hasmonean queen, 62, 77

Alexandria, city in Egypt, 17, 22, 27, 30, 81–2, 117, 142–3, 146; buildings in, 17, 29, 44; Julius Caesar and, 61; and Mauretanian Caesarea, 40–3

Alexandria, Donations of, 29, 65

Alexandrians, 23

Alexas, husband of Salome, 70, 72, 74–5

Algeria, 34, 37–8, 47, 159n32

Alkasar, site in Morocco, 47, 161n89

allied monarchs, 28, 35, 38, 52–5, 82, 87, 109, 111, 113; and Livia, 137, 144; obligations of, 44, 91, 93, 96, 107. *See also individual rulers*

Amastris, city on Black Sea coast, 16–17

Amastris, queen, 16–17

Amazons, 10–11

Ambibulus, M., prefect of Judaea, 76

Amenephtes, Egyptian pharoah, 126

Ammon, Egyptian god, 40

Ampsaga, river in northwest Africa, 34–5

Amynandros, king of Athamania, 132

Anahita, Persian goddess, 125

Anatolia, 11–13, 17, 99–100, 105, 114, 122. *See also* Asia Minor

Ancus Marcius, Roman king, 132

Anthedon, Judaean city, 93

Antigone, daughter of Berenike I, 19

Antigonos I, Macedonian king, 16
Antioch, city in Syria, 116, 142, 144
Antiochos III, Seleukid king, 21–2, 135
Antiochos VIII, Seleukid king, 116, 125
Antiochos IX, Seleukid king, 116
Antipas, tetrarch of Galilee and Peraia, 73–5, 149–52, 174n1
Antipatris, Judaean city, 62
Antipatros, Macedonian leader, 16, 18–19
Antipatros of Askalon, 61–3
Antipatros, son of Herod the Great, 67, 71–2
Antipatros, son of Salome, 67, 74
Antonia the Elder, daughter of M. Antonius, 139
Antonia the Younger, daughter of M. Antonius, 71, 78, 117, 129, 137, 139–42, 145, 148; and Cleopatra Selene, 41, 48
Antonia, mother of Pythodoris, 102–5, 114
Antonia Tryphaina, daughter of Pythodoris, 113, 115–19, 131
Antonii family, 31, 42, 105
Antonius, Gaius, Roman magistrate, 104
Antonius, Lucius, Roman magistrate, 104, 169n27
Antonius, Marcus, triumvir, 25, 30, 34, 45, 54, 66, 116, 120, 142; and Aba of Olbe, 122–3, 171n3; and Cappadocia, 49–50; children of, 27–32, 39, 41, 71, 103–4, 117, 129, 137, 141–2; and Cleopatra VII, 24, 27, 37, 63–5, 95, 122, 132, 136; death of, 30, 140, 142; and Donations of Alexandria, 29; and elder Glaphyra, 50–2; and Fulvia, 51, 136; and Herod the Great, 59, 62–5; and Octavia, 31, 139–40, 143; and Parthia, 124; and Pontos, 87; and Pythodoris, 102, 108–9, 111; Roman attitudes toward, 38, 88, 146
Antonius Euphorbos, physician, 42
Antonius Hybrida, C., Roman magistrate, 104
Antonius Merenda, T., Roman magistrate, 158n20
Antonius Musa, physician, 42, 124
Antonius Polemo, M., priest-king at Olbe, 114
Antony, Mark. See Antonius, Marcus

Aphrodite, Greek divinity, 19–20, 85, 93, 125
Appius Clausus, early Roman, 137
el-'Aqaba, Tell, site in Judaean hills, 62
Arabia, 44, 46, 55, 67
Archaianax, dynast of Pantikapaion, 81
Archelais, region in Jordan valley, 76
Archelaos (I), commander of Mithradates VI, 50
Archelaos (II), priest at Komana, 24, 50
Archelaos (III), priest at Komana, 50–1
Archelaos (IV) of Cappadocia, 38, 50–4, 109, 162n21; death of, 108, 111–14, 145; and Juba II, 46, 55–6; and Pythodoris, 56–7, 105–6, 111–12, 117, 145; summons to Rome of, 105, 107–8, 112–13
Archelaos (V), king of Rough Cilicia, 53
Archelaos, son of Herod the Great, 56, 72–6, 148, 162n37, 164n66
Archidamos II of Sparta, 19
Archiereia, Archiereus, 123
Aretas IV of Nabataea, 61
Arete, Phaiakian queen, 8, 19
Argonauts, 79, 106–7, 110
Ariarathes, kings so named, 49–50
Aristoboulos I, Hasmonean king, 59
Aristoboulos III, Hasmonean claimant, 59, 63
Aristoboulos, husband of younger Salome, 152
Aristoboulos, son of Herod the Great, 53–4, 67, 70–1, 131, 151
Aristoboulos, son of younger Salome, 152
Armenia, Armenians, 53–4, 89, 110, 112–14, 142
Armenia, Lesser, 30, 109–10, 152
Arsacids, Parthian royal line, 126
Arsinoë, mythological figure, 21
Arsinoë II, Ptolemaic queen, 19–21
Arsinoë IV, Ptolemaic princess, 24
art, 9, 18, 27, 40, 42, 48, 134, 149. *See also* sculpture
Artaxias I, Armenian king, 113
Artaxias III Germanicus, Armenian king, 113
Artaynte, Persian princess, 152
Artemis, Greek goddess, 100
Artemisia (I) of Halikarnassos, 13–14

Artemisia (II) of Halikarnassos, 14, 24, 156n25
Asandrochos, Bosporan king, 86
Asandros, Bosporan king, 82–9, 93, 94, 96, 166n17
Ascanius, king of the Latins, 132
Ashdod, Israeli city, 73
Asia, 79, 81, 91; Central, 85; Roman province of, 54, 104, 118
Asia Minor, 88–9, 99–100, 108–10, 114, 121–2, 144, 166n16; Antonius in, 51, 103; northern, 82, 87, southern, 49. *See also* Anatolia
Asiarch, title of Asian magistrate, 101
Asinius Pollio, Roman historian, 131
Askalon, Levantine city, 61–2, 66, 73–6, 78
Aspourgianians, peoples north of Black Sea, 88–9, 95, 106, 109
Aspourgos, Pontic king, 86, 89–90, 95, 166n24
Assyrians, 27, 49, 107, 127
Athamania, district of Greece, 132
Athens, Greek city, 45, 55, 57–8, 81, 117, 145
Atlantic Ocean, 34–5, 43, 56
Atossa, Persian queen, 11
Augustus, Roman emperor, 15, 42–3, 57–8, 76, 91, 145–6; and Aba of Olbe, 121–2; and Archelaos of Cappadocia, 54, 56, 112–13; and Bosporan kingdom, 83–95; cities named after, 38, 52–3, 107–8; and Cleopatra Selene, 33–5; eastern trip of, 69, 144; family of, 32, 45–6, 55, 69, 91, 129, 135–8; and Herodians, 55–6, 68–75, 131, 150; and Juba II, 34–5, 56–7; and Parthians, 123–4, 127; and Pontic kingdom, 108–16, 167n44; and royal children, 32; and Thracian kingdom, 117. *See also* List of Passages; Octavian
Ayaş, Turkish city, 52
Aydin, Turkish city, 101
Azotos, Judaean city, 73
Azov, Sea of, 79, 85

Baba, personal name, 163n20
Baba, Sons of, 65–7
Bakchios, project manager at Kyzikos, 118
basileia, 7–10, 16–17
basileus, 7–8, 15–16

basilissa, 7, 22, 39, 90, 108, 118–19, 125, 152; as honorific, 51–2, 119; origins of term, 15–17
Batanaea, district of southern Levant, 151
el-Beiyudat, Khirbet, locality in Jordan valley, 76
Berenike I of Judaea, 53, 67, 70–1, 74–5, 131, 142, 145, 151
Berenike I, Ptolemaic queen, 18–21, 157n43
Berenike II of Judaea, 119–20
Berenike II, Ptolemaic queen, 20–1
Berenike IV, Ptolemaic queen, 23–4, 50, 116
Berenike, locality on Red Sea, 19
Berenike, origins of name, 21
Berenike Trogodytike, on Red Sea, 19–20
Berenikeion, in Alexandria, 19
Berytos, Phoenician city, 71, 119
Black Sea, 49, 56, 79, 85, 87, 93, 106–12; coasts of, 16, 79, 81–2, 85, 94, 99–100, 105, 108–12, 116; origin of name, 169n50
Bocchus II of Mauretania, 34–5, 48
Bogudes II of Mauretania, 34–5
Boscoreale, Roman villa, 40, 42
Bosporos, kingdom of, 79–97, 111, 119, 167n63; and Livia, 90–3, 144; and Polemon, 87–9, 95, 109. *See also* Dynamis
Bosporos, straits so called, 79, 81, 94, 108
Britannicus, son of Claudius, 90
Bronze Age, 7, 73
Brutus, Marcus, tyrannicide, 118

Cádiz, Spanish city, 152
Caesarea in Mauretania, 36–8, 40, 43–4, 47–8
Caesarea of Herod the Great, 38, 69
Caesarea, places so named, 38, 93
Caligula, Gaius, emperor, 45, 118–19, 138, 142, 146, 150
Canidius Crassus, P., Roman official, 30
Cappadocia, Anatolian district, 38, 46, 49–53, 57, 69–71, 84, 106–7, 109–13
Carthage, Punic city, 34, 36–7
Catilius, Roman poet, 90, 167n48
Cato, M. Porcius, the Elder, Roman political leader, 132–3
Chairemon of Nysa, 100–2, 168n8

Chaldaians, ethnic group in Pontos, 106
Cherchel, city in Algeria, 37–8, 41
Chersonesos, city on northern Black Sea,
    85–6, 93
Christian Woman, Tomb of the, 47
Christians, 78, 118, 126, 152
Cicero, M. Tullius, Roman political
    leader, 104. *See also* List of Passages
Cilicia, Anatolian district, 52, 55, 108, 112,
    122–3, 171n89; Rough, 53, 121
Claudius, Roman emperor, 41, 45, 78, 139,
    141, 146, 170n86
Claudius Marcellus, C., husband of
    Octavia, 138
Claudius Nero, Ti., husband of
    Livia, 137
Clausus the Sabine, 137
Clausus (Claudius), Appius, 137
Cleopatra I, 21–2, 28, 103
Cleopatra II, 22–3, 125
Cleopatra III, 22–3, 106
Cleopatra IV, 23, 106
Cleopatra VI Tryphaina, 23, 116, 157n40
Cleopatra VII, 28–9, 34, 37, 40, 48, 55,
    83, 103, 146, 157n40; and Aba of
    Olbe, 122–3; and Antonia, 141; and
    Antonius, 24, 27, 29–30, 50, 66, 95,
    104, 132, 136; artistic representations
    of, 45; Cilician possessions of, 52,
    122; cult of, 18; death of, 30–1; and
    Herodians, 63–4, 66, 68, 77; and
    Julius Caesar, 24, 61, 82, 132–3; and
    Kostobaros, 65; linguistic abilities
    of, 21; and Livia, 143–4; and Octavia,
    140, 143; and Octavian, 142–3; reign
    of, 24–5; reputation of, 11, 38–9, 51,
    127, 137, 149; in Rome, 133–4, 144–5;
    territories of, 52, 100, 110
Cleopatra, Mauretanian name, 43, 48
Cleopatra, mythological figure, 21
Cleopatra, sister of Alexander the
    Great, 21, 28
Cleopatra Berenike III, 23
Cleopatra Selene, 18, 48, 146, 161n93;
    childhood of, 27–30, 129; children
    of, 44–6; and Cleopatra VII, 25, 29;
    coinage of, 39–40; death of, 46–8,
    55; and Dido, 37; as implementor
    of scholarship, 43–4; marriage of,
    33–6; on Nikopolis trophy, 32–3;

Ptolemaic heritage of, 17, 40, 48; as
    queen, 36–46; in Rome, 31, 131, 143;
    royal court of, 41–4
Cleopatra Thea, 125
Cleopatra Tryphaina, 116
Client monarchs. *See* allied monarchs
Clytaemnestra, wife of Agamemnon, 7–9,
    88, 155n2
coinage: of Amastris, 17; of Antonia
    Tryphaina, 119; of Aristoboulos of
    Armenia, 152; of Artaxias III, 113; of
    Asandros, 83, 166n17; of Cleopatra I,
    22; of Cleopatra Selene, 35, 39–40,
    42, 47, 158n11; of the Cyrenaica,
    30; of Dynamis, 84, 87–90, 93,
    96; of elder Salome, 75; of Juba
    II, 35, 39–40, 42, 47, 160n74; of
    Massinissa, 47; of Pharnakes II, 96;
    of Phraatakes, 125; of Polemon I, 114;
    of Polemon II, 119–20; Ptolemaic,
    20; of Ptolemy of Mauretania, 44–5,
    161n89; of Pythodoris, 108, 114–15;
    of Thea Mousa, 123–5; of younger
    Salome, 152
Colchis, 79, 81, 106–7, 110
Coma Berenices, constellation, 21
Coponius, Roman prefect, 76
Cornelia, Roman matron, 34, 131, 135–6,
    140, 142
Corniche des Dahra, Algerian
    toponym, 37
Crete, Greek island, 29–30, 158n11
Crimea, 85, 93
crocodiles, 30, 39
Croesus, Lydian king, 99
Cyprus, 17, 20, 22, 122
Cyrenaica, 17, 20, 22, 29–30, 34, 36, 39

Damascus, Syrian city, 16, 68
dancing girls, 152
Danube River. *See* Ister
Dardanos, city in Troad, 11
Dareios I, Persian king, 11
Dareios III, Persian king, 16
Daskyleion, city in northwest Anatolia, 11
dates, 74, 76, 78
Demetrios Poliorketes, Macedonian
    king, 16, 20
Demetrios, son of Demetrios
    Poliorketes, 20

Demosthenes, Athenian politician, 14.
    See also List of Passages
Dido, Carthaginian queen, 37
Diocaesarea, Cilician city, 123
Diomedes, Greek hero, 8
Dionysios of Herakleia Pontika, 16
Dioskourias, city on the Black Sea, 107
divorce, 47, 56, 58, 67, 93, 137, 140
Don River. *See* Tanais
dreams, 56–7
Drusilla of Mauretania, 45–6
Drusilla, sister of Gaius Caligula, 118
Drusus, grandson of Livia, 144
Drusus, son of Livia, 32, 137, 140–1
Dynamis, Bosporan queen, 79–97, 111, 129,
    145, 166n24; birth of, 82–4; children
    of, 86, 89; coinage of, 93, 96; and Livia,
    90–1, 144; marriages of, 83–4, 86–7, 95;
    and Polemon, 84, 88–91, 95, 109

echephron, 9
eclipses, 46
Edom, region of southern Levant, 60
Egypt, Egyptians, 59, 67, 73, 90, 116,
    167n48, 168n10; Antonia the younger
    and, 141–2; Cleopatra VII and, 24–5,
    38, 63; Cleopatra Selene and, 27–33,
    36, 38–40, 143; Germanicus and,
    144; incest in, 20, 126; indigenous
    aristocracy of, 31–2, 40; Juba II
    and, 43; Julius Caesar and, 82,
    133; prophetic thought in, 28; and
    Pyrrhos of Epeiros, 19; Roman
    acquisition of, 30–1, 35; royal women
    in, 17–25; sculpture of, 40; symbols
    of, 30, 39–40
Egyptian language, 21
Elaioussa-Sebaste, Anatolian city, 52,
    54–6, 162n21
Ephesos, Ionian city, 16
Epidauros, city in Peloponnesos, 117
Equitius, alleged nephew of Cornelia, 136
Ethiopia, 35
Euergetes, 103
Eunoë Maura, Mauretanian queen, 133
euphorbion, 42–3
Eurydike, Ptolemaic queen, 19

Fadia, daughter of Fadius, 103–4
Fadius, Q., Roman freedman, 103

Fasa'yil, locality in Jordan valley, 74
Fayum, Egyptian district, 141
Felix, M. Antonius, governor of
    Judaea, 45
fish, 85, 118
Flamininus, L. Quinctius, Roman
    magistrate, 152
Flaubert, Gustave, 152
France, 81
Fulvia, wife of Antonius, 51, 136, 139

Gadeira, Iberian city, 152
Gaius Caesar, grandson of Augustus, 46,
    55, 104
Gaius Caligula, emperor. *See* Caligula
Galatia, Anatolian region, 110
Galba, emperor, 120
Galilee, Sea of, 59, 150–1
Gaul, 55, 75–6, 150
Gaza, Levantine city, 65, 73, 93
Georgia, region on Black Sea, 106–7
Gepaipyris, Bosporan queen, 119, 167n63
Germanicus, son of Antonia the younger,
    90, 103, 113, 141–4
Giresun, Turkish city, 106
Glaphyra of Cappadocia, 38, 49–58, 104,
    106, 145, 171n89; death of, 56–7; and
    Fulvia, 51, 136; and Juba II, 46–7,
    55–6; and Herodians, 53–7, 67, 69–71,
    75, 111, 131, 151
Glaphyra the hetaira, 50–2
Glaphyrai, Thessalian town, 53
Gnaios, gemcutter, 42
Golan, region of Levant, 68
Golden Fleece, 106, 110
Gongylos, dynastic family at
    Pergamon, 12–13
Gracchus, Roman aristocrats so named,
    131, 135, 172n21
grain trade, 81, 85, 87
grapes, grapevine, 81, 107
Greece, 30, 34, 50, 55, 132, 144
gynaikokratia, 10, 15

Hades, 9, 46–7
Halikarnassos, Karian city, 13–14, 156n26
Hanno, Cathaginian explorer, 43
Hasmon, Judaean leader, 59
Hasmoneans, 59–67, 73, 77, 150
Hatshepsut, Egyptian queen, 21

Hecuba, wife of Priam of Troy, 7
Hekatomnids, dynasty at Halikarnassos, 13–15, 18, 21, 99, 156n26
Hekatomnos, Karian satrap, 14
Helen of Sparta, 7
Hellas, Pergamene ruler, 12–13
Hellespont, 11–12
hemp, 85
Herakles, Greek hero, 40–1
Herennius Capito, C., Roman procurator, 76
Hermonassa, Pontic town, 90, 108, 144
Herod the Great, 32, 55, 62, 75, 77, 87, 145, 147, 161n11; and Antonius, 63–4; and Archelaos of Kappadocia, 53–4; and Augustus (Octavian), 63, 66, 68, 71, 75; as builder, 38, 61, 74–5, 93, 150; children of, 53, 56, 66–7, 70–2, 131, 134, 150–1; and Cleopatra VII, 63–5; descendants of, 89, 112, 119, 151–2; and Glaphyra, 53–4; and Kostobaros, 65–7; last years and death of, 55, 67, 70–5; and Mariamme, 59, 63–5; and Nikolaos of Damascus, 30, 148; and Syllaios, 68–70
Herod, son of Salome the younger, 152
Herodians, 64–5, 67, 70, 76–8, 119–20, 149–52, 174n9; Archelaos of Cappadocia and, 53–7, 111–12; early years of, 59–63; intrigues at court of, 53–4, 57, 63, 66, 71, 77, 152; Josephus' account of, 90, 147–8; and Livia, 69, 90–1; and Roman elite, 131, 142; source of income of, 73; and Syllaios, 67–9
Herodias, Judaean princess, 149–51
hides, 85
Hieron II of Syracuse, 130, 132
Huns, 97

Iamneia, Judean town, 73
Ida, Trojan mountain, 11
Idrieus, Hekatomnid dynast, 14
Idumaea, Idumaeans, 56, 60–1, 63, 65–6
incest, 20, 125–7
India, 23, 43–4
Iol, Mauretanian city, 37–8
Ionia, Anatolian region, 87, 123
Iotape, princess of Media Atropatene, 30, 104, 169n26

Ischomachos, Athenian farmer, 15
Isis, Egyptian divinity, 19, 22, 25, 38, 40
Istros, European river, 116
Itanos, Cretan locality, 29
Ithaka, Greek island, 8–9

Jason, Greek hero, 79, 106–7, 110
Jericho, town in Jordan valley, 59, 62–3, 72, 74, 76
Jerusalem, 62, 64, 66, 87
Jesus of Nazareth, 151, 164n66, 174n9
Jewish Law, 56–7, 67, 151
Jews, 62, 147–8, 174n9
Jezebel, Israelite queen, 37
John the Baptist, 149–52
Jokasta, Theban queen, 126
Jordan, river of southern Levant, 59, 71, 74, 76, 150
Joseph, uncle of Herod the Great, 62–5
Josephus, Jewish historian, 76, 90, 147–8. See also List of Passages
Juba I of Numidia, 34
Juba II of Mauretania, 36, 39, 45, 48, 53, 112, 131, 143, 160n71, 160n74; and expedition to Arabia, 46–7, 55; and Glaphyra, 46–7, 55–7, 162n38; and marriage to Cleopatra Selene, 35, 140–1; scholarship of, 37, 42–4, 58; youth of, 33–4, 134, 139. See also List of Passages
Juba, possible son of Cleopatra Selene, 45
Judaea, 45, 53–4, 58, 64, 70, 72, 77, 131, 147; economy of, 73–4; and ethnarch Archelaos, 56; Greek and Roman customs in, 67; and Livia, 69, 90, 144
Judaism, 61, 65, 69, 170n86
Judas Maccabeus, Hasmonean leader, 59
Julia, daughter of Augustus, 32
Julian family, 132, 143
Julius Caesar, C., 29, 31, 34, 61, 101, 114, 126–7, 171n7; assassination of, 27, 49–50, 85, 118, 133; and Bosporos, 82–4; and Cleopatra VII, 24, 82, 132–3

Kabeira, Pontic city, 107–8
Kaisareia, in Bosporos, 93
Kaisareia, cities so named, 93, 145. See also Caesarea
Kaisareia, in Mauretania, 38
Kaisarion, son of Cleopatra VII, 29, 31, 133

Kallimachos of Kyrene, 21
Kalydonian Boar Hunt, 21
Kandaules, Lydian king, 10
Kanesh, Assyrian trading post, 49
Karia, Anatolian region, 13–15, 18, 99
el-Kebir, North African river, 159n32
Kerch, strait and town, 79
Komana, Pontic shrine, 24, 50, 107, 115
Konon, astronomer, 21
korasion, 151
Kostobaros, Idumaean
    aristocrat, 65–7, 70
Kotys VIII of Thrace, 113, 116–18
Kotys IX of Thrace, 118
Kotys, son of Polemokratia, 118
Krinagoras of Mytilene, 35, 43
Kültepe, Turkish site, 49
Kydnos, Anatolian river, 27
Kyniska, Spartan princess, 19
Kypros, mother of Herod the Great,
    61–2, 64, 77
Kyriaina, wife of Myron, 92
Kyzikos, Mysian city, 118–19, 144

Laodikeia, Pontic city, 108
Laodikeia, Syrian city, 63
Lepidus, M. Aemilius,
    triumvir, 155n1
Levant, 17, 52, 65, 68, 75; southern, 53, 73,
    76, 147, 164n56
Libya: ancient, 36, 45; modern, 17, 29
Licinius Crassus, M., Roman
    magistrate, 124
Linear B writing, 7
Livia Drusilla, wife of Augustus, 45, 73,
    112, 137, 146; and Antonia
    Tryphaina, 117–18; and Cleopatra
    VII, 142–3; and Dynamis, 90–3, 129,
    144; and Pythodoris, 108, 110, 113,
    129, 144–5; and Salome, 69–72, 75–8,
    129, 144
Livy, Roman historian, 141. *See also* List
    of Passages
Lot, biblical patriarch, 126
Lucius Caesar, grandson of Augustus, 104
ludi saeculares, 53
Lydia, Anatolia region, 99
Lygdamis, dynast of Halikarnassos, 13
Lysimachos, successor of
    Alexander, 16–17

Macedonia, Macedonians, 10, 15–19,
    21, 157n43
Machairous, Herodian fortress, 150–1
Magnesia, Ionian city, 51
Maiotis, portion of Black Sea, 79
Mania, Persian satrap, 11–14
marble, 38, 118, 145
Marcii Reges, Roman aristocratic
    family, 132
Marcius Rex, Q., Roman magistrate, 133
Mariamme, wife of Herod the Great, 59,
    63–7, 70
Marisa, Judaean city, 60–1
Masada, Hasmonean fortress, 62–3
Massenet, Jules, 152
Massinissa, king of Numidia, 34, 47, 130,
    132, 159n30
Mathianes, Bosporan personality, 93
matron, 34, 77–8, 131, 134–6, 140, 142–3
Mattathias, Hasmonean leader, 59
Mauretania, 20, 42, 44–5, 53, 55–8, 124,
    162n38; Cleopatra Selene and, 35,
    37, 40, 42, 48, 129; creation of allied
    kingdom of, 28, 34, 37–8, 140, 143;
    early history of, 34–5, 40–1, 47, 133;
    origin of Nile in, 36, 43
Mauretanian Royal Mausoleum, 47
Mausoleion, tomb of Mausolos,
    14–15, 156n23
Mausolos, satrap of Karia, 14
Meander, river and valley in southwest
    Anatolia, 51, 99–101
Media, Asian region, 30; Media
    Atropatene, 104
Medinet el-Haras, Egyptian locality, 19
Meidias, son-in-law of Mania, 12–13
Meleagros, Greek hero, 21
Merenptah, Egyptian pharoah, 126
Mesopotamia, 100
Messalla Corvinus, M. Valerius,
    Augustan intimate, 102
Methe, mythological figure, 42
Misenum, locality on Bay on Naples, 135
misogyny, 11
Mithradates III of Kommagene, 169n26
Mithradates of Pergamon, 82–4
Mithradates I of Pontos, 97
Mithradates VI of Pontos, 50, 81–2, 84, 88,
    100–2, 106–7, 110–11, 135; descendants
    of, 82–4, 86, 88, 91, 96, 107, 129

Mithradatic kingdom and dynasty, 87, 95–7, 101, 108–10

Moaphernes, governor of Colchis, 106

Morocco, 34

Mousa, name common in Italy, 124

Mousa of Parthia. *See* Thesmousa

Mukawir, site in Jordan, 150

Mylasa, Karian city, 14

Myron, Bosporan personalities, 92

Mytilene, city on Lesbos, 35, 87

Nabataea, Nabataeans, 61–2, 67–9, 77, 142, 150

Nausikaa, Phaiakian princess, 8

Nero, emperor, 54, 139, 146, 152

Nikolaos of Damascus, 30, 43, 72, 74, 76, 147–8

nikolas date, 76, 78

Nikopolis, city in Akarnania, 32–3

Niksar, Turkish town, 107

Nile River, 17, 35–6, 39, 43–4; First Cataract of, 17; Kanobic Mouth of, 17

Nitokris of Babylon, 10

Novorosiyirsk, Russian town, 94

Numidia, Numidians, 33–4, 36, 43, 48, 161n89

Nymphaion, Bosporan town, 91–2

Nysa, Karian town, 99–101, 105, 108, 168n5

Obodas, Nabataean king, 67

Octavia, sister of Octavian, 31–4, 117, 129, 136–40, 143

Octavian, triumvir, 29, 33, 51, 69, 122, 137–8, 142–3, 159n26; and Herod the Great, 59, 62–3, 66. *See also* Augustus

Odysseus, Greek hero, 7–9

Oedipus, mythological personality, 126

Olbe, Anatolian temple state, 114, 121–3, 170n67

olives, 33, 107

Olympias, mother of Alexander the Great, 15, 18

Olympic Games, 19, 55

Orestes, mythological personality, 21, 88

Ourania, Greek divinity, 125

Panathenaic Festival, 118

Pantaleon, Bosporan naval commander, 85, 166n24

Pantikapaion, Bosporan city, 79–81, 84–6, 89–93

Paraisades V of Bosporos, 81

Parthia, Parthians, 63, 108, 112, 114, 120, 123–7, 157n50, 171n16

Penelope, wife of Odysseus, 7–9, 16, 18, 21, 129, 155n9

Peraia, Levantine region, 71, 150

Pergamon, Mysian city, 12–13, 82, 144; Pergamon Altar, 32

Perikles, Athenian statesman, 132

Persia, Persians, 10–18, 49, 53, 110, 116, 126, 152, 169n50, 172n20

Perusine War, 136

Petubastes IV, Egyptian priest, 40–1

Phanagoreia, Bosporan town, 90–3, 144

Pharnabazos, Persian satrap, 11–12

Pharnakeia, Pontic city, 106

Pharnakes II, Bosporan king, 81–5, 91, 96

Phasael, brother of Herod the Great, 62, 74

Phasaelis, city in Jordan valley, 73–4, 76

Pheroras, brother of Herod the Great, 62, 70–1

Phila, Macedonian queen, 16

Philai, Egyptian town, 90, 167n48

Philip II, Macedonian king, 15–16, 19

Philip, husband of Berenike I of Judaea, 19

Philip, son of Herod the Great, 73–5, 151

Philistines, 73

Philometor, 102–3

Philoromaios, 84, 89–92

Philostratos, tutor of Cleopatra VII, 35

Phraatakes (Phraates V), Parthian king, 124–7

Phraates IV, Parthian king, 123–7, 171n7

Phrygian cap, 94

Phrygians, 49

Pixodaros, Hekatomnid dynast, 14, 156n22

Polemokratia, Thracian queen, 118

Polemon I of Pontos, 84, 86–90, 95, 102, 106, 108–12, 114, 169n40

Polemon II of Pontos, 114–15, 118–20, 170n86

Pompeii, Campanian city, 40

Pompey the Great (Cn. Pompeius), Roman magistrate, 50, 101, 107, 126

Pontos (Black Sea), 110

Pontos (territory), 24, 50, 53, 82, 84, 87–90, 95, 103, 105–20, 144

Port Sudan, Egyptian town, 19
portraits: of Antonia Tryphaina, 119; of
   Augustus, 64, 93, 108; of Cleopatra
   VII, 39–40; of Cleopatra Selene, 40,
   42; of Cornelia, 136; of Dynamis, 93;
   of Glaphyra, 55; of Hekatomnids,
   14; of Juba II, 55; of Livia, 91–2, 108,
   143; of Mariamme, 64; of Octavia,
   143; of Tiberius, 108; of M. Vipsanius
   Agrippa, 93
Poseidon, Greek divinity, 8, 85, 118
priestess-queen, 123
Prokles, Mysian dynast, 13
Ptolemies, Egyptian dynasty, 16, 20–1,
   28, 48, 57, 116, 123, 157n43; attitude
   toward women of, 15, 17–18, 20–4,
   29; collapse of, 24, 30–1, 40, 109, 148;
   and Mauretania, 36, 40–1, 43–5; and
   Romans, 23, 27, 34; territories of, 17,
   22, 25, 29–30, 59, 122
Ptolemy I, 16–19, 28, 31
Ptolemy II, 19–20, 43, 160n68
Ptolemy III, 20, 160n68
Ptolemy IV, 20, 160n68
Ptolemy V, 21–2, 28
Ptolemy VI, 22, 103, 125
Ptolemy VIII, 22–3, 29, 34, 116, 131, 135
Ptolemy IX, 23, 135
Ptolemy X, 23, 135
Ptolemy XI, 23
Ptolemy XII, 23–4, 50, 116, 157n40, 168n10
Ptolemy XIII, 24, 126, 157n40
Ptolemy XIV, 24, 126
Ptolemy XV, 31
Ptolemy Apion, 29
Ptolemy of Mauretania, 44–7, 58, 91, 96
Ptolemy Philadelphos, 29, 31
Ptolemy, use of name, 48
Pyrrhos of Molossia and Epeiros, 19
Pythion, uncle of Pythodoris, 101
Pythodoris of Pontos, 18, 83,
      99–120, 126, 146; and Archelaos of
      Cappadocia, 53, 56–7, 106–7, 111–12,
      145; descendants of, 114–20; family
      background of, 100–4, 107–8, 116,
      144, 168n8; and Polemon I, 87–8, 95,
      109, 114; and Romans, 108, 110–13, 129,
      144–5, 169n40; and Strabo, 103–7, 111,
      113–14; territories of, 100, 106–7, 111
Pythodoris II of Thrace, 119

Pythodoris, daughter of Antonius, 115
Pythodoros of Nysa, 101–4, 109, 168n10

queen, queenship: cultic aspects of, 19;
   as honorific, 118–19; and Penelope,
   8–10; problems with term, 7–8, 13–
   16, 155n1; Ptolemaic, 17–25, 40; and
   Romans, 48, 96, 107, 143; terms as
   used by Herodotos, 10, 13

Red Sea, 19, 43–4
Rhescuporis of Thrace, 117
Rhodes, Greek island, 14, 62, 66,
   100–1, 156n26
Rhoimetalkes, Thracian kings so
   named, 116–18
Rhoxane, wife of Alexander the Great, 18
Roman Republic and Empire, 20, 37,
   50–1, 67, 69, 81, 96, 115, 126, 145, 151,
   156n23; and allied monarchy, 34, 82,
   89, 91–2, 109–10, 122–3, 129–32, 144–
   5; annexation of Egypt by, 31; and
   Archelaos of Cappadocia, 48, 53, 55–
   6, 106, 108, 112–13; architecture of,
   48; aristocracy of, 13–14, 48, 55, 57,
   67, 105, 109, 131–2, 137; and Armenia,
   54; attitudes toward monarchy of,
   132–4, 137; attitudes toward women
   of, 10, 17, 129, 134–6, 140, 142–3;
   and Bosporan kingdom, 81–93; and
   Cappadocia, 49–50, 52; and Cilicia,
   55, 112, 123; and civil war, 34, 93,
   109; and Cleopatra VII, 25, 27, 29,
   129, 133, 143; and Cleopatra Selene,
   29, 31–3, 37, 43, 46, 48, 131, 143; and
   Crete, 29–30; and Cyrenaica, 30; and
   divorce, 67; global economy of, 41,
   73; and Herodians, 53, 61, 64, 68–9,
   71, 74–8, 131, 148; imperial family of,
   45, 90–1, 129, 147; and Kyzikos, 119;
   literature of, 43; and Mauretania,
   34–5; and Mithridates VI of
   Pontos, 81–2, 92; and Nysa, 99–102;
   obligations of, toward children,
   32; and Parthians, 108, 114, 124–7;
   polygamy and, 46; and Pontos,
   109, 111; and Ptolemies, 17, 21, 23–5;
   and Pythodoros of Nysa, 101–2;
   reputation of Antonius in, 39, 88,
   146; and Syria, 74; and Thrace, 116

Rome, buildings and topography of
city: aqueducts, 133; Ara Pacis, 32,
44, 96–7; Forum Julium, 143–4;
Mausoleum of Augustus, 48; Oppian
Hill, 137; Palatine Hill, 139–40,
145; Porticus Liviae, 137; Porticus
Octaviae, 137
Rome, city of, 21, 27–9, 35, 39–40, 45,
101, 105, 135, 139–40, 142; Bosporan
monarchs in, 89, 95–6; foreign
ambassadors in, 30, 35; Ptolemies in,
23–5, 116; royal children in, 31–4, 131
Russia, 79, 110

Sabines, Italian ethnic group, 134, 137;
Sabine women, 134, 136
Salamis, Battle of, 13
Salome, daughter of Herodias, 150–2
Salome, follower of Jesus of
Nazareth, 174n9
Salome, physician, 78
Salome, sister of Herod the Great, 59–78,
90, 129, 142, 145, 152; children of, 63,
67; and death of Herod the Great,
72–3; estates of, 73; and Glaphyra,
53–4, 70–1, 75; and Livia, 69, 71–2,
77–8, 144; and Mariamme, 64–6;
and marriage to Alexas, 70, 74;
and marriage to Joseph, 62–5; and
marriage to Kostobaros, 65–7; and
Syllaios, 68–71
Samaria, district and city of southern
Levant, 37, 56, 66
Samothrake, Greek island, 118
Sandahanna, Tel, Judaean site, 60–1
Sapaians, Thracian ethnic group, 116
satraps, 10–12, 14, 49
Savior Harbor, port on Red Sea, 19
Scribonius, Bosporan usurper, 83–4,
86–8, 90, 93, 95
sculpture: Augustus of Prima Porta, 124;
of Cleopatra VII, 39; of Cornelia,
136, 140; of the elder Artemisia, 13;
Egyptian, 40; of the Mausoleion, 14.
See also portraits
Sebaste, Cappadocian city. See
Elaioussa-Sebaste
Sebaste, cities so named, 145
Sebaste, Pontic city, 107
Sebastopol, city in Crimea, 93

Sebastopolis, city on Black Sea, 107
Sebastos, 107. See also Augustus
Selene, people so named, 48
Seleukids, 16, 31, 57, 99, 116, 122, 135;
collapse of, 59, 101, 109, 122; and
Ptolemies, 21–2, 28, 103, 125; royal
women of, 17, 21–2, 103, 125
Seleukos I, 31, 122–3
Seleukos IV, 22
Sempronia, Roman matron, 135–6
Seven Wonders of the World, 135–6
Shikma, Israeli river, 73
Silk Road, 85
Sinope, city on Black Sea, 84, 87
Sisenes, Cappadocian personality, 50–2
Smyrna, Ionian city, 102, 114
Socrates of Athens, 15
Sorek, Israeli river, 73
Spain, 35, 133, 150
Sparta, Greek city, 10, 18–19
Strauss, Richard, 149
Sukhumi, Georgian town, 107
Sultanhisar, Turkish town, 99
Susa, Elamite city, 171n16
Syllaios, Nabataean minister, 61–71, 77
Syria, 59, 63–5, 68–9, 142, 144; Roman
province of, 74, 76
Syrian Wars, 20–1

Taman, Russian city, 90–1
Tanais, Bosporan city and river, 79, 81–2,
85, 88, 93
Tangier, Moroccan city, 47
tapestry, 9
Tarraco, Iberian city, 35
Tarragona, Spanish city, 35
Tarsos, Cilician city, 27, 50, 122
Tauris, region on north shore of Black
Sea, 93
Teda, Israeli town, 93
Tel Aviv, Israeli city, 73
Teos, Ionian city, 91
Teukros, hero, 121
Teukros, name of priest kings at Olbe, 122
Themistokles, Athenian political leader, 132
Thesmousa (Thea Mousa), Parthian
queen, 123–4, 171n7
Theudion, brother-in-law of Herod the
Great, 71
Thrace, Greek region, 116–19

Thuoris, Egyptian queen, 21
Tibarenians, Anatolian ethnic group, 106
Tiber, river in Italy, 32, 133
Tiberius, emperor, 32, 45, 54, 99, 106,
    113, 137, 142, 167n44; and Antonia
    Tryphaina, 117; and Archelaos of
    Cappadocia, 58, 105, 108, 112–13;
    on coinage, 108, 114; and Livia,
    75–6, 173n36
Tigranes V of Armenia, 54, 89–90, 112
Tigranes VI of Armenia, 54
Tipasa, Algerian town, 47
Titus, emperor, 119
Tomyris, queen of the Massagetai, 10
Trabzon, Turkish town, 106
Trachonitis, Levantine region, 68–9
Tralleis, Anatolian city, 101, 105,
    107–8, 144
Trapezous, Pontic city, 106
Troad, Anatolian region, 11–13
Trojan War, 7–8, 14–15, 28, 121, 132
Troy, Anatolian city, 12, 99, 142
Tryphaina, Christian martyr, 170n86
Tula, Russian town, 79
Turkey, 49, 106, 121
Turranius, C., prefect of Egypt, 167n48

Tuthmosis I, Egyptian pharoah, 40
Tyro, beloved of Poseidon, 8

Urania, divinity, 125

Vaballathus, son of Zenobia of
    Palmyra, 126
Vergil, Roman poet, 37. See also List of
    Passages
Vienna, city in Gaul, 56, 75

Wilde, Oscar, 149, 152

Xenophon, Greek adventurer and scholar,
    12–13. See also List of Passages
Xerxes, Persian king, 11–13, 152

Zadaros, father of Mathianes, 93
Zela, Pontic city, 82–4, 167
Zenis, Persian satrap, 11
Zenobia, queen of Palmyra, 126
Zenon of Laodikeia, 108
Zenon, son of Pythodoris, 102, 113–14
Zenophanes, dynast, 122
Zenophanes, priest-king at Olbe, 122
Zeus Olbios, 121–2